PERSO

Personality Psychology: The Basics provides a jargon-free and accessible overview of the discipline, focusing on why not all individuals think, feel, speak, or act the same way in the same situation.

The book offers a brief history of the area, covering a range of perspectives on personality including psychodynamic, behaviourist, humanistic, and cognitive approaches. Also featuring fascinating case studies to richly illustrate the theories discussed, the text looks at influential theories and related research within each of the major schools of thought in personality psychology. Rigorously examining the fundamental principles of personality psychology, the author concludes by outlining the future of the area in relation to cutting edge research and potential future trends.

Exploring the major personality theories that seek to explain why people behave as they do in eight reader-friendly chapters, this is an essential introduction for students who are approaching personality psychology for the first time.

Stanley O. Gaines, Jr. (Senior Lecturer, Brunel University London) specialises in the fields of relationship science and ethnic studies. He has authored or co-authored more than 100 publications, including *Personality and Close Relationship Processes*, winner of the Distinguished Book Award from the International Association for Relationship Research in 2018. Moreover, he has served as principal investigator or co-investigator for studies that have been funded by organisations such as the American Psychological Foundation, Ford Foundation, Society for the Psychological Study of Social Issues, Fulbright Foundation, and the Economic and Social Research Council in collaboration with UKAid.

THE BASICS

The Basics is a highly successful series of accessible guidebooks which provide an overview of the fundamental principles of a subject area in a jargon-free and undaunting format.

Intended for students approaching a subject for the first time, the books both introduce the essentials of a subject and provide an ideal springboard for further study. With over 50 titles spanning subjects from artificial intelligence (AI) to women's studies, *The Basics* are an ideal starting point for students seeking to understand a subject area.

Each text comes with recommendations for further study and gradually introduces the complexities and nuances within a subject.

For a full list of titles in this series, please visitwww.routledge.com /The-Basics/book-series/B

PERSONALITY PSYCHOLOGY

THE BASICS

Stanley O. Gaines, Jr.

Routledge
Taylor & Francis Group

LONDON AND NEW YORK

First published 2020
by Routledge
2 Park Square, Milton Park, Abingdon, Oxon OX14 4RN

and by Routledge
52 Vanderbilt Avenue, New York, NY 10017

*Routledge is an imprint of the Taylor & Francis Group, an
informa business*

British Library Cataloguing-in-Publication Data
A catalogue record for this book is available from the
British Library

Library of Congress Cataloging-in-Publication Data
A catalog record has been requested for this book

ISBN: 978-0-367-17289-3 (hbk)
ISBN: 978-0-367-17290-9 (pbk)
ISBN: 978-0-429-05603-1 (ebk)

Typeset in Bembo
by Swales & Willis, Exeter, Devon, UK

To my son, Luther Gaines–White: You exist; therefore, I am.

CONTENTS

BOXES

PREFACE

During the 1979-80 academic year, I was enrolled as a first-year student at the University of Texas at Arlington (in the US). I was a pre-dental student within the BSc Biology programme but harboured dreams of pursuing a career in which writing would play a major role (though my father had steered me away from such a career; I had wanted to be a journalist prior to entering university). In the midst of seeking answers concerning my personal and professional dilemmas, I went to the main public library in Dallas and rummaged through various index cards (during the pre-Internet era!), looking up books in subjects such as Self and Identity. I found a book titled *Man's Search for Himself*, which Rollo May had published in 1953. May's book was already dated in many respects (e.g., the post-World War II emphasis on the imminent threat of nuclear annihilation seemed almost quaint, though admittedly unsettling). Although I did not know it at the time, I had begun a quest – not just for answers to the personal question of "Who Am I?" but also for a deeper understanding of human personality in general – that is reflected directly in the present book.

By the beginning of my third year in university, I had made a permanent move away from home and had taken three optional modules (or courses, as we would say in the US) in Psychology, thanks to the liberal education policies that govern much of higher education in the US. The third (and, as I assumed at the time, final) module was titled Psychology of Women, in which the students and professor explored gender roles. That module eventually convinced me to pursue psychology instead of dentistry as a career. It appears that the profession of dentistry has survived quite nicely without me! As for my eventually chosen profession, I have been blessed to work as a social psychologist for nearly 30 years. My undergraduate mentor, William Ickes, was especially important in helping me define myself as a social psychologist who examines individual differences in interpersonal behaviour (within and outside the context of close relationships).

As I write this Preface, I am taking a break from reading second-year undergraduate essays in social psychology. I am struck by the conviction with which most of the students proclaim that "the situation" inherently overwhelms "the person" in terms of influences on individuals' behaviour (although some of the students opt for an interactionist approach that acknowledges the joint effects of personality and environment on individuals' behaviour). I smile, because the primarily situationist sentiment that I encounter in the students' essays is reminiscent of social-psychological findings on the *actor-observer effect*, whereby individuals tend to attribute their own behaviour to situational influences but tend to attribute other people's behaviour to personality influences (E. E. Jones & Nisbett, 1972). As actors, you and I are intimately aware of the myriad ways that the social and physical environment facilitate or constrain our behaviour. However, as observers, you and I are prone to concluding "That's just the way he is/she is/they are" when we try to understand why other people behave as they do (Molouki & Pronin, 2015). In truth, situations vary in terms of their impact on an individuals' behaviour; and different individuals do possess different personalities, as is evident when the situation is "weak" enough to allow those differences to emerge (Snyder & Ickes, 1985).

This is the third book that I have written for Routledge (following Gaines, 1997, 2017), and the first book in which I have been able to devote substantial attention to all of the major schools of thought within personality psychology. I am indebted to Eleanor Reedy (Social Psychology Commissioning Editor, Routledge) for encouraging me to develop the present book as part of the *Basics* series at Routledge. Eleanor's inspiration and guidance have helped me greatly in writing a book on personality psychology that (hopefully) is informative and accessible to A-level/high school students, undergraduates, postgraduate students, and academics alike. In addition, I am grateful to Alex Howard (Editorial Assistant, Routledge Psychology) for helping me keep on track regarding the post-manuscript development process, and to Colin Morgan and the production team at Swales & Willis for their expert work on the final, publication-ready version of this book. Finally, I appreciate the support that Routledge Books in general have given to my scholarly work throughout my career.

At the beginning of this Preface, I alluded to the pivotal role that Rollo May's (1953) *Man's Search for Himself* played in my personal and professional development. As it happens, May was one of the major American figures within the *humanistic/existential* school of personality psychology (which, as we will learn in Chapter 4, addresses issues of being versus becoming). Moreover, in *Love and Will* (1969) – May's best-known work (Ewen, 1998) – one will find an interesting twist on French philosopher Rene Descartes's declaration, "I think, therefore I am." Rather than spoil the plot at this early stage, I shall comment further on that particular twist in Chapter 8. For now, I shall reveal that May's version of *existential psychology* (which contends that issues of being versus *non*being are as important as, if not more important than, issues on being versus becoming; Medina, 2008) serves as the basis for my own twist on Descartes's dictum, which readers will find in my Dedication to my son.

As we embark on our tour of personality psychology, we shall learn about several theories and lines of research from each of the major schools within the field (i.e., *psychodynamic, behaviouristic, humanistic/existential, trait, cognitive*, and *biological*). A cursory reading of the present book is likely to reveal that no particular theorist or researcher possesses a monopoly on The Truth (whatever that may be). However, a detailed reading of the present book is likely to reveal that each theory and line of research yields insight into the amazingly complex human psyche. I hope that you will find this intellectual journey to be thought-provoking, even challenging, no matter what stage of personal and professional development you have achieved (or wish to achieve). In spirit, I am with you.

INTRODUCTION

AN INTRODUCTION TO
PERSONALITY PSYCHOLOGY

> Personality, it is said, is an individual's unique way of perceiving his environment, including himself.
>
> Gordon W. Allport, *Pattern and Growth in Personality* (1961/1963, p. 274)

One of the most important lessons that one learns from the history of social psychology (which is covered in *Social Psychology: The Basics*; Frings, in preparation) is that interpersonal situations can exert considerable influence on individuals' thoughts, feelings, and behaviour (e.g., G. W. Allport, 1968/1985). By the same token, the history of social psychology acknowledges that not all individuals necessarily think, feel, or behave the same way in a particular interpersonal situation, at a particular point in time (e.g., E. E. Jones, 1985/1998). Indeed, throughout the history of social psychology, individual differences in *attitudes* (i.e., individuals' positive versus negative thoughts and feelings toward various persons, places, things, and other entities; Blair, Dasgupta, & Glaser, 2015) have been examined empirically as predictors of interpersonal behaviour (Ross, Lepper, & Ward, 2010).

Gordon W. Allport was a pioneer in the field of social psychology, especially regarding the conceptualisation and measurement of individuals' stereotyped thoughts and prejudiced feelings as potential influences on individuals' behaviour toward members of psychological outgroups (e.g., G. W. Allport, 1954/1979). In addition, G. W. Allport was a pioneer in the field of *personality psychology* (i.e., the study of the entire, functioning individual; McAdams, 1997), especially concerning the conceptualisation and measurement of *traits* (i.e., individuals' descriptions of their own psychological characteristics; Paunonen & Hong, 2015) and *values* (i.e., individuals' priorities in life as reflected in particular organised sets of beliefs; McAdams & Manczak, 2015) as predictors of individuals' behaviour toward members of psychological ingroups and outgroups alike (e.g., G. W. Allport, 1937/1951, 1955, 1961/1963). Thus, whether viewed from the vantage point of interpersonal relations (e.g., Gaines, 2016/2018) or intergroup relations (e.g., Gaines, 2017), G. W. Allport's *psychology of the individual* (C. S. Hall & Lindzey, 1970) – including, but not limited to, G. W. Allport's trait theory (Ewen, 1998) – offers a broad, expansive foundation for integrating various theories and results of empirical studies on individual differences in thoughts, feelings, and behaviour within particular social situations (see Funder & Fast, 2010).

In the present book, G. W. Allport's (1937/1951, 1955, 1961/1963) psychology of the individual serves as the primary theoretical framework for our review of the literature in personality psychology. We are aware that, by emphasising G. W. Allport's perspective on personality psychology, we run the risk of ignoring the conceptual road less travelled – most notably, Ross Stagner's *Psychology of Personality*, which presents a comparatively behaviouristic and experimental view of personality psychology across several editions (1937, 1948, 1961, 1974; see McAdams, 1997). However, G. W. Allport's and Stagner's respective orientations share certain basic assumptions about the proper subject matter of personality psychology. For example, the opening quote from G. W. Allport (1961/1963, p. 274) concerning the definition of personality in terms of individual uniqueness – notwithstanding G. W. Allport's pre-Women's Rights Era use of masculine pronouns to refer to all of humanity – directly cites Stagner's (1961) third edition of *Psychology of Personality* as a source of inspiration. In any event, with G. W. Allport as our conceptual guide, we shall strive to present a concise (yet comprehensive) review of personality psychology.

OVERVIEW OF THE PRESENT BOOK

One of the most fascinating aspects of personality psychology is the co-existence of several well-defined schools of thought, each of which includes two or more wide-ranging theories that – according to their respective creators – go a long way toward explaining why individuals behave as they do (Ewen, 1998). Certain schools of thought (i.e., psychodynamic, behaviourist, and humanistic/existential) are regarded as "classic" (Wiggins & Pincus, 1992); whereas other schools of thought (i.e., trait, cognitive, and biological) are regarded as "contemporary" or "emerging" (see Digman, 1990). In Chapters 2 through to 7 of the present book, we will learn more about the major schools of thought within personality psychology.

Readers of the present book will notice that we have "stacked the deck" in terms of the amount of space that we devote to *psychodynamic theories* that – following the lead of Sigmund Freud's (e.g., S. Freud, 1908/1925, 1931/1950) psychoanalytic theory – assume that unconscious motives exert considerable influence on individuals' behaviour (see Millon, 1996). Our expansive coverage of psychodynamic theories does not reflect a particular conceptual bias or predisposition toward those theories. Rather, our interest in psychodynamic theories can be understood in terms of the sheer impact that those theories have made within personality psychology (see also Ewen, 1998). Even Stagner – whose *Psychology of Personality* (e.g., Stagner, 1937), as we have already mentioned, serves as a behaviouristic alternative to G. W. Allport's *Pattern and Growth in Personality* (1937/1951) – placed special emphasis upon the psychodynamic school (e.g., Stagner, 1961).

EXAMPLES OF CORE CONSTRUCTS IN PERSONALITY PSYCHOLOGY

In order to understand core constructs in personality psychology from the standpoint of G. W. Allport's (1937/1951, 1955, 1961/1963) psychology of the individual, one must begin by examining William James's (1890/2010) seminal version of *self-theory* (see C. S. Hall & Lindzey, 1970). According to James, the *self* is an individuals' ongoing awareness that they are distinct from – yet interconnected with – various aspects of the physical and social worlds that they inhabit (see Swann & Bosson, 2010). Having been influenced by Charles Darwin's (1859) *theory of natural selection*, James (1890/2010) emphasised the biological origins of the self (e.g., the self is a product of the mind – which, in turn, is a product of the brain). However, James (1902) subsequently encouraged readers to decide for themselves whether they believe that the self ultimately is a product of biology or a product of divinity. (Within philosophy and theology, the older term of *soul* historically was used to describe the self as a divinely ordained entity; see Calkins, 1917, for a critique of the pre-psychology literature on the soul.)

In turn, according to James (1890/2010), two major components of the self can be identified – namely, (1) the *pure Ego*, or self-as-knower; and (2) the *empirical Me*, or self-as-known (G. W. Allport, 1955). G. W. Allport contended that the empirical Me – which G. W. Allport preferred to label as the *proprium* – is the aspect of the self that is directly accessible to individuals' consciousness. Having sidestepped the problems that plague James's conceptualisation of the pure Ego (e.g., if the pure Ego reflects upon the self, then what is the entity that presumably reflects upon the pure Ego, and so on; C. S. Hall & Lindzey, 1970), in *Personality: A Psychological Interpretation* (1937/1951), G. W. Allport promoted the empirical Me or proprium in *Pattern and Grown in Personality* (1961/1963) as the component of the self that encompasses and gives order to the wide array of traits, values, and other constructs that are part and parcel of individuals' personalities (Ewen, 1998).

Within the empirical Me or proprium, G. W. Allport (1955) accepted James's (1890/2010) further division into the *material self* (i.e., individuals' physical possessions, including their own bodies), *social self* (i.e., the roles and relationships within which individuals are embedded), and *spiritual self* (i.e., individuals' intelligence and personality characteristics). (The term "spiritual self", which James chose over potentially less soul-evoking terms such as "psychic self", does not appear to have been problematic for G. W. Allport, who shared James's (1902) interest in religion and spirituality; e.g., G. W. Allport, 1950.) G. W. Allport believed that, in everyday life, individuals do not experience components of the proprium as distinct from each other (C. S. Hall & Lindzey, 1970). Nevertheless,

G. W. Allport's own programme of research – which included the development of surveys to measure traits (e.g., G. W. Allport, 1928) and values (G. W. Allport, Vernon, & Lindzey, 1960; see also Vernon & G. W. Allport, 1931) – tended to prioritise aspects of the spiritual self (see Ewen, 1998).

With regard to James's (1890/2010) spiritual self, G. W. Allport (1937/1951, 1955, 1961/1963) drew a distinction between individual differences in *intelligence* (i.e., presumed cognitive ability) and individual differences in *personality* (i.e., a variety of psychological attributes that lie outside the domain of presumed cognitive ability; see C. S. Hall & Lindzey, 1970). As it turns out, G. W. Allport's psychology of the individual largely predates the emergence of cognitive psychology, which currently addresses theories and research on intelligence (see Gobet, in preparation). In any event, G. W. Allport viewed intelligence as a construct that should be considered separate from the subject matter of personality psychology (a view that is shared by many, but not all, of G. W. Allport's followers; see Ewen, 1998).

Unlike James (1890/2010), G. W. Allport (1937/1951, 1955, 1961/1963) wrote systematically about the relevance of several modern-day personality constructs to the spiritual self (see C. S. Hall & Lindzey, 1970). For example, G. W. Allport's psychology of the individual includes traits, values, attitudes, and *motives* (the latter of which can be defined as internal forces that direct individuals' behaviour; Sheldon & Schuler, 2015). In principle, one could add *affect* (i.e., individual differences in feelings at a particular point in time; Augustine & Larsen, 2015) – including *emotions* (i.e., feelings that tend to be directed toward particular entities) and *moods* (i.e., feelings that are not necessarily directed toward any particular entity; R. Brown, 1965) – to the list of major personality constructs. Nevertheless, G. W. Allport devoted the bulk of his scholarly efforts toward understanding traits in all of their complexity (Ewen, 1998).

Regarding traits, G. W. Allport (1937/1951, 1955, 1961/1963) made a distinction between *common traits* (which can be found in varying degrees among large numbers of individuals and are especially amenable to quantitative research methods) and *personal traits* (which, in principle, might be found only among one individual and are especially amenable to qualitative research methods; C. S. Hall & Lindzey, 1970). G. W. Allport acknowledged that the field of personality psychology in general might gravitate toward studies of common traits (as ultimately proved to be the case during the second half of the twentieth century; McAdams, 1997). However, G. W. Allport's psychology of the individual emphasised personal traits, as the psychological equivalent of fingerprints (i.e., no two individuals possess exactly the same combination of personal traits; Ewen, 1998).

Finally, with respect to personal traits, G. W. Allport (1937/1951, 1955, 1961/1963) distinguished among *cardinal traits* (i.e., single traits that essentially define the entire personalities of some individuals); *central traits* (i.e., five to ten traits that go a long way toward defining the personalities of most individuals); and *secondary traits* (i.e., an unspecified number of traits whose expression in the behaviour of some, if not most, individuals is heavily dependent upon the presence versus absence of situational influences; Ewen, 1998). G. W. Allport's best-known empirical work on traits (i.e., G. W. Allport, 1965) focused on several central traits (e.g., aggressive, autonomous, sentimental, self-centred) – or, alternatively, one cardinal trait (i.e., neurotic) – of an older woman ("Jenny") with whom a primary correspondent ("Glenn") was acquainted for more than twenty years, via more than 300 letters that the older woman had sent to the correspondent and his wife ("Isabel"), during an interval that spanned more than a decade after the correspondent's stint as a university roommate of the woman's son ("Ross"; see Hall & Lindzey, 1970; for further details on *Letters from Jenny*, see Box 1.1). Compared to cardinal traits and central traits, G. W. Allport de-emphasised secondary traits in practice (Zuroff, 1986).

BOX 1.1 INSIGHT INTO ONE WOMAN'S PERSONALITY: GORDON ALLPORT'S *LETTERS FROM JENNY* (1965)

One of the most exhaustive, empirically orientated studies of a particular individual's personality was Gordon Allport's *Letters from Jenny* (1965; for a review, see Wrightsman, 1981). Although authoritative reviews of *Letters from Jenny* (e.g., Ewen, 1998; C. S. Hall & Lindzey, 1970) have tended to follow G. W. Allport's practice of referring to "Jenny's" main letter-writing correspondent as "Glenn" (and referring to the correspondent's wife as "Isabel"), Winter (1997) revealed that the name "Glenn" was a pseudonym for Gordon Allport himself; and the name "Isabel" was a pseudonym for Gordon Allport's wife, Ada(!). In any event, the letters in question served collectively as a treasure trove of insight into "Jenny's" personality – not just for Gordon Allport, but also for successive generations of personality researchers (O'Dell, 1978).

In the hands of a less-capable researcher, *Letters from Jenny* (G. W. Allport, 1965) might have functioned as a mundane, unenlightening account of the final twelve years of "Jenny's" life, from middle to elderly adulthood. However, G. W. Allport's mastery of entire schools of thought within personality psychology is evident in the ease with which G. W. Allport shifts from an existential perspective to a psychodynamic and, subsequently, trait perspective in fleshing out the unique combination of psychological attributes that comprise "Jenny's" personality (see R. Brown, 1965, for a discussion of laypersons' and scientists' progression from describing individuals' behaviour to drawing conclusions with regard to individuals' personalities). Moreover, despite the increasingly paranoid content of "Jenny's" letters over time (especially in the years following the death of her son, "Ross"), G. W. Allport stopped short of labelling "Jenny" as psychotic. Instead, G. W. Allport opted to emphasise "Jenny's" basic dignity. Although we will not usually refer to G. W. Allport as a humanist (at least in terms of allegiance to a given school of thought), G. W. Allport's overarching optimism concerning human nature is obvious in the ultimately sympathetic portrait of "Jenny" that one finds in G. W. Allport's book (see also J. F. Brennan, 2003, for a description of G. W. Allport as a humanistic psychologist).

We hasten to add that G. W. Allport (1937/1951, 1955, 1961/1963) did *not* portray traits as the only constructs that were worth studying within personality psychology (C. S. Hall & Lindzey, 1970). Nonetheless, G. W. Allport's psychology of the individual does promote traits as the most relevant constructs for the development of personality psychology as a distinct branch of psychology (Ewen, 1998). By the latter half of the twentieth century, an overwhelming consensus among personality psychologists indicated that traits had emerged as the core constructs within their field (A. R. Buss, 1989).

EXAMPLES OF IMPORTANT (BUT NOT-YET-CORE) CONSTRUCTS IN PERSONALITY PSYCHOLOGY

So far, we have identified various core constructs within personality psychology, from the perspective of G. W. Allport's (1937/ 1951, 1955, 1961/1963) psychology of the individual. However, we have not said much about important, but not-yet-core, constructs in personality psychology (notwithstanding their core status in developmental psychology; e.g., C. R. Cooper & Denner, 1998). As a theoretical point of departure, we turn to Erik Erikson's (1959/1980, 1963/1995, 1968/1994) *ego psychology*, which serves as a conceptual bridge between James's (1890/2010) self-theory and G. W. Allport's psychology of the individual (see C. S. Hall & Lindzey, 1970). Erikson is best-known for his writings on *identity*, which Baumeister (1997) – drawing upon Erikson (e.g., Erikson, 1968/1994) – defined as "the [combination or aggregate of] definitions that are created for and superimposed on the self" (p. 682). Identity may be distinguished from the *self-concept* (i.e., individuals' conscious reflection upon themselves; Baumeister, 1998), in that identity is jointly constructed by self and society; whereas the self-concept ultimately is constructed by one's self (Baumeister, 1997).

In spite of G. W. Allport's (1954/1979) panoramic view regarding intergroup relations (Brewer & R. J. Brown, 1998), G. W. Allport's (1937/1951, 1955, 1961/1963) psychology of the individual focused on *personal identity* (i.e., the aggregate of definitions that are created for the self), rather than *social identities* (i.e., aggregates of definitions that are superimposed upon the self; see Baumeister, 1997). However, Henri Tajfel's (1981; Tajfel & Turner, 1986) *social identity theory* incorporated elements of G. W. Allport's (1954/1979) psychology of the individual (and, to a lesser extent, elements of Erikson's [1968/1994] ego psychology), in the process of arguing that *self-esteem* (i.e., individuals' positive versus negative attitude toward themselves; Blascovich & Tomaka, 1991) reflects the joint influence of individuals' personal and social identities (R. Brown, 1986). Thanks largely to Tajfel's efforts, social identity constructs have become increasingly prominent within the literature on the self (for a review, see Swann & Bosson, 2010).

Returning to Erikson's (1959/1980, 1963/1995, 1968/1994) ego psychology, Erikson's progressively sharp focus on *gender identity* and (especially) *ethnic identity* during the 1960s dovetails with the rise of the post-1950s Women's Rights and Civil Rights movements in the United States (see R. Brown, 1986, for a synthesis of the respective literatures on social identities and social movements). On the one hand, research on gender identity – exemplified by Janet Spence and Robert Helmreich's studies of individual differences in *gender-related traits* (e.g., Spence, Helmreich, & Holahan, 1979; Spence, Helmreich, & Stapp, 1974), *gender-role attitudes* (e.g., Spence, Helmreich, & Stapp, 1973), and *gender-role compliance* (e.g., Spence, Helmreich, & Sawin, 1980), among other gender-related constructs – has not always acknowledged the influence of Erikson's ego psychology (see Frable, 1997). On the other hand, research on ethnic identity – exemplified by Jean Phinney's studies of individual differences in *exploration* (i.e., individuals' thoughts about their ethnic groups) and *commitment* (i.e., individuals' feelings about their ethnic groups; e.g., Phinney, 1992; Phinney & Ong, 2007; R. Roberts et al., 1999) – clearly was influenced by Erikson's ego psychology, as interpreted by James Marcia (1966, 1967).

With respect to aspects of individuals' ethnic identity, Erving Goffman's (1963) *interactionist role theory* (see also Goffman, 1959) drew upon Erikson's ego psychology (without citing any specific writings by Erikson) in distinguishing among *racial*, *religious*, and *national identities* (referring to race-based, faith-based, and state-based social identities, respectively; see Verkuyten, 2005). In turn, Stanley Gaines and colleagues (Gaines, Marelich, Bunce, Robertson, & Wright, 2013) acknowledged the influence of Erikson's (1959/1980, 1963/1995, 1968/1994) ego psychology, as well as Goffman's interactionist role theory, on their research concerning individual differences in racial, religious, and national identities. Conceptually speaking, Gaines (2012) has devoted special attention to minority group members' racial identity, which might be influenced by intergroup processes, such as social perceivers' expressions of stereotyping, prejudice, and discrimination (see also Fiske, 1998).

Finally, among aspects of individuals' racial identity, Gaines and Reed (1994, 1995; Reed & Gaines, 1997) emphasised *Black identity* (i.e., African-descent persons' psychological attachment toward their racial group; Gaines, 2012) as an especially important type of racial identity within the United States (and, arguably, throughout various Western nations). Drawing upon Gaines and Reed's writings, Roberts Sellers and colleagues (Sellers, Smith, Shelton, Rowley, & Chavous, 1998) proposed a *multidimensional model of African American identity* (including *racial centrality*, *racial ideology*, *racial regard*, and *racial salience* as components). Furthermore, Sellers and colleagues (Sellers, Rowley, Chavous, Shelton, & Smith, 1997) conducted research on individual differences in three of the four components of African American identity (i.e., racial centrality, racial ideology, and racial regard).

Before leaving the topic of important, but not-yet-core, constructs in personality psychology, we note that — in and of themselves — gender and ethnic group memberships are *not* personality constructs. If one were to focus exclusively on individuals' birth sex and race (as was common in "differential psychology" during the early twentieth century; for reviews, see Markus, 2008; Unger, 1979), then one might argue that certain elements of gender and ethnicity comprise part of individuals' material selves (which, in turn, comprise part of the empirical Me or proprium; G. W. Allport, 1955; James, 1890/2010). However, if one were to broaden one's conception of gender and ethnicity beyond individuals' birth, sex and race (e.g., Frable, 1997; Howard, 2000), then one might contend that some elements of gender and ethnicity comprise part of individuals' social selves (which likewise comprise part of the empirical Me/proprium). In any event, gender and ethnic group memberships *per se* are best regarded as influences on (but not equivalent to) individuals' gender and ethnic identities, respectively (Swann & Bosson, 2010). In addition, gender and ethnic group memberships are linked to achievement-related motives (e.g., Helmreich & Spence, 1978) and cultural values (e.g., Gaines et al., 1997a), in that order.

PRELUDE TO CHAPTER 2

Perhaps no other school of thought has stimulated as much popular curiosity outside personality psychology, or generated as much scholarly controversy within personality psychology, as has the psychodynamic school (which we defined earlier in the present chapter).

Representative theories include (in order of appearance) the psycho-analytic theory of Sigmund Freud (1900/1965), which evolved from S. Freud's earlier work with Josef Breuer (e.g., Breuer & S. Freud, [1895/1995]; the analytical psychology of Carl Jung [1912/1916]; the individual psychology of Alfred Adler [1927/1957]); the "social-psychological" personality theories of Karen Horney (1922–37/1966), Harry Stack Sullivan (1953), Erich Fromm (1941), and Wilhelm Reich (1933/1980); the ego psychology theories of Anna Freud (1936/1966), Heinz Hartmann (1939), David Rapaport (1960), and Erik Erikson (1950); the object relations theories of Melanie Klein (1927), Donald Winnicott (1931), Ronald Fairbairn (1952), and Harry Guntrip (1969), as well as the attachment theory of John Bowlby (1969/1997); the "return-to-Freud" psychoanalytic theory of Jacques Lacan (1966/1977); the self-psychology theories of Heinz Kohut (1971) and Otto Kernberg (1967), neither of which should be confused with the aforementioned self-theory of James (1890/2010); and the personology of Henry Murray (1938). In Chapter 2, we shall examine psychodynamic theories, as well as research that addresses those theories.

CLASSIC SCHOOLS OF THOUGHT I

PSYCHODYNAMIC PERSPECTIVES ON PERSONALITY

In Chapter 1 of the present book, we learned that William James's (1890/2010) self-theory addresses individuals' consciously experienced mental lives in detail. As it turns out, James also was interested in aspects of individuals' *sub*conscious mental lives (Taylor, 1999). Nevertheless, James's self-theory generally is regarded as a theory of consciousness (Poll & Smith, 2003). In fact, one of the best-known post-Jamesian theories of the self – namely, William Swann's (1983) *self-verification theory* – is based on the assumption that individuals are not only aware of their own self-conceptions but prefer to maintain social and personal relationships with other persons who affirm those self-conceptions, even if those self-conceptions are negative (a prime example of the *Consistency Seeker* mode or metaphor of self-perception, whereby individuals presumably are motivated to seek information that is compatible with prior beliefs about themselves; Robins & John, 1997).

Compared to James's (1890) self-theory, psychodynamic theories historically have tended to prioritise *unconscious* (i.e., not readily accessible via consciousness, and possibly inaccessible) aspects of personality (Poll & Smith, 2003). Early psychodynamic theorists, such as Josef Breuer and his then-protégé, Sigmund Freud, promoted a "talking cure" that was meant to bring about catharsis or emotional release (e.g., Breuer & Freud, 1895/1995) in a manner that James's cognitively orientated psychotherapy was not originally intended to accomplish (Taylor, 1999). Despite Breuer's role as a founder of the psychodynamic school in personality psychology, Sigmund Freud eventually became world-renowned as the standard bearer of the psychodynamic school of thought and the closely associated therapeutic method of psychoanalysis (which involved confronting clients with their own unwanted motives, rather than releasing pent-up emotions *per se*; Tauvon, 2001).

In the present, "super-sized" chapter, we will review more than a dozen psychodynamic theories that owe an intellectual debt to Breuer's (e.g., Breuer & Freud, 1895/1995) original conceptualisation and application of the "talking cure" (see Millon, 1996). Also, we will examine the rise of feminist critiques against the psychodynamic school during the 1960s-era Women's Rights Movement in the United States and elsewhere, especially targeting the "masculine psychology" of Freud (1900/1965; see Stevens, 2008). Finally, we will consider attempts to reconcile feminism with psychodynamic perspectives from the 1970s onward (Walsh, Teo, & Baydala, 2014).

[*NOTE*: Some of the terminology in the present chapter might be objectionable to some readers, especially under-18 readers. Especially when we cover Sigmund Freud's (1900/1965) version of psychoanalytic theory, we will encounter certain sexually charged terms. The author apologises in advance for any discomfort that readers might experience when such terms appear in the text.]

BASIC ASSUMPTIONS UNDERLYING PSYCHODYNAMIC PERSPECTIVES

According to psychodynamic perspectives on personality, *motives* (essentially, individuals' answer to the question, "What drives you to do what you do?" – with the caveat that individuals might not be able to answer that question; Gaines, 2016/2018) are stable, unconsciously experienced aspects of personality that may be expressed in different behaviours across different individuals (McClelland, 1985/1987). Exactly *which* motives are the central drivers of individuals' behaviour is a matter of debate among psychodynamic theorists (Ewen, 1998). However, with the notable exception of Henry Murray (developer of a theory in 1938, known as "personology"; Hall & Lindzey, 1957), psychodynamic theorists generally agree that motives are highly similar across individuals (Millon, 1996).

Most (but not all) of the psychodynamic theorists whom we cover in the present chapter were practising psychotherapists (having been trained in the technique of psychoanalysis, even though most of those theorists eventually rejected the controversial assumption of infant sexuality that was central to the original psychoanalytic theory of Freud, 1900/1965; see Hall & Lindzey, 1957). The dominance of clinical practitioners within the psychodynamic school helped lead to a close identification of personality psychology with "abnormal" (subsequently re-labelled as clinical) psychology during the early part of the twentieth century (see McAdams, 1997). However, during the years that immediately preceded World War II, personologist Henry Murray (1938) championed a research-orientated approach that was credited for promoting studies of motives in a manner that was analogous to Gordon Allport's (1937/1951) advocacy of research on traits (Ewen, 1998).

During the course of the twentieth century, the psychodynamic school split into various factions (for a review, see Millon, 1996). For example, Sigmund Freud's (1900/1965) original (and sometimes labelled as "orthodox") version of psychoanalytic theory faced early challenges from two of S. Freud's most prominent former students – namely, Carl Jung's (1912/1916) analytical psychology and Alfred Adler's (1927/1957) individual psychology (not to be confused with Gordon Allport's [1937/1951] psychology of the individual). In turn, Adler's individual psychology inspired challenges from more socially orientated theories by three onetime followers – namely, Karen Horney's (1922-37/1966) feminine psychology, Harry Stack Sullivan's (1953) interpersonal theory, and Erich Fromm's (1941) didactic humanism (the character analysis of Wilhelm Reich [1933/1980] is also socially orientated but is not typically viewed as bearing Adler's influence; see Stevens, 2008). Meanwhile, Anna Freud (1936/1966) – Sigmund Freud's daughter – led a subschool of ego psychologists (including Heinz Hartmann,

1939; David Rapaport, 1960; and Erik Erikson, 1950) who retained many elements of orthodox psychoanalytic theory but highlighted the importance of the ego – rather than the id – to personality and social development. In a direct challenge to Anna Freud and other ego psychologists, Melanie Klein (1927) led a rival subschool of object relations theorists (including Donald Winnicott, 1931; Ronald Fairbairn, 1952; and Harry Guntrip, 1969; as well as John Bowlby, who developed a competing perspective that became known as attachment theory, 1969/1997). Finally, additional perspectives such as Jacques Lacan's (1966/1977) version of psychoanalytic theory, Heinz Kohut's (1971) and Otto Kernberg's (1967) versions of self-psychology, and Henry Murray's (1938) personology were quite distinct from each other but remain recognisable as psychodynamic perspectives on personality.

THE "BIG THREE" PSYCHODYNAMIC THEORIES

SIGMUND FREUD'S VERSION OF PSYCHOANALYTIC THEORY

Hoping to do for the then-fledgling science of psychology what Charles Darwin's (1859) theory of natural selection had done for the better-established science of biology, Sigmund Freud (1900/1965) developed the original version of *psychoanalytic theory*, which proposes that humans' behaviour – like the behaviour of (other) animals – is determined largely by the three "master motives" of sex, aggression and anxiety reduction (McClelland, 1985/1987). S. Freud believed that all motives reside within the *id*, which is present at birth and is an entirely unconscious component of individuals' personality structure (Ewen, 1998). From approximately one to three years of age, according to S. Freud, the *ego* (essentially, the "I" or subjective self in the self-theory of James, 1980/2010) emerges from the id and begins to act on behalf of the id, extending across the unconscious, preconscious and consciousness (and, thus, protecting individuals from fully comprehending the role of motives in their own behaviour; Schellenberg, 1978). Finally, from approximately three to five years of age, the *superego* arises from the ego, similarly extending across the unconscious, preconscious, and consciousness (and, thus, competing with the id for attention from the ego by promoting internalised morality; Hall & Lindzey, 1957).

Following the humanitarian atrocities of World War I, Sigmund Freud (1927) eventually revised his version of psychoanalytic theory so that (1) the sex motive was recast as *eros*, or the "life instinct"; and (2) the aggression motive was recast as *thanatos*, or the "death instinct" (whereas the anxiety-reduction motive was de-emphasised altogether; Ewen, 1998). Nevertheless, S. Freud maintained his belief that all persons possess the same motives and the same personality structure (Hall & Lindzey, 1957). In one of his final, major revisions to psychoanalytic theory, S. Freud (1933/1990) contended that individual *differences* in personality arise from differences in the degree to which one or two components of personality structure (i.e., id, ego, and superego) become dominant over the other component or components (e.g., dominance by the id leads to an *erotic* type; dominance by the ego leads to a *narcissistic* type; and dominance by the superego leads to a *compulsive* type; Millon, 1996).

As Howard Jones (2015) noted, William James's (1980/2010) self-theory had promoted the concept of *free will* (or *Volition*, as James put it), which grants individuals considerable leeway in choosing their own attitudes and setting themselves on a course toward mental health (versus mental illness). In stark contrast to James's self-theory, as Richards (1991) pointed out, Sigmund Freud's (1900/1965) psychoanalytic theory championed the concept of *psychic determinism*, whereby individuals' mental health versus mental illness is *not* amenable to change via individuals' conscious intentions. S. Freud believed that, beyond the age of five or six (an interval during which caregivers possess the capacity to shape individuals' personalities to a substantial degree), individuals' personalities are set in stone for the most part (Schellenberg, 1978).

Freud's (1905/1962) psychoanalytic theory includes a model that identifies five *psychosexual stages* of personality development (summarised in Ewen, 1998, p. 43). First, in the *oral* stage (from birth to approximately 18 months of age), primary erotogenetic zones are the mouth, lips, and tongue (with feeding as the source of conflict); personality characteristics reflecting the enduring influence of the oral stage during adulthood include smoking and eating, as well as passivity and gullibility (and their opposites). Second, during the *anal* stage of psychosexual development (from approximately 1 to 3 years of age), the primary erotogenetic zone is the anus (with toilet training as the source of conflict); personality characteristics reflecting the enduring influence of the anal stage in adulthood include orderliness, parsimoniousness, and obstinacy (and their opposites). Third, during the *urethral* stage (also from approximately 1 to 3 years of age), the primary erotogenetic zone is the urethra (with bedwetting as the source of conflict); personality characteristics reflecting the enduring influence of the urethral stage in adulthood include ambition (and its opposite). Fourth, during the *phallic* stage (from approximately 2 to 5 years of age), the primary erotogenetic zones are the penis and clitoris (with the *Oedipus complex* signifying opposite-sex sexual desires and same-sex aggressive desires in boys, and the *Electra complex* signifying opposite-sex sexual desires and same-sex aggressive desires in girls, as sources of conflict); personality characteristics reflecting the enduring influence of the phallic stage in adulthood include vanity and recklessness (and their opposites). Finally (and following a *latency phase* from approximately 6 to 12 years of age, when no major milestones are experienced in terms of personality development), during the *genital* stage (from adolescence to early adulthood), the primary erotogenetic zones are the penis and vagina (with the inevitable difficulties of life as the sources of conflict); personality characteristics reflecting the enduring influence of the genital stage (the goal of normal development in S. Freud's psychoanalytic theory) include a sincere interest in others, effective sublimations, and realistic enjoyments.

The numerous controversies that surround Sigmund Freud's (1905/1962) psychoanalytic theory are the stuff of legend (Hall & Lindzey, 1957). Consider S. Freud's claim that gay men suffer from "arrested development" (i.e., never progress as far as the genital stage), ostensibly because they experienced such high levels of love and affection from their mothers early in life that they ended up rejecting women in general as potential romantic partners, upon reaching adulthood (see McClelland, 1985/1987). One might think that, by the time that the American Psychiatric Association dropped homosexuality from its list of personality disorders in 1980, followers of S. Freud's psychoanalytic theory would have disavowed the claim about gay men's "arrested development" (see Millon, 1996). However, in a study of 90 gay men (most of whom were recruited from gay bars) and 109 heterosexual men (most of whom were recruited from university classes), Rubinstein (2010a) concluded that gay men scored significantly lower on *self-esteem* (i.e., individuals' realistic evaluation of themselves, whether positive or negative, which we covered in Chapter 1 of the present book) and significantly higher on *narcissism* (i.e., individuals' unrealistically positive evaluation of themselves; Swann & Bosson, 2010) than did heterosexual men – results that seemingly support S. Freud's (1905/1962) claim about gay men's problematic development. Rubinstein's results are tainted by the fact that most of the gay men, but *none* of the heterosexual men, were recruited from bars (e.g., it is not clear whether bar-frequenting heterosexual men would have scored differently from bar-frequenting gay men on measures of self-esteem or narcissism; Drescher, 2010). Interestingly, Rubinstein (2010b) responded to a separate critique (Hartmann, 2010) by proclaiming that he is a "very gay-friendly investigator and therapist" (p. 48) who was expecting *non*significant group differences and who would welcome disconfirming evidence regarding those differences.

Putting aside the issue of "arrested development" as a function of individuals' sexual orientation, for a theory that supposedly is rooted in the biological sciences, Sigmund Freud's (1900/1965) version of psychoanalytic theory is notably deficient (e.g., *libido*, or psychic energy that ostensibly surges through individuals and is popularly associated with id-directed sexual behaviour, currently lacks any basis in empirical fact; Ewen, 1998). However, the contributions of S. Freud's psychoanalytic theory to the *social* sciences are numerous (Schellenberg, 1978). For example, the *authoritarian* or *prejudiced personality* is a construct that Theodor Adorno and colleagues (Adorno, Frenkel-Brunswik, Levinson, & Sanford, 1950) developed on the basis of S. Freud's earlier concept of identification with the aggressor (i.e., in response to aggressive urges toward same-sex parents [as distinct from sexual urges toward opposite-sex parents], individuals are presumed to redirect their aggressive urges toward members of psychological outgroups within a given society; Snyder & Ickes, 1985); in Box 2.1, we will encounter Bob Altemeyer's (1981) Right-Wing Authoritarianism (RWA) Scale, which was influenced by Adorno et al.'s research. Furthermore, later in the present chapter, we will elaborate upon *narcissism* (a construct that also looms as important within the self-psychology theories of Kohut, 1971 and Kernberg, 1967). To put it simply, S. Freud's version of

BOX 2.1 ALTEMEYER'S (1981) RIGHT-WING AUTHORITARIANISM SCALE

As Freeman (2008) pointed out, Adorno et al.'s (1950) *The Authoritarian Personality* deals primarily with traditional Freudian themes, such as the transmission of authoritarianism from fathers to their resentful sons. In order to measure individual differences in the authoritarian personality (also known as the prejudiced personality), Adorno, Frenkel-Brunswik, Levinson and Sanford (1950) developed the 38-item California F (for pre-Fascist tendencies) Scale (Allport, 1954/1979). Results obtained by Adorno, Frenkel-Brunswik, Levinson and Sanford (1950) from a sample of 2000 participants in the United States indicated that scores on the California F Scale tended to be significantly and positively correlated with scores on anti-Semitism, ethnocentrism, and conservatism (Snyder & Ickes, 1985). However, the California F scale was plagued by methodological problems, especially *acquiescence bias* (i.e., a tendency for individuals to answer "Agree" without necessarily reading the content of specific items – a tendency that raises basic questions about construct validity when all of the items in a scale are worded such that "Agree" responses are always interpreted as reflecting high levels of the construct in question; Christie, 1991).

In order to overcome the methodological problems that beset Adorno's (1950) California F Scale, Bob Altemeyer (1981) developed the 30-item Right-Wing Authoritarianism (RWS) Scale that included equal numbers of negatively worded versus positively worded items (see Adair, Paivio, & Ritchie, 1996). Consistent with Adorno et al.'s original conceptualisation of the authoritarian personality, Altemeyer (1998) contended that right-wing authoritarianism reflects a combination of individuals' submission to authority figures and acceptance of conventional norms within a given society (Hewstone, Rubin, & Willis, 2002). Moreover, consistent with Allport's (1954/1979) elaboration regarding the authoritarian or prejudiced personality, Altemeyer (1994) argued that right-wing authoritarianism is expressed via individuals' negative stereotyping and prejudice toward members of socially defined groups who have been stigmatised within that society (Hilton & von Hippel, 1996). Finally, Altemeyer (1988, 1996) found that individuals who score high on right-wing authoritarianism are not only easily threatened but tend to react strongly to perceived threats (Sullivan & Transue, 1999).

Alongside *social dominance orientation* (SDO, or individuals' attitudes toward societal hierarchies that are based on demographic
characteristics such as biological sex, race, and age; Sidanius &
Pratto, 1999), right-wing authoritarianism as operationalised by
Altemeyer has helped to galvanise post-Civil Rights Era research
on intergroup relations (J. Jones, 1997).

psychoanalytic theory stands as the most influential theory of all time
within personality psychology (and, one might argue, across psychology
as a whole; Hall & Lindzey, 1957).

CARL JUNG'S ANALYTICAL PSYCHOLOGY

At one time, Sigmund Freud viewed Carl Jung as the natural successor to lead psychoanalytic theory beyond the early part of the twentieth century (Ewen, 1998). Instead, Jung became the first major
defector from psychoanalytic theory, strongly rejecting S. Freud's
(1900/1965) emphasis on infant sexuality (Hall & Lindzey, 1957).
Afterward, Jung (1912/1916) developed his own *analytic psychology* as
a competing psychodynamic theory of personality (Millon, 1996).
Jung placed less emphasis on S. Freud's "master motives" in general
and hinted at a different, largely unexplored need to fulfil one's
potential; this latter need eventually became known as the *self-
actualisation motive* among proponents of humanistic psychology (see
Chapter 4 of the present book).

In terms of personality structure, Jung's (1912/1916) analytical
psychology retained the constructs of id, ego, and superego from
S. Freud's (1900/1965) psychoanalytic theory, although Jung
renamed the id as the *personal unconscious*; renamed the ego as the *personal conscious*, and renamed the superego as the *persona* or *collective conscious* (Ewen, 1998). Jung's most original contribution to
understanding personality structure was the addition of the *collective
unconscious*, which is a repository of unconsciously experienced
images that all humans share (and, presumably inherit from pre-
human as well as human ancestors; Hall & Lindzey, 1957). The primary individual–difference construct in Jung's analytical psychology is
a de-sexualised version of the libido (e.g., Jung, 1921/1971), which

can flow inward (thereby leading to *introversion*) or outward (thereby leading to *extraversion*) with regard to a particular individual, at a particular point in time (McClelland, 1985/1987).

Like S. Freud's (1900/1965) version of psychoanalytic theory, Jung's (1912/1916) analytical psychology was promoted as a biologically orientated psychodynamic theory – a claim that is at odds with the lack of any empirical evidence that could trace the existence of a "collective unconscious" that supposedly was passed from pre-human species to *Homo sapiens* (Hall & Lindzey, 1957). However, Jung's (1921/1971) construct of introversion versus extraversion survives intact as part of a personality typology that is measured via the huge popular Myers-Briggs Type Indicator (MBTI; I. B. Myers, 1962), and in greatly modified form as one of a relatively small number of major traits that are consistently measured by various comprehensive questionnaires (as we will see in Chapter 5). All things considered, Jung's analytical psychology may be regarded as second only to S. Freud's psychoanalytic theory in terms of influence within personality psychology (Ewen, 1998).

ALFRED ADLER'S INDIVIDUAL PSYCHOLOGY

Like Carl Jung, Alfred Adler initially was a follower of Sigmund Freud's (1900/1965) psychoanalytic theory and rebelled against S. Freud's insistence that human beings act primarily on the basis of sexual urges from birth onward (Millon, 1996). However, Adler's (1925) *individual psychology* differs from Jung's analytical psychology *and* S. Freud's psychoanalytic theory by focusing less on the structure of personality (id, ego, and superego in Jung's and S. Freud's theories; and collective unconscious in Jung's theory), and more on the indivisibility of the individual's psyche (Ewen, 1998). Nevertheless, one can detect influences of Jung's and S. Freud's theories on Adler's theory (e.g., *complexes*, or combinations of unconsciously experienced images that are unique to the id of each individual; and *motives*, or unconsciously experienced psychological needs that exist within the id of all individuals; Hall & Lindzey, 1957).

Adler's (1925) individual psychology initially proposed that S. Freud's (1900/1965) psychoanalytic theory had placed too little emphasis upon the *aggression* motive (i.e., a need to inflict physical and/or psychological harm to other persons), relative to the *sex* motive (i.e., a need to become physically intimate with other persons; see McClelland, 1985/1987). Subsequently, Adler himself de-emphasised the aggression motive and shifted his attention toward the *power* motive (i.e., a need to exert influence over other persons; Ansbacher, 1978). Finally, Adler de-emphasised the power motive in favour of a *social interest* motive (i.e., a need to act on behalf of the common good; P. R. Peluso, J. P. Peluso, J. White, & Kern, 2004) that presumably was the "master motive" for all human beings at birth. Interestingly, Adler believed that individuals' experiences with caregivers from birth until approximately the age of five or six determined whether individuals' need for social interest would remain high or would wane by adulthood (Ansbacher, 1988).

Adler (1935) proposed a personality typology of "styles of life", based on individuals' combination of need for social interest and activity level by adulthood (Massey, 1988) – a typology that has not been very influential within personality psychology (despite attempts to measure styles of life via surveys by a few of Adler's followers; e.g., Curlette, Kern, & Wheeler, 1996; Wheeler, Kern, & Curlette, 1986). Nevertheless, Adler's (1932) individual psychology *did* popularise the concepts of *inferiority* and *superiority* complexes via his writings on the presumed effects of birth order on individuals' personality characteristics (Ewen, 1998). In turn, those complexes were central to Adler's "styles of life" typology (i.e., a *ruling* type was characterised by a superiority complex; *getting* and *avoiding* types were characterised by an inferiority complex; and an especially adaptive, *socially useful* type was not characterised by any particular complex; Massey, 1988). All in all, Adler's (1925) individual psychology is widely regarded as a pivotal theory that paved the way for even more overtly "social-psychological" personality theories within the psychodynamic school (Hall & Lindzey, 1957).

"SOCIAL-PSYCHOLOGICAL" PSYCHODYNAMIC THEORIES

KAREN HORNEY'S FEMININE PSYCHOLOGY

At a time when Sigmund Freud (1923/1927) was writing about women's supposedly arrested development in terms of personality (e.g., unable to progress to the "genital" or highest stage of psychosexual development), Adler (1927/1957) was championing women's rights, such as the right to vote (Ewen, 1998). Furthermore, Adler developed the concept of *masculine protest* to refer to women's (as well as men's) questioning of societal roles and stereotypes that deem women inferior to men (Bitter, Robertson, Healey, & Cole, 2009). Building upon (yet expanding beyond) Adler's concept of masculine protest, Karen Horney (1922-37/ 1966) developed her theory of *feminine psychology* as a direct challenge to S. Freud's "masculine psychology" (i.e., psychoanalytic theory; Hirsch, 2005).

Early in her 1922–37 lecture series, Horney did not dispute Sigmund Freud's (1923/1927) controversial contention that women suffer from "penis envy" – though Horney argued that, conversely, men suffer from "womb envy" (O'Connell, 1980). However, later in her 1922–37 lecture series, Horney rejected S. Freud's "anatomy is destiny" argument concerning gender and personality, eventually embracing the view that *societal discrimination* (rather than biology) was the cause of those psychological difficulties that women might experience to a greater degree than did men (Hall & Lindzey, 1970). Over time, Horney (1937) developed a typology of responses to interpersonal anxiety (i.e., *moving toward others*, resulting in a "compliant" type; *moving against others*, resulting in an "aggressive" type; and *moving away from others*, resulting in a "detached" type; Ewen, 1998) that presumably varied by gender as a function of societal influences (i.e., women were steered in the direction of moving toward others to a greater extent than were men; whereas men were steered in the directions of moving against others and moving away from others to a greater extent than were women; Rendon, 2008).

Despite the intuitive appeal of Horney's (1937) typology of neurotic responses to interpersonal anxiety, no single, agreed-upon measure of those constructs has emerged within personality psychology (although some of Horney's followers have tried to develop such a survey; e.g., Coolidge, Moor, Yamazaki, S. E. Stewart, & Segal, 2001). However, as the Women's Rights Movement gained momentum within the United States and elsewhere during the late 1960s, Horney's 1922–37 lecture series was (re)published as the book, *Feminine Psychology*, in 1967 (Hall & Lindzey, 1970). In turn, as Sandra Bem (1994) pointed out, that book helped inspire a re-evaluation of the way that gender-related traits were conceptualised and measured within personality psychology (most obviously in the development of the Bem Sex Role Inventory and gender schema theory by Bem, 1974, 1981; for details regarding S. Bem's work, see Chapter 5 of the present book). Taken as a whole, Horney's theory of feminine psychology was decades ahead of its time in its full-throated affirmation of the basic dignity of human beings, whether male or female (Ewen, 1998).

HARRY STACK SULLIVAN'S INTERPERSONAL THEORY

Like Horney's (1922-37/1966) feminine psychology, Harry Stack Sullivan's (1953) posthumously published *interpersonal theory* highlights the importance of the *anxiety-reduction* motive to a greater degree than do any of the "Big Three" psychodynamic theories (i.e., the psychoanalytic theory of S. Freud, 1900/1965; the analytical psychology of Jung, 1912/1916; and the individual psychology of Adler; 1927/1957; see McClelland, 1985/1987). Moreover, both Horney's feminine psychology and H. S. Sullivan's interpersonal theory cast anxiety as inherently *inter*personal (rather than *intra*personal, as was the case in S. Freud's psychoanalytic theory; Hall & Lindzey, 1970). However, Horney (1937) was more concerned about the implications of interpersonal anxiety for feelings of helplessness and danger; whereas H. S. Sullivan (1954) was more concerned about the implications of interpersonal anxiety for loss of self-esteem (Zerbe, 1990).

According to H. S. Sullivan's (1953) interpersonal theory, all individuals possess a need for *interpersonal intimacy* – a multifaceted need that is emotionally focussed at birth but eventually acquires a sexual dimension as well, once individuals embark on their developmental journey into adolescence (Hall & Lindzey, 1970). However, given that other persons serve as the primary sources of anxiety in individuals' lives, an especially adaptive process regarding humans' personality development is the emergence of the *self-system* (a structure that serves to reduce anxiety, not unlike the function of the ego in the psychoanalytic theory of S. Freud, 1900/1965; see Westen, 1992). Ideally, the self-system should enable individuals to distinguish among *good-me* (i.e., individuals' acknowledgement of their own socially desirable personality characteristics), *bad-me* (i.e., individuals' acknowledgement of their own socially undesirable personality characteristics), and *not-me* (individuals' acknowledgement of those personality characteristics that they do not possess; Ewen, 1998). However, in practical terms, the self-system might fail to distinguish between bad-me and not-me, thus making it difficult for individuals to identify those aspects of their personalities and corresponding social behaviour that could benefit from therapeutic intervention (Sullivan, 1954).

Based on his observations of clients in psychotherapy, H. S. Sullivan (1947/1966) developed a list of ten maladaptive personality types (i.e., *nonintegrative, self-absorbed, incorrigible, negativistic, stammering, ambition-ridden, asocial, inadequate, homosexual,* and *clinically adolescent*) – a list that never attracted much attention within personality psychology (in retrospect, the seemingly arbitrary inclusion of gay men, lesbians, and stutterers within a list of adaptive *or* maladapative types was not just "politically" incorrect, but also *scientifically* incorrect; Millon, 1996). Nevertheless, H. S. Sullivan's (1953) fundamental premise that all types of personality is inherently interpersonal (Hall & Lindzey, 1970) served as the primary inspiration for a circular or circumplex model of interpersonal traits in particular (Leary, 1957) and an interpersonal circumplex theory of personality in general (Wiggins, 1991) that we will examine further in Chapter 5 of the present book. All in all, not only did H. S. Sullivan specifically advocate the establishment of a science of interpersonal relations that would draw upon psychiatry and social psychology; but H. S. Sullivan's interpersonal theory arguably provides a comprehensive framework for conducting programmatic research on personality and close relationship processes within such a science (Gaines, 2007a, 2007b).

ERICH FROMM'S DIDACTIC HUMANISM

As we have seen, among two of the major neo-Adlerian personality theories – namely, Karen Horney's (1923-37/1966, 1937) feminine psychology and Harry Stack Sullivan's (1953, 1954) interpersonal theory – the inherently interpersonal nature of anxiety was a major theme. As it turns out, Erich Fromm's (1941,

1957) *didactic humanism* was yet another neo-Adlerian, "social-psychological" personality theory that focused on the interpersonal basis of anxiety (C. S. Hall & Lindzey, 1970). However, as T. Leary (1957) noted, Fromm's didactic humanism is unique in that it deals especially with the implications of interpersonal anxiety for individuals' experience of isolation and weakness.

The dual themes of *anxiety* and *alienation* are evident in Erich Fromm's (1941) didactic humanism, reflecting the joint influence of Sigmund Freud's (1900/1965) theory of psychoanalysis and Karl Marx's (1932/1990) theory of alienation upon Fromm's theory (McLaughlin, 1998b). According to Fromm, all individuals eventually experience aloneness – not only with regard to their social environment (i.e. other people), but also with regard to their physical environment (i.e., nature; Mann, 2000). In turn, Fromm's didactic humanism proposes that individuals ultimately develop one or more *escape mechanisms* (akin to defence mechanisms in the psychoanalytic theory of S. Freud (1900/1965); for details regarding defence mechanisms, see the upcoming section on the ego psychology of Anna Freud, 1936/1966, in the present chapter) for dealing with aloneness (Hall & Lindzey, 1970). Fromm's escape mechanisms include *authoritarianism, malignant aggression*, and *automaton conformity*; authoritarianism is the best-known example of the escape mechanisms (serving as the impetus for Fromm's ground-breaking, yet initially unpublished, pre-World War II-era qualitative research on the authoritarian personality; McLaughlin, 1999).

As McLaughlin (1998a) noted, Fromm's (1941, 1957) didactic humanism was rejected on ideological grounds by some psychologists during and after World War II, due to Fromm's overt embrace of Marxist philosophy. However, G. W. Allport (1954/1979) praised Fromm's didactic humanism for its attention to the role that societies can play in shaping the development of authoritarian (i.e., prejudiced) versus tolerant (i.e., unprejudiced) personalities (e.g., by engaging versus refusing to engage in scapegoating toward members of socially devalued groups). All in all, despite the lack of acknowledgement in some circles (e.g., Adorno, Frenkel-Brunswik, Levinson, & Sanford, 1950), Fromm's theory of didactic humanism and research on authoritarianism set the stage for an explosion of interest in the authoritarian personality throughout personality and social psychology after World War II (Christie, 1991).

WILHELM REICH'S CHARACTER ANALYSIS

We have already seen that Karen Horney's (1922-37/1966) feminine psychology and Erich Fromm's (1941) didactic humanism questioned the premise (which one finds in the psychoanalytic theory of Sigmund Freud, 1900) that society inevitably exerts a constructive influence on individuals' personality development (as a counterpoint to individuals' own motives as destructive influences; Hall & Lindzey, 1957). If one looks closely, then one will notice that Harry Stack Sullivan's (1953) interpersonal theory also questioned the assumption that society invariably plays a constructive role in individuals' personality development (particularly within the content of intergroup relations; Ewen, 1998). However, Wilhelm Reich's (1933/1980) *character analysis* goes beyond the other "social-psychological" psychodynamic theories in detailing the potentially *destructive* effects of society on personality development (Shapiro, 2002).

According to Reich's (1933/1980) character analysis, internally generated sexual tensions and externally generated political and economic inequalities can combine to produce a rigid *muscular armour* (i.e., a constricted manner in which individuals move their bodies, as if constantly preparing for "fight or flight"; Walsh, Teo, & Baydala, 2014). Reich controversially proposed that the development of muscular armour prevented individuals from releasing their *orgone* (a sexualised type of bodily energy, somewhat akin to *libido* as originally described by S. Freud, 1908/1925) – a condition that ostensibly required clinical intervention via massage therapy, if not overt sexual therapy (Stevens, 2008). Even Sigmund Freud's sexually orientated psychoanalytic theory never advocated such direct physical contact between clinicians and clients (see Klee, 2005). In fact, Reich's character analysis was so far outside the mainstream of psychodynamic theories (let alone practices) that one might reasonably question Reich's sanity (Pietikainen, 2002).

Reich's (1933/1980) character analysis has been lambasted as thoroughly unscientific (e.g., lacking a basis for disconfirmable hypotheses), even when compared with other psychodynamic theories (Stevens, 2008). However, Reich's character analysis is strongly reflected in the concepts of *oral*, *anal*, and *phallic characters* (corresponding to three of the four pre-genital stages on the psycho-sexual development model of S. Freud, 1908/1925) that are generally associated with Sigmund Freud's version of psychoanalytic theory (Millon, 1996). Moreover, Walsh and colleagues (Walsh, Teo, & Baydala, 2014) regarded Reich's character analysis as a political-economic theory that rivalled Fromm's (1941) didactic humanism or "social-political theory" in the degree to which it fused Marxist and (Sigmund) Freudian principles together.

EGO PSYCHOLOGY THEORIES

ANNA FREUD'S VERSION OF EGO PSYCHOLOGY

According to Sigmund Freud's (1923/1927) psychoanalytic theory, in the process of navigating between (1) the id's promotion of sexual and aggressive urges toward parents and (2) the superego's prohib-ition against those same urges toward parents, the ego typically employs one or more *defence mechanisms* to try and reduce individuals' anxiety (Tauvon, 2001). S. Freud focused primarily on the defence mechanism of *repression*, or the ego's attempts to banish unwanted sexual and aggressive urges from consciousness (Baumeister, Dale, & Sommer, 1998). However, S. Freud mentioned several additional defence mechanisms in his writings, without attempting to provide a single, comprehensive list (even though repression appeared to be insufficient to manage anxiety on its own; Carlin, 2010). Fortunately, for psychodynamic theorists and practitioners, Anna Freud (1936/1966) brought together all of the defence mechanisms from S. Freud's varied writings into one coherent list, as part of A. Freud's *ego psychology* (Kernberg, 1994).

Unlike Sigmund Freud's (1923/1927) psychoanalytic theory, Anna Freud's (1936/1966) ego psychology depicted the ego as highly competent in navigating intrapersonal conflicts that involved conflicting messages from the id and the superego (Millon, 1996). Anna Freud's initial list of defence mechanisms employed by the ego included (1) *denial*, (2) *displacement*, (3) *intellectualisation*, (4) *projection*, (5) *rationalisation*, (6) *reaction formation*, (7) *regression*, (8) *repression*, and (9) *suppression*; A. Freud subsequently added (10) *sublimation*, (11) *identification with the aggressor*, and (12) *altruism* (the latter three of which S. Freud had not explored in detail, P. F. Kernberg, 1994). Westen and Chang (2000) pointed out that A. Freud (1958) was especially concerned with the defence mechanisms that individuals use during adolescence, which is a time of sexual awakening.

Notwithstanding Anna Freud's (1936/1966) efforts toward documenting all of the ways that the ego might reduce (and, perhaps, eliminate) individuals' intrapersonal anxiety, no single, agreed-upon survey exists that could measure most (if not all) of the defence mechanisms (although a small number of A. Freud's followers have attempted to do so; e.g., Joffe & Naditch, 1977). However, to the extent that the relatively new field of neuropsychoanalysis has revived academicians' and practitioners' interest in defence mechanisms (including, but not limited to, repression; Boag, 2006), the measurement of A. Freud's complete list of defence mechanisms remains a worthy conceptual and empirical goal within the psychodynamic school of personality psychology (see Davison & MacGregor, 1998). In summary, A. Freud's ego psychology functions as a viable alternative to "id psychology" (i.e., the psychoanalytic theory of S. Freud, 1900/1965) without requiring a full-scale rejection of S. Freud's core constructs (Millon, 1996).

HEINZ HARTMANN'S VERSION OF EGO PSYCHOLOGY

By definition, Anna Freud's (1936/1966) version of ego psychology is defensive in its orientation (i.e., focussed on the means by which the ego manages individuals' intrapersonal conflict; Kernberg, 1994). Comparatively speaking, Heinz Hartmann's (1939) version of *ego psychology* is more adaptive in its orientation (i.e., focussed on the degree to which the ego operates autonomously from the id and ego, within a conflict-free sphere; Wallerstein, 2002). Furthermore, in H. Hartmann's version of ego psychology, the ego is present at birth (rather than emerging from the id at 1–3 years of age) and possess adaptive abilities (e.g., adapting to internal as well as external reality; Redfearn, 1983).

According to H. Hartmann's (1939) version of ego psychology, various *conflict-free capacities* (e.g., visual perception, memory, motor coordination, language, skills, talents) eventually develop into *ego functions* that operate independently from the id drives of eros and thanatos (Danzer, 2012). This is not to say that ego functions necessarily are entirely disconnected from id drives; it is possible for id drives to create intrapersonal conflict by disrupting the normal development of ego functions (Blatt & Auerbach, 2000). Nevertheless, given that ego functions are shaped partly by biological maturation and partly by social (i.e., cultural and family) influences in H. Hartmann's ego psychology, constructive social influences may counteract negative biological (e.g., id-based) influences on ego-function development (Gammelgaard, 2003). In turn, entire societies can play a role in directing constructive social influences on individuals' ego-function development (Mitchell & Harris, 2004).

Unlike the other psychodynamic theories that we have encountered so far, H. Hartmann's (1939) version of ego psychology has stimulated little (if any) empirical research on personality constructs (see Millon, 1996). However, Dixon-Gordon and colleagues (Dixon-Gordon, Turner, & Chapman, 2011) pointed out that *brief adaptive psychotherapy* (a short-term, insight-based form of therapy) is based on H. Hartmann's ego psychology (especially drawing upon H. Hartmann's concept of adaptation). On a related note, results of a study by Winston et al. (1994) indicated that brief adaptive psychotherapy yielded significantly greater social adjustment and a significant reduction in clients' psychological symptoms, compared to clients' waiting for (but not yet receiving) any type of treatment. Overall, Karasu (2001) concluded that psychotherapy in the tradition of H. Hartmann's (1939) version of ego psychology can aid individuals (1) by bolstering individuals' ego strength and (2) by bolstering individuals' adaptation to internal and external reality − a clear set of contributions to the psychodynamic school, and to personality psychology as a whole.

DAVID RAPAPORT'S VERSION OF EGO PSYCHOLOGY

Initially, David Rapaport was known largely for his translation of Heinz Hartmann's *Ego Psychology and the Problem of Adaptation* (1939) from German to English, in 1958. Rapaport shared H. Hartmann's goal of developing an ego psychology theory that would serve as the conceptual framework for a general, comprehensive science of human behaviour (Kleiger, 1993). Eventually, Rapaport (1960) developed his own version of *ego psychology*, incorporating elements of cognitive as well as psychodynamic theories of personality (Holt, 2005).

Schafer (1999) pointed out that Rapaport's (1960) version of ego psychology was reflected in Rapaport's approach to psychological testing, which focused on implications of test results for understanding clients' various ego functions (e.g., memory, perception). For example, prior to Rapaport's methodological innovations, psychodynamically orientated clinicians frequently relied on a single test – namely, the Rorschach Inkblot Test (Rorschach, 1924) – as a *projective* (i.e., indirect) means toward diagnosing individuals' personality disorders (especially as reflecting the influence of motives that presumably reside within the id; see Millon, 1996). However, Rapaport and colleagues (Rapaport, Gill, & Schafer, 1945) introduced a series of tests – both *objective* (i.e., direct) and projective – to diagnose individuals' faulty cognitive processes (presumably arising from the ego) as well as personality disorders (Marcus, 1999). By the mid-to-late 1980s, the resulting "Rapaport Method" had become the standard test battery in psychiatric hospital settings (Sweeney, Clarkin, & Fitzgibbon, 1987).

Kleiger (1993) noted that the "Rapaport Method" (Rapaport, Gill, & Schafer, 1945) influenced John Exner's development of his own method, the Comprehensive Rorschach System (1986) – a method that, ironically, has overtaken the "Rapaport Method" in popularity among clinical psychologists. Interestingly, in a small-scale study within the United States, Blais and colleagues (Blais, Norman, Quintar, & Herzog, 1995) found that the "Rapaport Method" and the "Exner Method" produce different diagnoses of clients, despite the similarity in much of the Rorschach (1924) material that is contained within the two methods. Nevertheless, the Rapaport system is distinguished by its compatibility with a strong theory (i.e., the ego psychology of Rapaport, 1960) – a testament to the conceptual and methodological sophistication of Rapaport's work (Sugarman & Kanner, 2000).

ERIK ERIKSON'S VERSION OF EGO PSYCHOLOGY

Like Heinz Hartmann (1939), Erik Erikson (1950) created a version of *ego psychology* that emphasised ego development as occurring in a more adaptive manner than Anna Freud (1936/1966) had assumed

(Danzer, 2012). In addition, like H. Hartmann's earlier version, Erikson's version of ego psychology addressed direct societal influences on individuals' ego development (rather than indirect influences via the superego), to a greater extent than Anna Freud's earlier version of ego psychology had done (Millon, 1996). However, unlike H. Hartmann's earlier version, Erikson's version of ego psychology explicitly promoted a *lifespan approach* to ego development, emphasising individuals' potential for psychological growth throughout their lives (Ewen, 1998).

Atalay (2007) contended that Erikson's (1950) version of ego psychology can be considered a "psychology of crisis", because it proposes that individuals either succeed or fail at resolving specific crises during each of Erikson's "Eight Stages of Man". Capps (2012) added that, in a refinement of the "(St)ages of Man", Erikson (1959/1980) identified eight *virtues* or sets of character strengths that emerge from individuals' successful crisis resolution: (1) *Hope* (ideally, during individuals' infancy), (2) *will* (preschool age), (3) *purpose* (elementary school age), (4) *competence* (secondary school age), (5) *fidelity* (adolescence), (6) *love* (young adulthood), (7) *care* (middle adulthood), and (8) *wisdom* (elderly adulthood). Constantinople (1969) devised the 60-item Inventory of Psychosocial Development to measure individual differences in success (5 items) versus failure (5 items) in resolving the first six psychosocial conflicts (i.e., *establishing interpersonal trust, establishing self-control, making further strides toward independence, adjustment to schoolteachers' demands, establishing a sense of who they are as unique persons* [i.e., *identity*], and *establishing a sense of who they are in relation to significant others*) that Erikson (1950) had proposed; subsequently, Whitbourne and Waterman (1979) expanded Constantinople's Inventory of Psychosocial Development to 80 items, adding success versus failure in resolving the final two conflicts (i.e., *mature enactment of societal roles that require caring for other persons,* and *achieving a sense of peace and tranquillity concerning previous successes and failures throughout life*; Ewen, 1998).

Results of the aforementioned studies by Constantinople (1969) and Whitbourne and Waterman (1979) – which were conducted on the same set of participants, ten years apart – revealed that Erikson's (1950) model concerning individuals' progression through the eight stages of psychosocial development was supported for men, but not for women (Ewen, 1998). However, both studies yielded individual differences in crisis resolution at each stage (regardless of gender) as Erikson would have predicted, leading Whitbourne and Waterman (1979) to conclude that crisis resolution was influenced by societal change (as distinct from biological maturation) to a greater degree among women than was the case among men. Furthermore, as we noted in Chapter 1 of the present book, research on *ethnic identity* – a particular aspect of identity that Erikson (1968/1994) discussed at length – has blossomed since the early 1990s (Frable, 1997). When one considers the levels of interest that many cultural psychologists have displayed toward Erikson's construct of ethnic identity as operationalised via the Multigroup Ethnic Identity Measure (MEIM) by Phinney (1992; see Chapter 1 of the present book) and via the Ethnic Identity Scale (EIS) by Umana-Taylor and colleagues (Umana-Taylor, Yazedijan, & Bamaca-Gomez, 2004; see Box 2.2 of the present chapter), one realises that Erikson's (1968/1994) ego psychology remains highly relevant to contemporary psychology, outside as well as within personality psychology (see Umana-Taylor, 2012).

OBJECT RELATIONS AND ATTACHMENT THEORIES

MELANIE KLEIN'S VERSION OF OBJECT RELATIONS THEORY

So far, every psychodynamic theory that we have reviewed in the wake of Sigmund Freud's version of psychoanalytic theory has rejected S. Freud's (1900/1965) initial premise that sexuality was the primary motive underlying infants' behaviour toward their mothers. Melanie Klein's (1927) version of *object relations theory* continues the trend away from an emphasis on infant sexuality, focusing on the quality of the mother-offspring relationship (whereby the mother usually is the "object" of the offspring's emotions, and the pattern of interaction that develops between the mother and the offspring over time constitutes "relations"; Lubbe, 2008). According to Klein's object relations theory, the mother can simultaneously be the target of her offspring's love, *and* the target of her offspring's hate (with love and hate present in infants at birth; Debbane, 2011). One recurrent (albeit controversial) theme that one might detect from individuals' from childhood to

BOX 2.2 UMANA-TAYLOR ET AL.'S (2004) ETHNIC IDENTITY SCALE

In Chapter 1 of the present book, we learned that Jean Phinney and colleagues (Phinney, 1992; Phinney & Ong, 2007; Roberts et al., 1999) drew heavily upon Erikson's (1959/1980, 1963/1995, 1968/1994) ego psychology as interpreted by Marcia (1966, 1967) in developing their Multigroup Ethnic Identity Measure (MEIM). In a now-classic review article that preceded the wave of research regarding ethnic identity during the 1990s, Phinney (1990) alluded briefly to Henri Tajfel's (1981; Tajfel & Turner, 1979) *social identity theory*, which proposes that individuals' self-esteem is influenced jointly by (1) individuals' unique or personal identity, as well as (2) one or more aspects of individuals' group-related or social identity (Verkuyten, 2005). However, social identity theory was not strongly reflected in the development of Phinney's MEIM (Umana-Taylor, 2012).

In order to integrate concepts from Tajfel's (1981; Tajfel & Turner, 1979) social identity theory with concepts from Erikson's (1959/1980, 1968/1994, 1963/1995) ego psychology within one survey, Adriana Umana-Taylor and colleagues (Umana-Taylor, Yazedjian, & Bamaca-Gomez, 2004) developed the 17-item Ethnic Identity Scale (EIS; for a review, see Cokley, 2007). Umana-Taylor and colleagues kept Phinney's (1992; Phinney & Ong, 2007; Roberts et al., 1999) cognitive construct of *exploration*, added the cognitive construct of *resolution* (i.e., individuals' conscious reflection upon what their ethnicity means to them), and reframed Phinney's affective construct of commitment as *affirmation* (Umana-Taylor, 2012). Results of factor analyses yielded support for Umana-Taylor et al.'s three hypothesised dimensions, although Phinney and Ong (2007) observed an important methodological confound. All of the affirmation items were worded in a *negative* direction; whereas all of the exploration and resolution items were worded in a *positive* direction (thus raising the possibility that Umana-Taylor et al.'s hypothesised distinction between resolution and affirmation should be re-interpreted as a negativity/positivity distinction; see Kim & Mueller, 1978, concerning valence effects in factor analyses). Perhaps the most balanced appraisal that one can make is that, just as Phinney's own MEIM was designed partly as a rebuttal to perceived problems with pre-existing measures of ethnic identity (particularly racial identity; Helms, 2007), so too was Umana-Taylor et al.'s EIS designed partly as a rebuttal to perceived problems with the MEIM; further research (ideally conducted outside Umana-

Taylor's research programme) will be needed so that personality psychologists can properly evaluate the conceptual and empirical potential of the EIS.

adulthood, from the standpoint of Klein's (1927) theory, is the *splitting* of conflictual pairs of emotions toward a particular object (i.e., individuals' love and hate toward their mothers, such as the distinction between mothers' "good breast" and "bad breast"; Mandin, 2007).

Rusbridger (2012) noted that, in Klein's (1927) version of object relations theory, children may experience anxiety from id-related conflict between (1) the "life instinct" of eros (which gives rise to children's love toward their mothers) and (2) the "death instinct" of thanatos (which gives rise to children's hatred toward their mothers). Klein's (1927) object relations theory emphasises thanatos over eros, unlike Sigmund Freud's (1920/1961) revised psychoanalytic theory (in which eros is at least as important, if not *more* important, in comparison to Thanatos; Juni, 2009). Klein believed that thanatos is revealed in the destructiveness that one commonly observes in children's play; such destructiveness presumably reflects unconscious *phantasy* (not to be confused with consciously experienced *fantasy*) on the part of the child (Grotstein, 2008). By the time that individuals reach adulthood, they run the risk of developing the *paranoid-schizoid position* (a mental state in which individuals erroneously perceive other persons as *part-objects*, rather than whole persons); Millon (1996) noted that the modern-day *schizoid personality disorder* (i.e., a psychological disorder that is marked by a sharp break between individuals' perceptions and reality) is a **D**iagnostic and **S**tatistical **M**anual of Mental Disorders (i.e., DSM) category that bears the influence of Klein's object relations theory.

Klein's (1927) version of object relations theory casts child psychoanalysis (with children's play providing raw data) as analogous to adult psychoanalysis (with free associations providing raw data) – a stance that many of Klein's onetime followers (most notably Bowlby, 1969/1997) found difficult to accept (see H. Steele

& M. Steele, 1998). Post-World War II-era research has tended to focus on adults' (as opposed to children's) object relations, such as the development of the Quality of Object Relations Scale (QORS) by Piper and colleagues (e.g., Azim & Piper, 1991; Piper, Debbane, Bienvenu, & Garant, 1984). Nevertheless, van Dijken and colleagues (van Dijken, van der Veer, van Ijzendoorn, & Kuipers, 1998) noted that Klein's (1927) version of object relations theory planted the conceptual seeds of John Bowlby's (1969/ 1997) attachment theory (which we will cover later in the present chapter). Overall, Klein's object relations theory has been praised for (1) emphasising mother-child relationships and (2) expanding the boundaries of child psychoanalysis beyond free associations and the content of dreams (Millon, 1996).

DONALD WINNICOTT'S VERSION OF OBJECT RELATIONS THEORY

According to Melanie Klein's (1927) version of object relations theory, individuals can adopt the "depressive position" (i.e., mature, realistic acceptance that other persons can trigger multiple, even contradictory emotions) as a psychologically healthy means toward neutralising the "paranoid-schizoid position" (which, as we learned in the preceding subsection, results from individuals' fragmentation of their mental representations concerning mothers; Shulman, 2010). In turn, Donald Winnicott's (1931) version of *object relations theory* retains Klein's "paranoid-schizoid position" but recasts Klein's "depressive position" (a term that was confusing, because it did not actually refer to the chronic mood disorder of depression) as *capacity for concern* (Nussbaum, 2006). Winnicott's concept of capacity for concern is more overtly interpersonal than was Klein's concept of the depressive position (which was essentially *intrapersonal*; Chescheir & Schulz, 1989). However, Winnicott contended that individuals may lose their capacity for concern, in the absence of sufficient nurturance from caregivers (especially mothers) over time; this loss of capacity for concern may serve as a precursor to the development of an antisocial tendency (although Winnicott was *not* referring to antisocial personality disorder *per se*; Millon, 1996).

In Klein's (1927) as well as Winnicott's (1931) versions of object relations theory, the ability to distinguish between internal reality (e.g., individuals' fragmented mental representations of their mothers) and external reality (e.g., actual, whole mothers in the world surrounding individuals) is a hallmark of individuals' mental health, among children (including infants) as well as adults (Chescheir & Schulz, 1989). Particularly within Winnicott's (1931) version of object relations theory, external objects (e.g., actual mothers in the real world) can provide an essential *holding environment* that includes psychological as well as physical nurturance for individuals (Stewart, 2003). According to Winnicott, when infants experience a consistently supporting holding environment, infants' *true self* not only develops but also thrives; whereas the lack of a supportive holding environment can promote the development of a *false self* that acts as a protective, yet dysfunctional, layer around (and blocking access to) the true self (Parker & Davis, 2009).

Merkur (2010) pointed out that Winnicott's (1931) version of object relations theory has been embraced more readily by clinicians than by academicians – a fact that might explain why Winnicott's version is not as well-known as Klein's (1927) version of object relations theory within personality psychology. However, Millon (1996) pointed out that in Winnicott's object relations theory, *schizoid personality disorder* can be readily identified as a prime example of mental illness resulting from individuals' prolonged failure to distinguish between internal reality and external reality. Furthermore, results of an academic study of *transitional objects* (Winnicott's term for teddy bears and other toys that can serve as targets of children's affection, at least over the short term) by Eytan Bachar and colleagues (Bachar, Canetti, Galilee-Weisstub, Kaplan-DeNour, & Shalev, 1998) indicate that individuals who reported attachment to transitional objects during childhood promoted significantly higher levels of optimal bonding with their mothers than did individuals who reported *lack* of attachment to transitional objects during their pre-adolescent years (although individuals who reported prolonged attachment to transitional objects during adolescence experienced significantly lower general well-being, and significantly more psychiatric problems, than did individuals who reported *lack* of attachment to transitional objects during adolescence). All in all, among many clinicians and academicians,

Winnicott's (1931) version has emerged as the most highly regarded post-Kleinian version of object relations theory (Spillius, 2009).

RONALD FAIRBAIRN'S VERSION OF OBJECT RELATIONS THEORY

Most of the psychodynamic theories that we have encountered thus far (including all of the ego psychology theories and object relations theories) have adopted the personality structure of id, ego, and superego that Sigmund Freud's (1923/1927) version of psychoanalytic theory and Anna Freud's (1936/1966) version of ego psychology had proposed. However, William Ronald Dodds (usually shortened to Ronald) Fairbairn's (1952) version of *object relations theory* does away with the concepts of id and superego, arguing that the ego is the sole aspect of individuals' personality structure that exists at birth (Sherby, 2007). Having turned for inspiration to Melanie Klein's (1927) earlier version of object relations theory (which, as we noted earlier in the present section, emphasised infants' internal representation of significant others or "objects"), Fairbairn casts infants' psychic energy or libido (residing within the ego) as *object-seeking* – an interpretation that one will not find in Klein's theory (or, for that matter, the theories of S. Freud or A. Freud; see Stephenson, 2012).

In Fairbairn's (1952) version of object relations theory, the primary function of the ego is to meet individuals' need to develop and maintain satisfying relationships with other persons (Sherby, 2007). However, according to Fairbairn's theory, it is easy for caregivers to *fail* to meet (and difficult for caregivers to succeed in meeting) infants' need for developing and maintaining satisfying relationships all (or even most) of the time; since infants cannot tolerate having caregivers who fail to meet their need for satisfying relationships, infants initially split caregivers (figuratively and unconsciously, of course) into (1) *good external objects* and (2) *bad internal objects*, subsequently splitting bad internal objects into (2a) *frustrating/rejecting objects* and (2b) *exciting/alluring objects* (Celani, 2001). Finally, infants unconsciously split their own egos as follows: (1) A *central ego*, which relates to the external or ideal object; (2) an *antilibidinal ego*, which relates to the rejecting object; and (3) a *libidinal ego*, which relates to the exciting object – a process that results in an *endopsychic structure* of personality (Grotstein, 1993).

Celani (2001) noted that Fairbairn's (1952) version of object relations theory paid special attention to *schizoid personality*, which supposedly is a consequence of infants' ego splitting but does *not* necessarily lead to individuals' experience of schizophrenia as a personality disorder later in life – a controversial claim, due to its implication that individuals might be "schizoid" but not at risk for psychopathology. However, regardless of the lack of precision with which Fairbairn used the term "schizoid", Millon (1996) credited Fairbairn's version of object relations theory with helping to establish contemporary psychiatrists' and clinicians' understanding of schizoid personality disorder as an *asocial* type. Overall, Fairbairn developed a version of object relations theory that differed markedly from Sigmund Freud's (1927) psychoanalytic theory and Klein's (1927) earlier version of object relations theory (Grotstein, 1993).

HARRY GUNTRIP'S VERSION OF OBJECT RELATIONS THEORY

As Crastnopol (2001) noted, Harry Guntrip was one of Ronald Fairbairn's most famous clients in psychotherapy; yet Guntrip did not believe that Fairbairn was of sufficient help – a negative outcome that eventually led Guntrip to become one of Donald Winnicott's most famous clients(!). However, Klaif (1985) pointed out that Harry Guntrip's (1969) version of *object relations theory* (also known as *person ego theory*) draws upon the object relations theories of both Fairbairn (1952) and Winnicott (1931), as well as the ego psychology of Erikson (1950). Guntrip is known especially for adding a fourth component to Fairbairn's endopsychic structure of central ego, antilibidinal ego, and libidinal ego – namely, the *regressed ego* (which does not relate to *any* object, whether internal or external; Celani, 2001). Just as the ego as a whole can split, so too can the libidinal ego split, with one portion evolving into the regressed ego (Sussal, 1992).

In Guntrip's (1969) version of object relations theory, the regressed ego can lead to individuals' disengagement from other persons (Hartman & Zimberoff, 2004). Guntrip did not believe that the formation of the regressed ego was part of individuals' normal personality/social development; rather, Guntrip argued that severe disappointment and trauma can trigger such abnormal development (Sussal, 1992). In any event, according to Guntrip, not only may the actions of the regressed ego lead to *schizoid personality disorder*; but schizoid personality disorder, in turn, can serve as the basis for individuals' development of additional personality disorders (Steinberg, 2010). Guntrip himself had been diagnosed as suffering from schizoid personality disorder; Guntrip was psycho-analysed initially by Fairbairn, and subsequently by Winnicott (Crastnopol, 2001). Guntrip viewed Winnicott as more "maternal" than was Fairbairn – a personality difference between the two psycho-therapists that, in Guntrip's opinion, accounted for the fact that Fairbairn was unsuccessful, whereas Winnicott was successful, in treating Guntrip (although Guntrip may have idealised Winnicott excessively; Slochower, 2011).

Some critics have depicted Guntrip's (1969) version of object relations theory as little more than an elaboration or amplification of Fairbairn's (1952) version of object relations theory (see Celani, 2001). However, over time, Guntrip managed to convince Fair-bairn that Guntrip's (1969) concept of regressed ego represented a substantive addition to Fairbairn's (1952) endopsychic structure (Crastnopol, 2001). Ironically, due to Guntrip's exceptional skills as a writer, Guntrip's version of object relations theory may have been even more effective at capturing the psychodynamics of the schizoid personality than was Fairbairn's earlier version of object relations theory (Millon, 1996).

JOHN BOWLBY'S ATTACHMENT THEORY

Klein's (1927) version of object relations theory eventually com-peted with Anna Freud's (1927/1975) version of ego psychology for dominance among psychodynamic theorists and practitioners within the UK, after both Klein and Anna Freud emigrated to London in the midst of World War II (and following the death of Sigmund Freud; Chodorow, 2004). In fact, open hostility erupted between Melanie Klein and Anna Freud within the British Psycho-Analytical Society, with many members of the Society feeling that they must choose sides (Prado de Oliviera, 2001). Among those psychodynamic theorists and practitioners who favoured Klein's perspective over A. Freud's perspective but did not wish to be perceived as overtly rejecting A. Freud (which conceivably could make them and their students vulnerable to retaliation from ego psychologists), two relational perspectives emerged within the resulting British Independent or "Middle Group" during the years that followed World War II: (1) Post-Kleinian object relations theories (e.g., Fairbairn, 1952; Guntrip, 1969; Winnicott, 1931); and (2) John Bowlby's (1969/1997, 1973/1998a, 1980/1998b) *attachment theory* (Hall, 2007). Unique among the theories that were developed by members of the British Independent Group, Bowlby's attachment theory was influenced jointly by *ethology* (i.e., the science of animal behaviour) and psychoanalysis (MacDonald, 2001).

In an early version of his attachment theory, Bowlby (1953) rejected Klein's (1927) premise that thanatos (the "death instinct") governed infants' behaviour toward mothers, instead arguing that a *need for emotional intimacy* was the primary motive underlying infants' behaviour – a need that was somewhat akin to eros (the "life instinct") as championed by S. Freud (1920/1961), but without the sexual connotations (H. Steele & M. Steele, 1998). Furthermore, Bowlby rejected Klein's insistence on interpreting children's play behaviour as an expression of children's latent hostility toward their mothers, instead opting to collect large-scale empirical data on the negative effects of long-term separation from mothers on children's personality and social development (Van Dijken, van der Veer, van Ijzendoorn, & Kuipers, 1998). Based on the results of observational research with children in hospitals, Bowlby proposed that (1) most caregivers consistently fulfil infants' need for emotional bonding, which leads infants to become *securely attached* to their caregivers; yet (2) some caregivers do *not* consistently meet infants' need for emotional bonding, which leads those infants to become *insecurely attached* to their caregivers (Bretherton, 1992). Afterward, building upon Bowlby's attachment theory, Mary Salter Ainsworth and colleagues (Ainsworth, 1963, 1967; Ainsworth, Blehar, Waters, & Wall, 1978) developed the "strange situation" experimental paradigm (whereby infants were briefly separated from their mothers and, having been reunited with mothers, displayed different behavioural responses to their mothers) that led to the identification of three *infant attachment styles*: (1) *Secure* (i.e., easily comforted following mothers' return, presumably due to mothers' consistent provision of love and affection toward the infants); (2) *anxious-ambivalent* (i.e., alternating between pulling toward and pushing away from mothers, an insecure style that presumably is due to mothers' inconsistent provision of love and affection); and (3) *avoidant* (i.e., rejecting mothers, an insecure style that presumably is due to mothers' consistent failure to provide love and affection; Hazan & Shaver, 1994a, 1994b). Subsequently, Hazan and Shaver (1987) developed a self-report measure of *adult attachment styles* (i.e., *secure*, or trusting toward romantic partners; *anxious-ambivalent*, or distrustful toward romantic partners because of concerns that their partners will not display as much love or affection toward them, compared to their displays of love and affection toward partners; and *avoidant*, or distrustful toward romantic partners because of concerns that the individuals themselves are unable or unwilling to display love or affection toward their partners; Bartholomew, 1990). Finally, Bartholomew and Horowitz (1991) expanded the scope of adult attachment styles to cover close relationships in general (rather than romantic relationships in particular, which Hazan and Shaver had covered), reconceptualised the anxious-ambivalent attachment style as *preoccupied*, and distinguished between *fearful* and *dismissing* forms of avoidant attachment styles (with the dismissing-avoidant style reflecting an insecure type because of individuals' denial that they possess a need for emotional intimacy, even though all individuals possess such a need; Mikulincer & Shaver, 2016).

Initially, Bowlby's (1953) attachment theory was rejected by other psychodynamic theorists and practitioners – not just by Klein (and, for that matter, A. Freud), but also by his fellow members of the so-called "Independent" or "Middle Group" (Van Dijken, van der Veer, van Ijzendoorn, & Kuipers, 1998). However, Bowlby's (1969/1997, 1973/1998a, 1973/1998b) attachment theory has been credited with exerting considerable influence upon contemporary clinicians' diagnoses of *dependent personality disorder* (a dysfunctional, submissive behavioural pattern; Millon, 1996). In addition, Bowlby's theory emerged as the best-known theory of personality development within the field of relationship science (Finkel, Simpson, & Eastwick, 2017) and has inspired the development of numerous surveys, most notably the Experiences in Close Relationships (ECR) questionnaire (Brennan, Clark, & Shaver, 1998) as a measure of attachment orientations (see Box 2.3 for details). In summary, Bowlby clearly charted a different conceptual and empirical course than even his fellow Independent Group members could have imagined concerning personality development (e.g., Ainsworth & Bowlby, 1992).

OTHER MAJOR PSYCHODYNAMIC THEORIES

JACQUES LACAN'S VERSION OF PSYCHOANALYTIC THEORY

Thus far, in the present chapter, we have encountered numerous English-language psychodynamic theories that – according to Quinodoz (2010) – represent culturally "Anglicised" translations of Sigmund Freud's (1900/1965) original, German-language version of psychoanalytic theory. Similarly, one could argue that French-language psychodynamic theories represent culturally "Gallicised" translations of S. Freud's theory (see Kurzweil, 1981). Jacques Lacan's (1966/1977) version of *psychoanalytic theory* is the best-known French-language psychodynamic theory (Stevens, 2008).

According to Lacan's (1966/1977) version of psychoanalytic theory, ego psychologists (e.g., Anna Freud, Heinz Hartmann, Erik Erikson) and object relations theorists (e.g., Melanie Klein, Donald Winnicott, Ronald Fairbairn, Harry Guntrip) had strayed too far from Sigmund Freud's (1900/1965) original version of psychoanalytic theory (Cohen, 2005). In contrast, Lacan proposed a "return to Freud" – not *Anna* Freud's (1923) ego psychology, but rather *Sigmund* Freud's pre-1905 psychoanalytic theory (i.e., when Sigmund Freud was still concerned primarily with distinctions among the unconscious, preconscious, and conscious; Walsh, Teo, & Baydala, 2014). Lacan was especially interested in the *unconscious* as the "ideal worker" within individuals' personality structures (e.g., the unconscious generates *dreams* as means toward unthinking and unquestioning fulfilment of individuals' desire, at least while individuals are asleep; Rocha, 2012). Lacan believed that the problem of the unconscious is the *problem of discourse with the Other* (e.g., *language* does not perfectly convey individuals'

BOX 2.3 K. A. BRENNAN ET AL.'S (1998) EXPERIENCES IN CLOSE RELATIONSHIPS QUESTIONNAIRE

Earlier in the present chapter, we learned about the typology of secure, anxious/ambivalent, and avoidant attachment styles that Hazan and Shaver (1987) developed concerning adults' personality characteristics, in response to the three-group typology that Ainsworth and colleagues (Ainsworth, Blehar, Waters, & Wall, 1978) had created regarding infants' behavioural responses to reunion with their mothers after having been separated for several minutes. Also, we learned about the distinction between fearful-avoidant and dismissing-avoidant attachment styles in adulthood that Bartholomew and Horowitz (1991) proposed, following Bartholomew's (1990) four-category typology. Technically, Bartholomew and Horowitz promoted the measurement of each adult attachment style along a continuum, which yields four separate scores (i.e., secure, anxious-ambivalent/preoccupied, fearful-avoidant, *and* dismissing-avoidant) – rather than the categorical approach of Hazan and Shaver, which yields one score for each individual (see also Bartholomew, 1994, for a critique of then-existing measures of attachment styles).

By the late 1990s, several teams of researchers had concluded that a minimum of two separate dimensions (i.e., *attachment anxiety* and *attachment avoidance*) emerged from factor analyses of various attachment surveys that contained continuous items (Holmes, 2000). Consistent with the movement toward continuous surveys in adult attachment research, Kelly Brennan and colleagues (K. A. Brennan, Clark, & Shaver, 1998) created the 36-item Experiences in Close Relationships (ECR) Questionnaire, with each item scored along a 7-point range (although the survey has undergone several minor refinements over time; for a review, see Mikulincer & Shaver, 2016). In general, when measured via the ECR and related surveys, attachment avoidance is a significant negative predictor of relationship-promoting behaviour, and a significant positive predictor of relationship-threatening behaviour; whereas attachment anxiety is not consistently related to relationship-promoting or relationship-threatening behaviour (Gaines, 2016/2018). Particularly when one considers the extent to which attachment avoidance undermines aspects of *interdependence* or mutual influence within close relationships (i.e., high attachment avoidance is reflected in low levels of satisfaction with the relationship, high levels of perceived alternatives to the relationship, low levels of investment in the relationship, and low levels of accommodation toward partners' destructive behaviour; Etcheverry, Le, Wu, & Wei, 2013), the ECR displays enormous potential in enabling relationship scientists to demonstrate the relevance of attachment orientations to precursors of relationship stability over the long term (see Finkel, Simpson, & Eastwick, 2017, for a conceptual rationale that links attachment orientations with interdependence processes).

desire to other persons – partly because individuals do not fully understand their own desire, and partly because language is an inherently social medium that can lead to misunderstanding when individuals attempt to communicate with other persons; Gillett, 2001).

Lacan (1966/1977) has been criticised for writing in such an opaque manner that readers must struggle to decipher essential arguments within his version of psychoanalytic theory (Stevens, 2008). However, Jardim and colleagues (Jardim, Costa Pereira, & de Souza Palma, 2011) successfully applied Lacan's version of psychoanalytic theory to understanding the origins of schizophrenia, interpreting a case study (along with fictional examples from novels) in terms of individuals' failure to achieve an integrated ego from infancy onward. Also, McSherry (2013) contended that various forms of personality disorder (including, but not limited to, schizophrenia) can be understood readily in terms of Lacan's theory. In conclusion, Lacan has been hailed as "the French Freud" (Kurzweil, 1981) for his innovative attempts to re-interpret Sigmund Freud's (1900/1965) earlier version of psychoanalytic theory for post-World War II-era readers.

HEINZ KOHUT'S VERSION OF SELF-PSYCHOLOGY

As we noted earlier in the present chapter, ego psychologists from Anna Freud (1936/1966) onward have depicted the ego as more capable in handling id-superego conflicts that Sigmund Freud's (1923) "id psychology" (i.e., S. Freud's version of psychoanalytic theory; Ewen, 1998) had acknowledged. According to Heinz Kohut (1971), the next logical step in the evolution of psychodynamic perspectives on personality was to propose a *self-*

psychology that traces the development of the entire self (including, but not limited to, the concepts of id, ego, and superego) from its infantile state of fragmentation and fragility to its (optimally) adult state of cohesion and resilience (Millon, 1996). Kohut's version of self-psychology elevates *narcissism* (a construct that we have encountered on more than one occasion within the present book) to the status of a key construct; in order for individuals to develop in a psychologically healthy manner, it will be necessary for them to transcend the immature, "I am the centre of the universe" mindset that characterises narcissism, and to progress toward a mature acceptance of the fact that the universe does not revolve around them (Stevens, 2008). Part of the developmental challenge for individuals will be to accept their actual position within the universe without descending into debilitating doubt over the meaning of their existence (Walsh, Teo, & Baydala, 2014).

In his version of self-psychology, Kohut (1971) agreed with Sigmund Freud's (1914/1953) belief that narcissism is *not* an inherently unhealthy attitude (and, thus, not automatically pathological; Schipke, 2017). However, Kohut disagreed with S. Freud concerning the *origins* of narcissism during childhood (i.e., Freud contended that narcissism results from libido or psychic energy flowing from the id to the ego, during the initial differentiation of ego from id early in life; whereas Kohut argued that narcissism results from parents' failure to engage in *mirroring*, which would involve displays of empathy toward young children's struggle to shift away from their original "centre-of-the-universe" position, and toward a more realistic view of themselves; Rhodewalt, 2012). Furthermore, Kohut disagreed with S. Freud over *psychotherapeutic treatment* of narcissism during adulthood (i.e., S. Freud believed that clinicians should force narcissistic clients to confront their previously unconscious self-love; whereas Kohut thought that clinicians should monitor narcissistic clients for potential depression and should provide the empathy that parents had failed to give the clients during childhood; Millon, 1996). Perhaps the most far-reaching difference between Kohut's and S. Freud's perspectives was that (unlike S. Freud) Kohut offered hope for many narcissistic clients who formerly had been dismissed as untreatable by clinicians (Son, 2006).

Kohut's (1971) version of self-psychology has been criticised for assuming (incorrectly) that individuals' failure to achieve a mature sense of self invariably reflects high levels of narcissism (Afek, 2018). By the same token, Kohut's version of self-psychology has been praised for providing a more sophisticated portrait of narcissism (distinguishing between the components of *grandiosity concerning self* and *idealisation of significant others*) than S. Freud (1914/1953) had offered (i.e., narcissism primarily as self-love; Meronen, 1999). Moreover, the Narcissistic Personality Inventory (NPI) as developed by Raskin and colleagues (e.g., Raskin & Hall, 1979; Raskin & Terry, 1988) and profiled in Box 2.4, was based largely on insights from Kohut's theory (notwithstanding S. Freud's theoretical contributions; Rhodewalt, 2012). Overall, Kohut's version of self-psychology paved the way for a renaissance in post–World War II-era theorising, research, and clinical applications regarding narcissism (Walsh, Teo, & Baydala, 2014).

OTTO KERNBERG'S VERSION OF SELF-PSYCHOLOGY

As we saw in the preceding paragraphs, S. Freud's (1914/1953) version of psychoanalytic theory and Kohut's (1971) version of self-psychology have greatly influenced psychodynamic perspectives on narcissism. Another psychodynamic theory that deserves acknowledgement concerning its coverage of narcissism is Otto Kernberg's (1967) theory, which Walsh and colleagues (Walsh, Teo, & Baydala, 2014) labelled as a separate version of *self-psychology*. Given that O. Kernberg (e.g., Kernberg, 1975) and Kohut (e.g., Kohut, 1977) increasingly formulated their respective views in opposition to each other over time (Tonkin & Fine, 1985), perhaps it stands to reason that O. Kernberg's theory would be regarded as a version of self-psychology. However, O. Kernberg's theory defies a clear label, drawing upon ego psychology theories (in the tradition of Freud, 1936/1966) as well as object relations theories (in the tradition of Klein, 1927) while distancing itself from Kohut's version of self-psychology (Millon, 1996).

Otto Kernberg (1975) took issue with Kohut's (1971) depiction of narcissism as mostly a *sub*clinical phenomenon (which had implied that narcissism usually was not harmful to individuals or

BOX 2.4 RASKIN AND C. S. HALL'S (1979) NARCISSISTIC PERSONALITY INVENTORY

According to Richard Robins and Oliver John (1997), several distinct modes or metaphors of self-perception can be found within personality psychology. Especially relevant for the present chapter is the *Egoist* metaphor, which presumes that human beings in general possess a self-enhancement motive that leads them to seek positive information about themselves via social interaction (see also Millon, 1996). In turn, the construct of narcissism arguably captures the essence of the Egoist metaphor more faithfully than does any other personality construct (W. K. Campbell & S. M. Campbell, 2009). Sigmund Freud's (1914/1953) version of psychoanalytic theory, Heinz Kohut's (1971) version of self-psychology, and Otto Kernberg's (1967) version of self-psychology all indicate that an exaggerated sense of one's positive qualities is central to the construct of narcissism (Rhodewalt, 2012).

Shortly before the American Psychiatric Association formally added narcissistic personality disorder to its list of mental disorders in the third edition of the Diagnostic and Statistical Manual (DSM-III, 1980), Robert Raskin and Calvin S. Hall (1979) developed the 40-item Narcissistic Personality Inventory (NPI) to measure individual differences in narcissism (Millon, 1996). Subsequently, using a principal components analysis of data from a very large US sample, Raskin and Terry (1988) identified seven interrelated yet distinct components of narcissism measured by the NPI: (1) *Authority*, (2) *exhibitionism*, (3) *superiority*, (4) *vanity*, (5) *exploitativeness*, (6) *entitlement*, and (7) *self-sufficiency*. Despite Raskin and Terry's identification of seven components of narcissism, most researchers have interpreted the NPI (Raskin & Hall, 1979) as a measure of a single dimension (indeed, results of reliability analyses support calculation of a single score; see Nunnally & Bernstein, 1994). In terms of predictive validity, narcissism as measured by the NPI consistently emerges as a significant negative predictor of relationship-maintaining behaviour, and as a significant positive predictor of relationship-threatening behaviour (Gaines, 2018). Although one may question the forced-choice nature of the items (whereby participants must choose between two statements about themselves for each item), the NPI currently is the most popular measure of subclinical narcissism in personality and social psychology (Rhodewalt, 2012).

significant others; Walsh, Teo, & Baydala, 2014). Instead, O. Kernberg's version of self-psychology presents narcissism as a frequent clinical phenomenon (Rhodewalt, 2012). Otto Kernberg's conceptualisation of narcissism lends itself readily to the DSM designation of *narcissistic personality disorder*, reflecting an egoistic pattern in which individuals place their own needs above the needs of significant others (Millon, 1996). One reason for the difference between O. Kernberg's and Kohut's pathologising versus normalising stances on narcissism apparently lies in the demographic differences between the populations whom the two therapists served (i.e., O. Kernberg's clients were more likely to be institutionalised, and less likely to be employed in high-paying professions, than were Kohut's clients; Sperry, 2003).

Unlike Kohut (1977), Otto Kernberg was not cited as one of Sigmund Freud's intellectual "progeny" in an overview by Stevens (2008). However, Millon (1996) credited O. Kernberg (1967, 1970) with developing one of the most original and influential conceptual accounts of narcissistic personality disorder that one can find among psychodynamic perspectives on personality. Furthermore, O. Kernberg's theory ranks alongside Kohut's version of self-psychology and S. Freud's (1914/1953) version of psychoanalytic theory in terms of influencing the development of the aforementioned Narcissistic Personality Inventory (NPI; Raskin & Hall, 1979; Raskin & Terry, 1988), with clinicians more likely to use the NPI to diagnose narcissism as an outright disorder, and academicians more likely to use the NPI to measure narcissism as an overly positive self-attitude among nonclinical populations (Rhodewalt, 2012). All in all, O. Kernberg's perspective is comparable to Kohut's theory in terms of the prominence that it gives to narcissism as a personality construct (Sperry, 2003).

HENRY MURRAY'S PERSONOLOGY

So far, we have encountered a variety of psychodynamic theories that propose a small number of major motives (usually no more than 2–3 motives) that presumably are reflected in individuals' behaviour. However, one might reasonably ask whether 2–3 motives really can explain human behaviour in all of its complexity (McClelland, 1985/1987). According to Henry Murray's (1938) *personology*, individuals differ in more than 20 motive dimensions (unlike other psychodynamic theories that assume individual *similarities* in relevant motives; Hall & Lindzey, 1970); this large number of motives reflects Murray's interest in studying the whole person (not unlike Allport, 1937/1951).

Ewen (1998) provided a list of Murray's (1938) motives, which includes (but is not necessarily limited to) *abasement, achievement, acquisition/conservance, affiliation, aggression, autonomy, blameavoidance, construction, contrariance, counteraction, defendance, deference, dominance/ power, exhibition, exposition, harmavoidance, infavoidance, nurturance, order, play, recognition, rejection, sentience, sex/erotic, similance, succorance*, and *understanding/cognizance*. Unlike Sigmund Freud's (1900/ 1965) version of psychoanalytic theory, Murray's personology focuses on psychological needs that were not assumed to be present and functioning within individuals at birth but, rather, emerged gradually over time (Hall & Lindzey, 1957). In addition to motives or needs, situational influences (which Murray termed collectively as *press*) must be taken into account; needs and press work together to produce repeated behavioural sequences over time (which Murray termed *thema*; McClelland, 1985/1987).

Despite Murray's (1938) insistence that more than 20 motives were required for researchers to do justice to the enormous variability in behaviour that one finds among individuals, personologists have devoted an inordinate amount of attention to the achievement motive, or *need for achievement* (nAch) – a construct that has proven to be controversial (e.g., unlike men, women as a whole were initially deemed to be lacking in the need for achievement; for examples, see McClelland, 1966; McClelland, Atkinson, Clark, & Lowell, 1953). However, some personologists have expanded the scope of their research to include the *need for power* (Y axis) and *need for intimacy* (X axis) as higher-order motives that incorporate eight of the lower-order motives from Murray's list within a circular or circumplex model (i.e., *dominance, aggression, autonomy, rejection, infavoidance, abasement, nurturance*, and *affiliation*, starting from the 12 o'clock position and working one's way anticlockwise at approximately 45-degree angles; e.g., Wiggins, 1997; Wiggins & Broughton, 1985). Although the Thematic Apperception Test (TAT) was developed by Christiana Morgan and Henry Murray (1935) as a projective measure of individuals' motives in general, Dan McAdams and colleagues (e.g., McAdams, 1980; McAdams & Bryant, 1987) have opted to collect interview data and code participants' responses for the needs of power and intimacy in particular (Gaines, 2016/2018). All things considered, Murray's personology offers a solid conceptual framework for conducting research on individual differences in motives (though methodological issues with the TAT remain problematic; Hyde & Kling, 2001).

CRITIQUE OF PSYCHODYNAMIC PERSPECTIVES

Earlier in the present chapter, we learned that Sigmund Freud, 1953 held a negative attitude toward gay men, proclaiming that they suffered from "arrested development" when compared to heterosexual men. As it happens, S. Freud took a similarly dim view toward *all* women, whether lesbian or heterosexual: Women could either (1) admit that they harboured "penis envy" (thus accepting their supposedly inferior status and making the best of a bad situation by attempting to become mothers), or (2) deny that they harboured "penis envy" (thus trying unsuccessfully to become like men and rejecting their own femininity; Margolis, 1984). Obviously, S. Freud's theory placed women in a catch-22 situation (i.e., damned if you do, damned if you don't; Walsh, Teo, & Baydala, 2014). We have already seen that Karen Horney (1922–37/1966) actively challenged S. Freud's "masculine psychology" by promoting her own, feminine psychology. In addition, Clara Thompson (1953) advocated a "psychology of women" more than a decade before the modern-day Women's Rights Movement in the US and other Western nations sparked widespread interest in such a topic among scholars and students (see Enns, 1989).

One of the more intriguing responses to feminist critiques of Sigmund Freud's (1908/1925) psychoanalytic theory – and, to a large degree, feminist critiques of the psychodynamic school in general – has been the attempt by some writers to seek reconciliation between feminism and psychoanalysis (Walsh, Teo, & Baydala, 2014). One of the best-known feminist psychoanalysts is Nancy Chodorow (1978), who argued that S. Freud and his followers may have been right to call attention to girls' negative feelings toward their mothers and positive feelings toward their fathers, but wrong to attribute those sets of feelings to an "Electra complex" (in all fairness, a term that S. Freud did not particularly like; Ewen, 1998). Rather, according to Chodorow, girls might simply respond to well-established connectedness toward their mothers by seeking greater levels of autonomy from their mothers (which, in turn, might result in establishing greater connectedness toward their fathers; Stevens, 2008). Thanks to efforts by Chodorow and other feminist psychoanalysts, members of the psychodynamic school of personality have become increasingly sensitised toward their own gender biases in the post-Women's Rights Era (e.g., emphasising the quality of the mother-child relationship, to the relative exclusion of other caregiver-child relationships; Margolis, 1984).

PRELUDE TO CHAPTER 3

Despite the differences that we have observed between William James's (1890/2010) self-theory and Sigmund Freud's (1900/1965) version of psychoanalytic theory, both theories can be classified as *mentalist*, due to their emphasis on conscious and unconscious within-person influences on individuals' behaviour (Kihlstrom, 2004). Conversely, the *behaviourist* school – which alternatively has been depicted as part of personality psychology (e.g., Hall & Lindzey, 1978) or as an alternative to personality psychology (e.g., Ewen, 1998) – emphasises *outside*-person influences on individuals' behaviour (Moore, 2013). Representative theories include (in order of appearance) the reflexology of Ivan Pavlov (1926/1928), the connectionism of Edward Thorndike (1911), the classical conditioning theory of John B. Watson (1916), Edward Tolman's (1932) stimulus-stimulus theory, the drive reduction theory of Clark Hull (1943), the operant reinforcement theory of B. F. Skinner (1938), the stimulus-response theory of Neal Miller and John Dollard (1941), the social learning theory of Julian Rotter (1954), and the social learning theory of Albert Bandura and Richard Walters (1963). In Chapter 3, we shall examine behaviourist theories and relevant research in detail.

CLASSIC SCHOOLS OF THOUGHT II

BEHAVIOURIST PERSPECTIVES ON PERSONALITY

Many (if not most) historians of science have concluded that Wilhelm Wundt was the founder of modern-day psychology, during the late 1800s (J. F. Brennan, 2003). After all, Wundt published the ground-breaking *Principles of Physiological Psychology* in 1874 (reprinted in 1910) and established the world's first psychological laboratory in 1879 (Wade, Sakurai, & Gyoba, 2007). However, some historians of science would assert that the real founder of modern-day psychology was Ivan Pavlov, during the early 1900s (Walsh, Teo, & Baydala, 2014). In particular, Pavlov's landmark publication of *Lectures on Conditioned Reflexes: Twenty-Five Years of Objective Study of the Higher Nervous System* in 1926 (reprinted in 1928) documented the evolution of Pavlov's own programme of research from a focus on digestive physiology (for which he won the Nobel Prize in 1904) to an emphasis on classical conditioning (a cornerstone of early behaviourism in psychology; Todes, 1997).

Pavlov (1926/1928) initially viewed his physiologically orientated "reflexology" (which dealt with dogs' *conditioned* responses to environmental cues regarding the imminent availability of food, as built upon dogs' *unconditioned* responses to the food itself) as distinct from psychology (J. F. Brennan, 2003) but eventually aligned his reflexology with psychology (Walsh, Teo, & Baydala, 2014).

Technically speaking, Pavlov's reflexology is a forerunner to the behaviourist school within personality psychology, rather than a behaviourist theory of personality *per se* (Ewen, 1998). Nevertheless, Pavlov's theory and research provided much of the conceptual and methodological framework that led to the emergence of the behaviourist school (C. S. Hall & Lindzey, 1978).

In the present chapter, we will consider behaviourist perspectives on personality, which are inspired to varying degrees by Pavlov's (1926/1928) reflexology. We will learn that behaviourist theories – especially B. F. Skinner's (1938) operant reinforcement theory, which reflects Skinner's principle of *environmental determinism* (i.e., throughout individuals' lives, behaviour can be explained completely by influences that exist outside the individuals; Schellenberg, 1978) – have been criticised for their relative neglect of within-person influences on behaviour. However, we will also learn about certain neo-behaviourist responses – particularly Daryl Bem's (1972) self-perception theory – that acknowledge the usefulness of personality constructs as related to (but not necessarily causing) individuals' behaviour.

BASIC ASSUMPTIONS UNDERLYING BEHAVIOURIST PERSPECTIVES

A central premise among behaviourist perspectives on personality is the conviction that, in order to understand why individuals speak and act as they do, one must consider the impact of the social and physical environments within which persons engage in particular forms of speech and action (Ewen, 1998). At a minimum, behaviourist theories pose important conceptual challenges to Sigmund Freud's principle of *psychic determinism* (i.e., beyond the age of 5 or 6, the speech and action of individuals can be explained completely by influences that exist within those individuals; Schellenberg, 1978). However, behaviourist theories vary in terms of their (de-) emphasis on personality constructs as causes or antecedents of individuals' speech and action (C. S. Hall & Lindzey, 1978).

As noted by J. F. Brennan (2003), behaviourism developed partly as a response to *functionalism* (concerned with the "how" and "why" of consciousness, or individuals' mental processes), which was associated with the self-theory of William James (1890/2010) and the instrumental pragmatism of John Dewey (1909). In turn, functionalism had developed partly as a response to *structuralism* (concerned with the "what" of consciousness, or individuals' mental organisation), which was associated with the content psychology of Edward Titchener (1902) and the content psychology of Titchener's mentor, Wilhelm Wundt (1911/1973). Both structuralists and functionalists identify the mind (which, of course, is not directly observable) as the proper object of study for a science of psychology; whereas behaviourists identify observable behaviour as the proper object of study for a science of psychology (Walsh, Teo, & Baydala, 2014).

One can make a broad distinction between (1) those behaviourist theories that address the impact of the physical environment on individuals' speech and action; and (2) those behaviourist theories that address the impact of the social environment on individuals' speech and action (see Ewen, 1998). The connectionism of Edward Thorndike (1911), the classical conditioning theory of John B. Watson (1916), the stimulus-stimulus theory of Edward Tolman (1932), and the drive reduction theory of Clark Hull (1943) deal almost exclusively with the physical environment; whereas the operant reinforcement theory of B. F. Skinner (1938), the stimulus-response theory of Neal Miller and John Dollard (1941), the social learning theory of Julian Rotter (1954), and the social learning theory of Albert Bandura and Richard Walters (1963) deal partly (if not primarily) with the social environment (see C. S. Hall & Lindzey, 1978). In the present chapter, we will review all of the aforementioned behaviourist theories from the vantage point of personality psychology.

THEORIES THAT ADDRESS THE PHYSICAL ENVIRONMENT

EDWARD THORNDIKE'S CONNECTIONISM

Like Ivan Pavlov's (1926/1928) reflexology, Edward Thorndike's (1911) *connectionism* addresses relatively simple patterns of participants' learning via the associations that they make regarding events that occur close in time to each other, especially among animal participants (Elkind, 1999). However, unlike Pavlov's reflexology (which is concerned primarily with the interval of time that elapses between experimenters' presentation of conditioned and unconditioned *stimuli* to participants), Thorndike's connectionism focuses mainly on the interval of time that elapses between participants' *responses* and the outcomes that those participants experience (Wasserman & R. R. Miller, 1997). Consequently, Thorndike's connectionist theory and related research helped to establish the field of *comparative psychology* (which examines similarities and differences in the capacity for thinking across species; Blaser & Bellizzi, 2014).

John Donahoe (1999) labelled Thorndike (1905) as a "selectionist connectionist" (p. 451), emphasising the impact of Charles Darwin's (1859) theory of natural selection upon Thorndike's theory. To the extent that an organisms' response to a particular stimulus is followed closely in time by *reinforcement* (i.e., an event that yields pleasure), one would expect organisms to emit that associated response again if/when the stimulus appears again – a principle that is known as the *law of effect* (Thorndike also proposed, but subsequently dropped the proposal, that *punishment* exerted a similarly strong effect in preventing organisms from emitting an associated response again; J. F. Brennan, 2003). Furthermore, to the extent that response-reinforcement sequences repeatedly occur across time, one would expect organisms' association between those events to be strengthened – a principle that is labelled as the *law of exercise* (Thorndike also proposed, but eventually dropped the proposal, that *lack* of repeated response-reinforcement sequences necessarily would lead to organisms' weakened associations between those events over an extended interval of time; Walsh, Teo, & Baydala, 2014). Thorndike's law of effect and law of exercise influenced the development of B. F. Skinner's (1938) operant reinforcement theory, which we will cover later in the present chapter (see also Sheehy, 2004).

Thorndike's (1905, 1911) connectionism is *hereditarian* in its assumption that members of certain so-called racial groups (i.e., persons of African descent) generally possessed a lower innate capacity for learning, compared to members of other so-called racial groups (e.g., persons of European descent) – a perspective that has been criticised, not just as "politically incorrect", but (perhaps more importantly) as *scientifically* incorrect (see Popkewitz, 2011).

By the same token, Thorndike's (1917) connectionist theory and law of effect have been credited with helping to lay the conceptual foundation for modern-day *educational psychology*, which is concerned with the methods by which teachers can help *all* students learn effectively, regardless of students' racial or other ethnic group memberships (see Chase, 1998). Notwithstanding questions about the status of Thorndike's theory as a *bona fide* behaviourist theory (e.g., J. F. Brennan, 2003), Thorndike's connectionism has been hailed as an important precursor to the behaviourist theories of John B. Watson (1913) and B. F. Skinner (1938), both of which we will cover shortly.

JOHN B. WATSON'S CLASSICAL CONDITIONING THEORY

Rilling (2000) noted that John B. Watson (1916) developed *classical conditioning theory* (which involves the acquisition of *elicited responses* that originally occurred after the introduction of unconditioned stimuli but subsequently occur after the introduction of conditioned stimuli as well; Kirsch, Lynn, Vigorito, & R. R. Miller, 2004) largely as a response to Sigmund Freud's (1900/1965) psychoanalytic theory. J. B. Watson initially admired S. Freud's psychoanalytic theory but believed that individuals' *transference of emotions* (an important process within clinical settings, whereby clients may safely express emotions toward therapists after having been made aware that the emotions in question were originally experienced toward – but never had been expressed toward – their parents or other caregivers earlier in life; T. Davis, 2007) could be explained by appealing to principles of conditioned reflexes (associated with the reflexology of Ivan Pavlov, 1926/1928), rather than defence mechanisms (see Arlow, 2002). J. B. Watson was interested especially in the potential elicitation and generalisation of the "free-floating fear" that is known as anxiety (see Field & Nightingale, 2009).

Guided by classical conditioning theory (e.g., J. B. Watson, 1916), John B. Watson and Rosalie Rayner (1920) conducted one of the most controversial experiments in the history of psychology – namely, their conditioning of the approximately 11-month-old infant known as "Little Albert" to experience anxiety when presented with previously non-anxiety-inducing stimuli (starting with a white rat and adding various white, furry objects thereafter; LeUnes, 1983). As it turns out, J. B. Watson and Rayner were not the first behaviourists to apply classical conditioning techniques to a child (Windholz & Lamal, 1986). However, the ethical lapses in J. B. Watson and Rayner's study (not the least of which was the researchers' apparent use of prior knowledge that "Little Albert" reacted quite negatively to loud noises, which would explain the researchers' subsequent choice of the repeated banging of a gong as their unconditioned stimulus; see Sheehy, 2004) were so egregious – even by pre-World War II standards – that this particular study is a standout because of its precise application of behaviourist principles *and* its problematic methodology (Beck, Levinson, & Lyons, 2009).

Perhaps the most regrettable aspect of J. B. Watson and Rayner's (1920) classical conditioning study was the fact that – having induced anxiety in "Little Albert" regarding several harmless objects – the researchers never attempted to de-condition the infant (who already was suffering from a cognitive impairment at the time of their experiment, as the researchers may have been aware; Fridlund, Beck, Goldie, & Irons, 2012). One of J. B. Watson's students, Mary Cover Jones (1924a), eventually developed a behaviour modification protocol for use with another young child (Kornfeld, 1989); M. C. Jones' pioneering work is profiled in Box 3.1. Perhaps the most neutral evaluation that one can offer concerning J. B. Watson's classical conditioning theory (e.g., J. B. Watson, 1916) and related research (e.g., J. B. Watson & Raynor, 1920) is that J. B. Watson clearly implemented a "behaviourist manifesto" (as originally presented by J. B. Watson, 1913) but offered a version of behaviourism that is questionable in terms of its ultimate benefit to science, especially when one considers the physical and psychological stress that Watson and Raynor inflicted upon "Little Albert" (Walsh, Teo, & Baydala, 2014).

EDWARD TOLMAN'S (1932) STIMULUS-STIMULUS THEORY

Pavlov's (1926/1928) reflexology, Thorndike's (1911) connectionism, and J. B. Watson's (1913) classical conditioning theory collectively served as precursors to Neal Miller and John Dollard's (1941) stimulus–response theory (to be reviewed later in the

BOX 3.1 M. C. JONES'S (1924a, 1924b) BEHAVIOUR MODIFICATION PROGRAMME

After hearing John B. Watson give a lecture on classical conditioning theory and practice, Mary Cover Jones set out to remove the "free-floating fear" of anxiety toward particular stimuli in the physical environment (i.e., rabbits) that already had been manifested by a 3-year-old boy who was known as "Little Peter" (Malone, 2014). With the blessing of J. B. Watson, M. C. Jones (1924a) conducted the first known study of *behaviour modification*, whereby M. C. Jones began by bringing a rabbit into the same experiment room as "Little Peter" (but without allowing any contact between the rabbit and the child) and subsequently guided "Little Peter" through a series of progressively challenging scenarios (e.g., giving candy to the child while the rabbit was in the room, allowing the rabbit to nibble at the child) that ended with "Little Peter" touching the rabbit without becoming anxious (Gieser, 1993). Over time, M. C. Jones became known for her caring attitude and behaviour toward "Little Peter" and other research participants – a stance that was consistent with her eventual nickname, "the mother of behaviour therapy" (Mussen & Eichorn, 1988).

In a follow-up study, M. C. Jones (1924b) identified anxiety-provoking stimuli in a sample of children and pursued an eclectic range of techniques on a trial-and-error basis, with the effect that some (but not all) techniques proved to be effective at eliminating the children's anxiety levels (see McClelland, 1985/1987). Among the most successful techniques was *systematic desensitisation*, in which other (and increasingly similar) stimuli were paired with the originally anxiety-provoking stimuli across successive trials (Gieser, 1993). Due to the innovative methodology and oft-encouraging outcomes of M. C. Jones's behaviour modification programme, followers have adapted M. C. Jones's techniques for use in measuring behavioural avoidance among children (e.g., Castagna, T. E. Davis, & Lilly, 2017), combining behaviour therapy with electroencephalogram (EEG) feedback in rehabilitating former felons (e.g., von Hilsheimer & Quirk, 2006), and combining cognitive-behavioural therapy with drug therapy in treating several personality disorders (e.g., M. Davis, Barad, Otto, & Southwick, 2006), among many applications. Overall, M. C. Jones's behaviour modification programme can be regarded as the logical extension (and impressive complement) to J. B. Watson's classical conditioning programme (Fancher & Rutherford, 2017).

present chapter) – a theory that addresses within-organism events that serve as intermediaries between environmental events and organisms' observable behaviour (C. S. Hall & Lindzey, 1978). However, according to Edward Tolman's (1932) *stimulus-stimulus theory*, the environmental events and within-organism events in question are far more complicated than stimulus-response theory and its precursors had realised (Still, 1986). At a minimum, organisms (usually rats in Tolman's research; e.g., Tolman, 1938) routinely encounter a series of environmental events in their daily lives, each of which may trigger within-organism events (and, perhaps, require outward behaviour from the individual along the way; Mackintosh, 1986).

Combining portions of J. B. Watson's (1913) classical conditioning theory with aspects of Kurt Koffka's (1935) *Gestalt psychology* (which posits that the perceptual whole is greater than the sum of its parts; Walsh, Teo, & Baydala, 2014), Tolman's (1948) stimulus-stimulus theory proposes that various organisms display *purposiveness* (i.e., intentionality) in the process of responding to a series of environmental events as problem-solving exercises (Good & Still, 1986). Tolman's (1932) stimulus-stimulus theory is especially noteworthy for suggesting that rats, humans, and organisms from many other species may construct internal "maps" over time, enabling them to navigate their physical environments in a manner that may or may not be rewarding over the short term but can lead to rewards over the long term (D. E. Leary, 2004). Although the concept of "maps" has led some reviewers to label Tolman's theory as "cognitive behaviourism" (J. F. Brennan, 2003), a more nuanced reading of stimulus-stimulus theory reveals that the concept of *demand* (i.e., internal drive) – which can be activated in organisms, via experimenter's manipulation of the environment in a way that creates deprivation (keeping in mind ethical considerations for the species in question) – is as important to Tolman's theory as is cognition (and the cognitive capacity of rats need not be presumed to equal the cognitive capacity of humans; Feest, 2005).

Tolman (1924) selectively bred his laboratory rats in a manner that may have produced an unusually intelligent strain (Dewsbury, 2000) – a practice that has been cited as anticipating the rise of behaviour genetics (e.g., Innis, 1992), for better or worse (we will cover this controversial area of personality psychology in more detail, when we cover biological perspective in Chapter 7). On a more overtly positive note, Tolman's (1932) stimulus–stimulus theory has been credited with anticipating the rise of cognitive perspectives in psychology (J. F. Brennan, 2003). All things considered, Tolman's theory stands as a major contributor to the literature on behaviour and learning, within and beyond personality psychology (C. S. Hall & Lindzey, 1978).

CLARK HULL'S DRIVE REDUCTION THEORY

David McClelland (1985/1987) gave credit to Edward Thorndike's (1911) connectionism and Edward Tolman's (1932) stimulus–stimulus theory for exploring the survival value that biologically based needs might confer to organisms' learning processes across a variety of species. In addition, McClelland cited Clark Hull's (1943) *drive reduction theory* (which argues that potential behaviour is the product of habit strength, inborn needs, learned needs, external stimuli, and incentives; Walsh, Teo, & Baydala, 2014) as a major advance in behaviourists' attempts to make their learning-orientated research as methodologically precise as possible. Hull's drive reduction theory (also known as *hypotheticodeductive theory*; J. F. Brennan, 2003) is mathematically driven, employing algebraic formulae as testable sets of predictions concerning the interplay between internal and external influences on organisms' behaviour (Sheehy, 2004).

One of the most novel constructs in Hull's (1943) drive reduction theory is *habit strength*, or the degree to which individuals not only have (1) developed and maintained associations between the introduction of external stimuli and individuals' behavioural response but also have (2) received rewards for specific responses to specific stimuli (C. S. Hall & Lindzey, 1978). According to Hull, unless stimuli and responses follow each other closely in time and are rewarded quickly, individuals are unlikely to form a given habit in the first instance (J. F. Brennan, 2003). Once individuals form particular habits, to the extent that individuals experience an increase in rewards over time (following individuals' response to the stimuli in question), individuals' habit strength will tend to rise; to the extent that individuals experience a decrease in rewards over time, individuals' habit strength will tend to fall (Walsh, Teo, & Baydala, 2014).

Hull's (1943) drive reduction theory has been criticised for assuming (incorrectly, as it turns out) that *all* behaviour in *all* species is as mindless (i.e., completely lacking in forethought and insight) as is the behaviour of laboratory rats in tightly controlled experimental scenarios (J. F. Brennan, 2003). Nevertheless, Hull's theory has received praise for offering a considerably more sophisticated account of learning than John B. Watson's (1913) better-known theory of classical conditioning had offered (Walsh, Teo, & Baydala, 2014). Especially as elaborated by Kenneth W. Spence (1956) – who addressed many of the empirical shortcomings of Hull's theory in practice – drive reduction theory paved the way for more explicitly social-psychological theories of behaviour, such as Neal Miller and John Dollard's (1941) stimulus-response theory (which we will cover later in the present chapter).

THEORIES THAT ADDRESS THE SOCIAL ENVIRONMENT

B. F. SKINNER'S OPERANT REINFORCEMENT THEORY

If J. B. Watson (1913) served as the primary proponent of "classical behaviourism" during the early 1900s, then B. F. Skinner (1950) emerged as the main advocate of "radical behaviourism" by the mid-1900s (Ewen, 1998). In contrast to all of the preceding behaviourist theories that we have encountered so far, Skinner's (1938) *operant reinforcement theory* proposes that many (if not most) behaviours that organisms emit are voluntary, even arbitrary – *not* elicited by stimuli (C. S. Hall & Lindzey, 1978). In fact, some behaviours (e.g., a pigeon's pecking a bar) are often emitted *before* stimuli (e.g., birdseed to be released by the bar) is presented to organisms; yet stimuli may reinforce previously occurring behaviour (Clavijo, 2013). Furthermore, to the extent that an organism experiences a stimulus that follows a response as rewarding, the organism will continue to emit the response that yielded the stimulus – an example of *positive reinforcement* (Schellenberg, 1978). Accordingly, Skinner focused on *operant conditioning*, whereby organisms can be guided toward acquiring entirely new sequences of behaviour, depending on the degree to which organisms continue to experience stimuli as rewarding (Sheehy, 2004).

In terms of research, Skinner (1938) was known primarily for his application of operant reinforcement theory to the manipulation of pigeons' and rats' behaviour, respectively (Walsh, Teo, & Baydala, 2014). However, in *Verbal Behavior*, Skinner (1957) attempted to explain the most uniquely human of all behaviours – namely, *speech* – in terms of operant conditioning principles (Salzinger, 2008). According to Skinner, individuals' speech can be rewarded by audience members (thus making individuals' speech more likely to occur in the future), versus *not* rewarded – or even punished – by audience members (thus making individuals' speech less likely to occur in the future; Goddard, 2012). Thus, regardless of the complexity of the behaviour in question (and regardless of the species whose members' behaviour is under consideration), Skinner believed that the same mechanistic processes can be observed across organisms (J. F. Brennan, 2003).

Schellenberg (1978) went so far as to proclaim that Skinner (1953) was one of the "masters of social psychology" (as the title of Schellenberg's book indicates), alongside Sigmund Freud (1922), George Herbert Mead (1934/1967), and Kurt Lewin (1936). Actually, one might question whether S. Freud deserves to be included in a list of "masters of social psychology" (given S. Freud's belief in psychic determinism), although S. Freud's concept of *sublimation* (a defence mechanism that ideally redirects adults from the individually centred pursuit of sexual and aggressive motives to the more socially centred pursuit of love-related and work-related goals; see Sheehy, 2004) helps to explain why S. Freud would appear on such a list. As for Skinner, if one approaches social psychology primarily from a *sociological* standpoint (prioritising the impact of entire societies on individuals' behaviour), then one might reasonably conclude that Skinner should be regarded as a "master of social psychology" (e.g., Homans, 1961); but if one approaches social psychology primarily from a *psychological* standpoint (prioritising the impact of specific others on individuals' behaviour), then one might justifiably exclude Skinner from a shortlist of "masters of social psychology" (e.g., U. G. Foa & E. B. Foa, 1974). Of course, one need not impose such a rigid distinction between sociological and psychological social psychology (see Stryker & Statham, 1985); Skinner's (1938) operant reinforcement theory has been embraced by sociologists and psychologists alike (see Berscheid, 1985).

Should B. F. Skinner (1957) be regarded as a *personality* psychologist? If one assumes that individuals' patterns of behavioural stability and behavioural change can be understood without recourse to the self and its components (including personality constructs), then one could readily include Skinner among the ranks of personality psychologists (e.g., C. S. Hall & Lindzey, 1978); but if one assumes that individuals' patterns of behavioural stability and change *cannot* be understood without recourse to the self and its components, then one would be hard-pressed to label Skinner as a personality psychologist (e.g., Ewen, 1998). Unlike J. B. Watson (1924), Skinner never expressed any interest in understanding the antecedents of subjective states (e.g., presumed causes of individuals' anxiety; see Schellenberg, 1978). Given that Skinner is widely recognised as the best-known intellectual descendant of J. B. Watson (Clavijo, 2013), the thoroughness with which Skinner's radical behaviourism rejects "mentalism" is all the more striking (see Goddard, 2012). Perhaps the most accurate statement that one can make regarding Skinner's contributions to personality psychology is that – for all intents and purposes, Skinner (1938) believed that (1) behavioural stability is *de facto* personality stability; and (2) behavioural change is *de facto* personality change (Butt, 2004).

We hasten to add that the fields of social psychology and personality psychology overlap to a substantial degree, in terms of subject matter (following Gaines, 2016/2018). For example, in the process of defining social psychology as the study of the influence that actual, implied, or imagined others' presence might exert upon individuals' thoughts, feelings, and behaviour, G. W. Allport (1968/1985) identified the personality construct of *attitudes* (as we learned in Chapter 1 of the present book, individuals' thoughts and feelings toward a particular entity) as the major construct in social psychology. Although Skinner (1957) did not advocate the study of attitudes *per se*, intellectual followers such as Daryl Bem (1965, 1967, 1972) have argued that individuals acquire attitudes largely by reflecting upon their own behaviour (thus setting up a counterintuitive scenario whereby attitudes are interpreted as *consequences*, rather than antecedents, of individuals' behaviour; Schellenberg, 1978). We will comment further upon D. Bem's self-perception theory as a successor to Skinner's operant reinforcement theory, near the end of the present chapter.

Not only has Skinner's (1957) operant reinforcement theory been challenged on the grounds that it is inadequate as an explanation for the production of human language in particular (e.g., Chomsky, 1959); but Skinner's theory also has been challenged on the grounds that it dismisses the usefulness of *all* personality constructs (including such consciously experienced constructs as traits, values, and attitudes) as potential predictors of human behaviour in general (a dismissal that arguably helped to fuel the cognitive revolution in psychology; see Haslam, Smillie, & Song, 2017). By the same token, even Skinner's critics have acknowledged that operant reinforcement theory seems to explain certain aspects of language production (Goddard, 2012) and does not rule out the possible existence of personality constructs (Clavijo, 2013). Notwithstanding the provocative nature of Skinner's (1974) radical behaviourism, one can commend Skinner for retaining a sense of optimism concerning human behaviour as largely amenable to change via academicians' application of operant reinforcement principles (as distinct from clinicians' and academicians' application of psychodynamic or other "mentalistic" principles; Butt, 2004).

NEAL MILLER AND JOHN DOLLARD'S STIMULUS-RESPONSE THEORY

During the interval between the First and Second World Wars, the behaviourist school succeeded in prompting psychologists *en masse* to re-define their discipline as the science of behaviour (rather than the science of the mind; Hebb, 1960). However, by the time that the Second World War had begun to wreak large-scale havoc within and beyond academia, some behaviourists already were seeking to re-incorporate certain "mentalistic" constructs within their theories (Mandler, 2002). One of the earliest examples of the resulting neo-behaviourist perspective on personality was Neil Miller and John Dollard's (1941) *stimulus-response theory*, which drew jointly upon Sigmund Freud's (1900/1965) psychoanalytic theory and Ivan Pavlov's (1927) reflexology (Ewen, 1998). According to stimulus-response theory, behaviour can be understood as direct responses to within-individual influences, which (in turn) can be understood as direct responses to outside-individual influences (thus predicting that within-individual influences will mediate the impact of outside-individual influences on behaviour; C. S. Hall & Lindzey, 1978).

Probably the best-known aspect of Dollard and Miller (1950) stimulus-response theory was the *frustration-aggression hypothesis*, which holds that – when others are perceived as having prevented individuals from achieving a particular goal – individuals' drive toward aggression (following the drive theory of Hull, 1943) will be activated, leading the individuals to behave in an antisocial manner toward the others in question (Eibl-Eibesfeldt, 1977). Dollard, Miller, and colleagues (Dollard, Doob, Miller, Mowrer, & Sears, 1939) argued that (1) when one observes individuals behaving in an antisocial manner, one can be reasonably confident that the individuals have already concluded that they were frustrated by others; and (2) when individuals believe that they have been frustrated by others, one can be reasonably confident that individuals subsequently will behave in an antisocial manner toward the others in question (C. S. Hall & Lindzey, 1978). Consistent with the frustration-aggression hypothesis, Hovland and Sears (1940) reported empirical support for the frustration-aggression hypothesis in their secondary analysis of cotton prices and anti-Black lynchings in the US South (i.e., as the price of cotton went down over the years, Whites' lynchings of Blacks went up in the American South, suggesting that Black Americans appeared to be scapegoats for some White Americans' economic frustration; see J. M. Jones, 1997).

In a re-analysis using modern-day statistical methods, Hepworth and West (1988) found that the magnitude of the correlation between cotton prices at one point in time and anti-Black lynchings at a later point in time was smaller than Hovland and Sears (1940) had initially calculated. In addition, Hepworth and West uncovered a close-to-significant negative correlation between cotton prices and Whites' lynchings of other *Whites* that Hovland and Sears (1940) had neither predicted nor detected (see G. W. Allport, 1954/1979, p. 257, regarding "scapegoats for special occasions"). Nevertheless, Hepworth and West *did* replicate Hovland and Sears's overall finding that regional economic difficulties were reflected in Whites' subsequent lynching of Blacks, to a significant degree (a testament to the "prejudice problematic", as described by Dixon & Levine, 2012). Overall, Miller and Dollard's (1941; Dollard & Miller, 1950) stimulus–response theory and frustration-aggression hypothesis have (Dollard et al., 1939) received considerable support (for a review, see Marcus-Newhall, Pedersen, Carlson, & Miller, 2000).

JULIAN ROTTER'S VERSION OF SOCIAL LEARNING THEORY

Miller and Dollard (1941) initially alluded to social learning as a potential influence on individuals' behaviour but did not make social learning a major concept in their subsequent work (e.g., Dollard & Miller, 1950). To a large extent, Miller and Dollard agreed with Hull's (Hull, Hovland, Ross, M. Hall, Perkins, & Fitch, 1940) perspective on social learning as a simple process of association (e.g., "monkey see, monkey do"). In contrast, Julian Rotter's (1954) version of *social learning theory* – which draws partly upon Miller and Dollard's stimulus–response theory – addresses the role that watching other people receive (or fail to receive) reinforcement plays in individuals' formation of beliefs about the likelihood that their own behaviour will be reinforced (C. S. Hall & Lindzey, 1978). Funder (2001) noted that Rotter (1954) identified *expectancy* or expectations about potential, future reinforcement (rather than associations involving past reinforcement) as one major influence on individuals' behaviour. Weiner (2010) added that the *value* attached by individuals to potential, future reinforcement is the other major influence on individuals' behaviour in Rotter's version of social learning theory. As a result, according to Rotter, expectancy x value = behaviour (i.e., individuals' behaviour reflects individuals' belief about future outcomes, combined with the importance that individuals place upon those outcomes; Strickland, 1989).

Rotter (1966) eventually concluded that individuals differ in their beliefs about causality and control – that is, *locus of control* is assumed to vary across persons (Lefcourt, 1991). Rotter contended that individuals may be *internal* (i.e., perceive their successes or failures in life as due to their own efforts) versus *external* (i.e., perceive their successes or failures on life as due to external factors, such as impersonal fate or powerful others) in their locus of control (Carton & Nowicki, 1994). Accordingly, Rotter (1966) developed the Locus of Control Scale to measure individual differences in this construct, asking participants to answer a series of questions in which they were required to agree with one of a pair of statements (with one statement expressing an internal locus of control, and the other statement expressing an external locus of control; Strickland, 1989). Using a prototype of the Locus of Control Scale, Gore and Rotter (1963) found that persons with an internal locus of control were more likely than persons with an external locus of control to commit themselves to the US Civil Rights Movement (a finding that is consistent with the view that – having learned about other Americans "making a difference" by getting involved in the struggle for social equality – many individuals apparently decided that they, too, could help to make social change a reality, as would be expected from the social learning theory of Rotter, 1954).

In a critique of Rotter's social learning theory (1954) and conceptualisation of locus of control (1966), Carton and Nowicki (1994) pointed out that the causes or *antecedents* of individual differences in locus of control are not well understood, other than that "external" children report higher levels of stress than do "internals" (possibly because that parents of "internals" are more consistent than are parents of "externals", in terms of offering rewards when the children behave well and withholding rewards when the children behave badly). Also, due to concerns about the rigidity of Rotter's internal-external dichotomy, Levenson (1974) developed an alternative to Rotter's (1966) Locus of Control Scale that did not force participants to choose "external" over "internal" items or vice versa (as we shall see in Box 3.2, a change that allowed Levenson to identify three separate locus of control dimensions). Nevertheless, Rotter's original Locus of Control Scale remains the most popular measure of this construct (Lefcourt, 1991) and has consistently yielded results concerning the *consequences* of internal versus external locus of control (e.g., "internal" adults tend to perform significantly better on academic assessments than do "external" adults; Carton & Nowicki, 1994). All things considered, Rotter's social learning theory has emerged as one of the most influential neo-behaviourist theories of personality (Funder, 2001).

BOX 3.2 LEVENSON'S (1974) INTERNALITY, CHANCE, AND POWERFUL OTHERS SCALES

In spite of the popularity of Julian Rotter's (1966) Locus of Control Scale (undoubtedly owing to the simple, unidimensional nature of the underlying construct), some critics have noted that Rotter never conducted factor analyses of the scale (thus leaving questions unanswered regarding the construct validity of the survey across samples; e.g., West & Finch, 1997). Partly due to questions about Rotter's methodology, subsequent researchers have developed alternatives to the Locus of Control Scale (R. Brown, 1986). One of the best-known alternatives is Hanna Levenson's (1973a) multidimensional version, which measures three distinguishable aspects of locus of control: (1) *Internality*, (2) *control by chance events*, and (3) *control by powerful others* (with the latter two dimensions representing external influences that have originated within individuals' physical and social environments, respectively; Lefcourt, 1991).

In a series of studies, Levenson (e.g., Levenson, 1973a, 1973b, 1974) linked internality, control by chance events, and control by powerful others to a variety of behavioural outcomes in the spheres of work, politics, and interpersonal relations (with internality frequently leading to psychologically adaptive outcomes, and control by chance and powerful others frequently leading to psychologically maladaptive outcomes; for a review, see Levenson, 1981). Moreover, Walkey (1979) obtained independent support for Levenson's internality, chance, and powerful others dimensions (scores on chance and powerful others tend to be significantly and positively correlated with each other; whereas scores on internality are not consistently related to scores on the two external dimensions). However, apparently disregarding Levenson's results, Rotter (1975) continued to conceptualise locus of control in terms of opposite (i.e., internal versus external) types. Overall, Rotter's unidimensional perspective emerged as the dominant view regarding locus of control (R. Brown, 1986). Nevertheless, Levenson's multidimensional perspective on locus of control has been praised as a viable alternative to Rotter's view (Lefcourt, 1991).

ALBERT BANDURA AND RICHARD WALTERS'S VERSION OF SOCIAL LEARNING THEORY

Compared to Miller and Dollard's (1941) stimulus–response theory, Rotter's (1954) version of social learning theory represents a move away from Sigmund Freud's (1920/1961) version of psychoanalytic theory (C. S. Hall & Lindzey, 1978). As Grusec (1992) noted, Albert Bandura and Richard Walters's version of *social learning theory* (1963) continued the move away from Freudian constructs. W. F. White (1993) added that, according to Bandura and Walters's (1963) social learning theory, most of what individuals learn is acquired from observing other persons' behaviour (along with the rewards versus punishments that those other persons receive). However, Bandura and Walters were not particularly interested in examining the construct of locus of control that Rotter (1966) had popularised (see Funder, 2001). Rather, Bandura and Walters cast their social learning theory as a direct response to Miller and Dollard's (1950) stimulus–response theory – specifically, in testing the frustration–aggression hypothesis (as articulated by Dollard, Doob, Miller, Mowrer, & Sears, 1939).

Albert Bandura, Dorothea Ross, and Sheila Ross's (1961) classic study of the effects of modelling on children's displaced aggression (i.e., the "Bobo doll" study) was an important precursor to the development of Bandura and Walters's (1963) social learning theory (Ewen, 1998). Children who not only were prevented from playing with attractive toys (i.e., subjected to frustration, in the terms of Miller & Dollard, 1941) but also had observed an adult model reacting to frustration by acting aggressively toward a large Bobo doll were significantly more likely to engage in aggressive behaviour of their own toward the hapless Bobo doll than were children who either (1) saw a model acting *non*aggressively in response to frustration or (2) did not see a model in advance (Sheehy, 2004). Thus, contrary to Miller and Dollard (1941) stimulus–response theory and frustration–aggression hypothesis (Dollard, Doob, Miller, Mowrer, & Sears, 1939), Bandura and colleagues found that frustration *did* not lead inevitably to aggression (C. S. Hall & Lindzey, 1978). Indeed, as Markus and Zajonc (1985) pointed out, Bandura and Walters's version of social learning theory has been described as a stimulus–*organism*–response theory, because of the importance that it places upon individuals' capacity for consciously processing information from the environment before deciding on a course of action.

E. E. Jones (1985/1998) criticised Bandura and Walters's (1963) version of social learning theory (among other neo-behaviourist theories) for failing to acknowledge the role that models often play in deliberately seeking to shape observers' behaviour. However, W. F. White (1993) credited Bandura and Walters for attending to individuals' capacity for self-rewards and self-punishments as distinct from the rewards and punishments that they may receive from other persons. Finally, in Bandura and Walters's version of social learning theory, children as well as adults have the capacity to grasp the concepts of rewards and punishments (including self-rewards and self-punishments) – capacities that Hull (1943) and Miller and Dollard (1941) had not anticipated (see C. S. Hall & Lindzey, 1978). All in all, Bandura and Walters's theory helped set the stage for even more overtly cognitive theories of personality (e.g., the social-cognitive theory of Bandura, 1986, which we will cover in Chapter 6) in the aftermath of the cognitive revolution in psychology (see Sheehy, 2004).

CRITIQUE OF BEHAVIOURIST PERSPECTIVES

Is it as easy for psychologists to banish the self and its contents (e.g., all of the personality constructs that one will find in the present book) from empirical consideration as some behaviourists (especially Skinner, 1938) would have us believe? By and large, personality psychologists would respond with an emphatic "No!" to such a question (see Ewen, 1998). Surely human beings possess selves (James, 1890/2010), however unaware individuals might be regarding particular contents of their selves at a particular point in time (S. Freud, 1900/1965). Surely the self and its contents are linked to individuals' behaviour (G. W. Allport, 1961/1963), however dependent individuals' behaviour might be upon situational influences (G. W. Allport, 1937/1951).

One of the most creative attempts to reconcile behaviourism (most notably operant conditioning theory; Skinner, 1938) with "mentalism" (most notably self-theory; James, 1890/2010) is Daryl Bem's (1965, 1967, 1972) *self-perception theory* (which proposes that individuals infer their attitudes partly by speculating on the reasons why they behave as they do toward specific physical and social stimuli; Schellenberg, 1978). In practice, D. Bem's self-perception theory does not explain the formation of *all* attitudes (or the consequences of *all* behaviours; S. T. Fiske & S. E. Taylor, 1991). Nonetheless, D. Bem's theory complements Leon Festinger's (1957) *cognitive dissonance theory* (which posits that discrepancies between individuals' attitudes and behaviour result in anxiety, which individuals may seek to reduce by changing their attitudes over time; Petty & Brinol, 2015) by explaining that no presumption of prior discrepancy-generated anxiety is necessary for one to understand how particular attitudes are formed (Molouki & Pronin, 2015). More generally, D. Bem's self-perception theory embodies the *Scientist* mode or metaphor of self-perception (which is based on the assumption that individuals are motivated to acquire the most accurate information that they can acquire about themselves; Robins & John, 1997) and might ultimately be applied to other aspects of the self.

PRELUDE TO CHAPTER 4

In *Societal Structures of the Mind*, Uriel G. Foa and Edna B. Foa (1974) contended that psychodynamic therapists (in the tradition of S. Freud, 1900/1965) tend to deny respect (if not affection) to their clients; whereas it is not clear whether behaviourist therapists (in the tradition of Skinner, 1938) give or deny the interpersonal resources of affection and respect to their clients. In stark contrast, according to U. G. Foa and E. B. Foa, *humanistic* therapists (in the tradition of Rogers, 1961) tend to give affection as well as respect to their clients – a testament to the "Third Force" that Abraham Maslow (1954) envisioned for humanism as a counterpoint to the psychodynamic and behaviourist schools in personality psychology (Sappington, 1989). Within the school of humanism include, representative theories include (in order of appearance) the love-oriented aspects of Erich Fromm's (1957) didactic humanism (as distinct from the hate-orientated aspects; e.g., Fromm, 1941); Kurt Goldstein's (1939) organismic psychology, Charlotte Buhler's (1968) version of humanistic psychology, Abraham Maslow's (1968) version of self-actualisation theory, and Carl Rogers's

(1961) version of self-actualisation theory. [In addition, within the related school of *existentialism*, representative theories include (in order of appearance) Jean-Paul Sartre's (1943/1956) version of existential philosophy, Simone de Beauvoir's (1947) version of existential philosophy, Frantz Fanon's (1952/1967) version of existential psychology, and Rollo May's (1953) version of existential psychology.] In Chapter 4, we will examine these theories and associated research – alongside alternative perspectives from the emergent *positive psychology* movement (i.e., Diener, Emmons, Larsen, & Griffin, 1985; Ryan & Deci, 2000b; Ryff, 1989) – in greater detail.

HUMANISTIC AND EXISTENTIAL PERSPECTIVES ON PERSONALITY

In Chapter 3, we referred to Erich Fromm's (1941) social-psychological personality theory as "didactic humanism" (following C. S. Hall & Lindzey, 1957; see also Brookfield, 2002). However, Fromm preferred the term *existential humanism* as a label for his theory (Cortina, 2015). The latter term captures Fromm's belief that – despite the allure of authoritarianism as a means toward escaping the demands of freedom (with the negative consequence of succumbing to hatred toward entire groups of stigmatised persons; G. W. Allport, 1954/1979) – individuals ideally should embrace freedom by choosing to enter and maintain particular close relationships (e.g., Fromm, 1957). Fromm's resulting typology of ways of loving (i.e., individuals' attitudes toward various types of close relationships) is reflected in John Alan Lee's (1973) typology of colours of love (i.e., brotherly love, or friendship love; motherly love, or selfless love; erotic love, or passionate love; self-love, or love turned inward; and love of one's Creator, or religious love). In turn, J. A. Lee's typology is reflected in Clyde Hendrick and Susan Hendrick's (1986; C. Hendrick, S. S. Hendrick, Foote, & Clapion-Foote, 1984; C. Hendrick, S. S. Hendrick, & Dicke, 1998) typology of love styles, or attitudes toward love (i.e., eros, or passionate love; agape, or selfless love; pragma, or practical love; storge, or friendship love; mania, or obsessive love; and ludus, or game-playing love; see Djikic & Oatley, 2004). With the exception of ludus (which clearly undermines pro-relationship behaviour), love styles either promote pro-relationship behaviour (i.e., eros, possibly agape) or – at a minimum – do not work against individuals' relationship-maintaining behaviour (i.e., pragma, storge, and mania; Gaines, 2016/2018).

Fromm's (1941, 1957) didactic (or, alternatively, existential) humanism ultimately emerged as a seminal influence on theories, research, and practice in humanistic psychology and existential psychology (D. Hoffman, 2003). Perhaps the most obvious example of Fromm's influence on the two (sub)fields was the role that Fromm played as psychoanalyst and mentor for Rollo May, who subsequently helped to introduce much of the English-speaking world – especially the United States – to European existentialist theories of philosophy (e.g., May, Angel, & Ellenberger, 1958; see Buxton, 2005). May's knack for integrating constructs from humanistic psychology and existentialist psychology undoubtedly was nurtured by Fromm's didactic/existential humanism (see Peng, 2011).

In the present chapter, we shall examine personality theories from the perspectives of humanistic psychology and existential psychology, respectively. Notwithstanding the differences between the two perspectives (most notably concerning humans' awareness of their own mortality, which is emphasised more prominently within existential psychology than it is emphasised within humanistic psychology; C. S. Hall & Lindzey, 1970), we shall refer to "humanistic/existential psychology" as a school of thought that is unified by the belief that human nature essentially is positive or constructive (see Ewen, 1998). Along the way, we shall also consider contributions from the modern-day positive psychology movement, which has been cast as more empirically rigorous than humanistic/existential psychology (e.g., Seligman & Csikszentmihalyi, 2000) but nonetheless owes a considerable intellectual debt to humanistic/existential psychology (e.g., K. J. Schneider, 2011b).

BASIC ASSUMPTIONS UNDERLYING HUMANISTIC AND EXISTENTIAL PERSPECTIVES

According to humanistic/existential psychology, the whole person – not the gene, cell, or even brain of the person – is the proper unit of analysis for personality psychology (E. Taylor, 2000). Implicit in this core belief is the assumption that human behaviour cannot be reduced entirely to mechanistic processes involving individuals' brains working in isolation from individuals' physical and social environments (the latter of which typically includes interaction with other human beings; see E. Taylor, 1991). Rather, in order to understand why humans behave as they do, one must begin with the individual person and sub-sequently consider information about the person's behaviour as a function of various forces within the person *and* various forces out-side the person (E. Taylor, 2010).

Furthermore, just as the human mind is integral to the body (especially the brain) within which it resides, according to human-istic/existential psychology, so too is human consciousness an essential aspect of the mind that gave rise to it (a stance that distin-guishes the humanistic/existential school from the psychodynamic and behaviouristic schools of thought within personality psych-ology; K. J. Schneider, 2011a). Like freedom, consciousness is never absolute; human beings operate within physical and psycho-logical constraints that necessarily place limits on their awareness of the world (Greening, 1992). Nevertheless, among mortal entities on Earth, humans' capacity for awareness of their physical and social environments seems to be unrivalled (although some critics might contend that human beings are not sufficiently aware of [other] animals' awareness to claim outright superiority in this regard; e.g., Adams, 2010).

Finally, just as human consciousness is part and parcel of the mind from which it arose, in the view of humanistic/existential psychology, so too is the self a vital aspect of the consciousness from which it was derived (a perspective that likewise distinguishes the humanistic/existential school from the psychodynamic and behaviourist schools; Slife & Barnard, 1988). Among human beings, it is not just the case that individuals are aware of their physical and social environments; individuals are aware that *they* are the ones who possess such awareness (although the self may be far more elusive than any other aspect of individuals' daily experience; Puhakka, 2000). If any of the constructs that we have covered so far in the present chapter qualifies as uniquely human, then the self (and its by-product, the self-concept) would seem to be such a candidate (Sleeth, 2006).

Before covering specific theories in detail, we acknowledge that some critics (e.g., DeCarvalho, 1990) have distinguished between (1) the process of "becoming" (part of the being versus becoming dichotomy) as determined by a self-actualisation motive, from the standpoint of humanistic personality theories (e.g., Buhler, 1968; Goldstein, 1939, 1940; Maslow, 1962, 1968; Rogers, 1951, 1961); and (2) the process of "becoming" as freely sought by individuals, from the standpoint of existential personality theories (e.g., de Beauvoir, 1947; 1949/2009; Fanon, 1952/1967; 1961/1963; May, 1953, 1969; Sartre, 1943/1956; 1953/1996). However, other critics (e.g., McDonald & Wearing, 2013) do not draw such a distinction between humanistic and existential theories. In any event, throughout the present chapter, we will pay close attention to the manner in which "becoming" is described within various humanistic and existential theories.

HUMANISTIC THEORIES OF PERSONALITY

KURT GOLDSTEIN'S ORGANISMIC PSYCHOLOGY

According to Kurt Goldstein's (1939) *organismic psychology*, unity among the mind, body, and soul promotes individuals' physical and mental health; whereas discord among mind, body, and soul places individuals' physical and mental health at risk (Noppenney, 2001). Goldstein overtly drew upon William James's (1890/2010) self-theory – not just in promoting mind-body unity, but also in emphasising the construct of soul (a controversial construct throughout the history of psychology, as we observed in Chapter 1 of the present book). Having specialised in the rehabilitation of former World War I-era German soldiers whose brain injuries had resulted in *aphasia* (i.e., severe impairment in spoken and/or written language; York, 2009), Goldstein (1940) proposed that all human beings – whether brain-damaged or not – possess a motive or psychological need toward *self-actualisation* (i.e., the need to achieve or fulfil one's own potential; Fisher, 1949).

Notwithstanding the universality of self-actualisation as a psychological need among human beings, Goldstein's (1939, 1940) organismic psychology does *not* assume that all humans are equally successful in meeting that need (C. S. Hall, Lindzey, & Campbell, 1998). Various aspects of individuals' *environment* (which Goldstein conceived as the objective world; C. S. Hall, Lindzey, Loehlin, & Manosevitz, 1985) can enable or impede individuals' quest for self-actualisation. Details regarding the ways in which the environment can influence individuals' success versus failure in striving to fulfil their innate potential are provided by C. S. Hall and Lindzey (1978).

Goldstein (1939, 1940) has been criticised for basing an entire theory of personality on the physical and psychological experiences of a highly atypical group of individuals (i.e., former soldiers who suffered from aphasia; C. S. Hall, Lindzey, Loehlin, & Manosevitz, 1985). By the same token, Goldstein's organismic psychology in general (and construct of the self-actualisation motive in particular) is reflected directly in the subsequent self-actualisation theories of Maslow (1968) and Rogers (1961) – both of which have been applied to studies of non-clinical populations (see C. S. Hall, Lindzey, & Campbell, 1998). Furthermore, Goldstein's theory helped to revive psychologists' interest in James's (1890/2010) self-theory at a time when James's influence was in decline (e.g., James's focus on conscious experience had been criticised by psychodynamic theorists and behaviourists alike; see E. Taylor, 1999).

CHARLOTTE BUHLER'S VERSION OF HUMANISTIC PSYCHOLOGY

From the standpoint of Charlotte Buhler's (1968) version of *humanistic psychology*, the entire self is amenable to development, throughout individuals' life span (DeRobertis, 2015). Although Buhler (e.g., Buhler & Allen, 1972) acknowledged the influence of Goldstein's (1939) organismic psychology (DeRobertis, 2006), Buhler's version of humanistic psychology did not propose the existence of a single, all-encompassing master motive (i.e., self-actualisation). Compared to Goldstein, Buhler was more concerned with individuals' *intentionality* (i.e., the set of ideas that individuals possess regarding the goals that they embrace, combined with the set of ideas that individuals possess regarding the ways that they might go about fulfilling those goals) – rather than any particular motive – as a guiding force in individuals' self-development (see Jacobsen, 2007).

At first glance, one might detect a passing similarity between Buhler's (1968; Buhler & Allen, 1972) version of humanistic psychology and Erikson's (1959, 1963/1995; 1968/1994) ego psychology in terms of a shared concern with individuals' lifelong personality development. Indeed, given the greater prominence of Erikson's ego psychology (e.g., Ewen, 1998; C. S. Hall & Lindzey, 1970), one might ask what (if any) unique insight Buhler's version of humanistic psychology has to offer regarding the self, beyond the insight that Erikson's ego psychology already offers. In response, one is struck by Buhler's attention to the entire, unified self – not the oft-fragmented personality structure of id, ego, and superego that appears so often in Erikson's theory (DeRobertis, 2006).

Buhler's (1968; Buhler & Allen, 1972) version of humanistic psychology has been neglected, relative to other humanistic theories of personality (DeRobertis, 2006) – a situation that might lead one to question the importance of Buhler's theory. However, it may be more plausible for one to speculate that Buhler's status as one of the few prominent women in humanistic psychology (see E. Taylor, 2000) may have been responsible for personality psychologists' tendency to overlook Buhler's conceptual contributions to the field. Taken in its proper historical context, Buhler's version of humanistic theory serves as a solid bridge between humanistic and existential perspectives on personality (DeRobertis, 2006).

ABRAHAM MASLOW'S VERSION OF SELF-ACTUALISATION THEORY

Abraham Maslow's (1962, 1968) version of *self-actualisation theory* proposes that the self-actualisation motive is the most prized, yet least often fulfilled, of all human needs (Ewen, 1998). Unlike Goldstein's (1939, 1940) organismic psychology, Maslow's version of self-actualisation theory postulates the existence of several needs (i.e., physiological, safety, love/belonging, esteem/respect, and self-actualisation) that individuals typically experience as hierarchical (e.g., before one can satisfy one's safety needs for shelter and protection, one must attend to one's needs for food and water).

Nevertheless, Maslow's version of self-actualisation theory clearly bears the influence of Goldstein's organismic psychology (C. S. Hall & Lindzey, 1970).

In order to identify individuals who (in his opinion) had fulfilled their need for self-actualisation, Maslow (1954/1987) amassed qualitative "data" (e.g., biographical information) from historical as well as then-living public figures, in addition to his observations regarding the personalities of several of his own friends and acquaintances (C. S. Hall & Lindzey, 1970). This unusual data set served as a primary basis for Maslow's contention that some individuals defy the odds and progress through the entire hierarchy of needs over time (McClelland, 1985/1987). Although one might readily question the objectivity of Maslow's "study" (e.g., the criteria for inclusion versus exclusion of particular individuals were not stated clearly in advance of data "collection"; Ewen, 1998), Maslow acknowledged the methodological flaws in his own "research" and argued that detailed knowledge about individuals' personalities required unconventional as well as conventional research methods (Wertz, 2015).

Guided by Abraham Maslow's (1954) version of self-actualisation theory, Everett Shostrom (1964) developed the Personal Orientation Inventory (POI) to measure individual differences in achieved self-actualisation. As Tosi and Lindamood (1975) observed, the POI consists of 150 items, with 127 of those items belonging to one subscale, termed *inner-directedness* (i.e., the degree to which individuals live in a manner that reflects their beliefs, even if it means placing individuals at odds with significant others); the remaining 23 items belong to a second subscale, termed *time competence* (i.e., the extent to which individuals live in the here and now, rather than the past or the future; but see Forest and Sicz, 1980, concerning errors in the scoring manual of Shostrom, 1974, regarding time competence). Criticisms regarding forced-choice format and high intercorrelations among supposedly independent subscales of Shostrom's POI were so frequent and so consistent that Shostrom eventually developed a new survey, the Personal Orientation Dimensions (POD; Shostrom, 1975). Nevertheless, Friedman (2008) noted that (despite its psychometric problems) Shostrom's original POI remains the best-known measure of individual differences in achieved self-actualisation.

More recently, Robert Taormina and Jennifer Gao (2013) developed a 72-item inventory to measure individual differences in satisfaction of all five of the needs within Maslow's (1962) hierarchy (12 items measuring satisfaction of the self-actualisation need, 15 items apiece measuring satisfaction of the physiological, safety, love/belonging, and esteem/respect needs). All five of Taormina and Gao's scales proved to be valid (in terms of construct validity) and reliable (in terms of internal consistency) within a large sample of individuals in China, even though the scales initially were written in English. Taormina and Gao obtained significant positive correlations among scores on all five of the need satisfaction scales, with the highest correlations emerging among pairs of needs that were closest to each other conceptually within Maslow's need hierarchy. In addition, Taormina and Gao reported that scores on family support, traditional values, and life satisfaction were significantly and positively correlated with satisfaction of all five of the needs within Maslow's hierarchy. Finally, Taormina and Gao found that *neuroticism* or emotional instability was significantly and negatively correlated with satisfaction of all five needs within Maslow's hierarchy. [We will learn more about neuroticism when we cover the trait school of thought in Chapter 5.]

In one of the most novel (and, to some extent, controversial) applications of Maslow's (1962) version of self-actualisation theory, Eli Finkel and colleagues (Finkel, Hui, Carswell, & Larson, 2014; Finkel, Larson, Carswell, & Hui, 2014) presented and revised a *suffocation model of marriage* in the United States, reimagining Maslow's hierarchy of needs as "Mount Maslow". Finkel et al. contended that, from the mid-1800s to the present time, individuals within the United States have placed increasing demands on their marriages – shifting from an emphasis on satisfying individuals' lower-order needs (physiological, safety), to satisfying love/belongingness and esteem/respect needs, to satisfying higher-order needs (esteem, self-actualisation). Finkel and colleagues (Finkel, Cheung, Emery, Carswell, & Larson, 2015) argued that the not-so-good news is as follows: American marriages have never been at a higher risk of breakdown, due to the demands for individuals' higher-order need satisfaction that simply cannot be met in many (if not most) instances – hence, Finkel et al.'s use of the term "suffocation model" to describe contemporary marriages in the US. Nevertheless, Finkel and colleagues (2015) concluded that the good news is as follows: Those American marriages that *do* survive the increased demands for individuals' higher-order need satisfaction tend to be more fulfilling than virtually any marriages in earlier eras.

Guest (2014) noted that Maslow (1969) had described a sixth set of needs – that is, *ego-transcendent* needs that are spiritual, not self-interested – in order to understand what might motivate those lucky few individuals who had become self-actualised. Unfortunately, Maslow died in 1970, before having a chance to develop the concept of self-transcendent needs more fully. Few humanistic psychologists seem to be aware of Maslow's (1969) concept of ego-transcendent needs, which could explain the lack of systematic research on these latter needs. However, Koltko-Rivera (2006) pointed out that Maslow's evolving thoughts concerning ego-transcendent needs (also known as "metaneeds") led him to serve as one of the founders of the Journal of Transpersonal Psychology. At any rate, Maslow's version of self-actualisation theory (including the original hierarchy of needs) arguably is the best-known and most influential of all theories within the humanistic/existential school of personality psychology (see Moss, 2015).

CARL ROGERS'S VERSION OF SELF-ACTUALISATION THEORY

In Carl Rogers's (1951, 1961) version of *self-actualisation theory*, the need for self-actualisation is the only master motive that individuals possess at birth (Ewen, 1998). Unlike Goldstein's (1939, 1940) organismic psychology, Rogers's version of self-actualisation theory also proposes that individuals acquire the *need for positive regard from others* and the *need for self-regard* in the years following infancy (C. S. Hall & Lindzey, 1970). Nonetheless, like Maslow's (1962, 1968) version, Rogers's version of self-actualisation theory pays homage to Goldstein's organismic theory (McClelland, 1985/ 1987).

Rogers's (1951, 1961) version of self-actualisation theory arose from Rogers's experience as a counselling psychologist (Warner, 2009). Based on his work with clients who were facing everyday problems (as distinct from the clients whose cases involving moderate-to-severe psychological impairment provided much of the source material for psychiatrists and clinicians, especially within the psychodynamic tradition; Millon, 1996), Rogers concluded that most individuals already possess the social and psychological tools that they need to resolve their own problems (C. S. Hall & Lindzey, 1970). Moreover, Rogers became convinced that – above all else – counsellors should provide *unconditional positive regard* to their clients (thus helping clients meet their needs for positive regard from others, self-regard, and self-actualisation; Ewen, 1998). Consistent with Rogers's belief in a clients' ability to work through their difficulties with little to no overt guidance from counsellors, Rogers used terms such as *client-centred therapy*, *person-centred therapy*, and *nondirective therapy* to describe his approach to psychotherapy (Kensit, 2000).

One problem that arises for students of Rogers's (1951, 1961) version of self-actualisation theory is the lack of precision that characterises some of Rogers's writings (Tudor, 2010). For example, the terms *self* and *self-concept* – which, as we learned in Chapter 1 of the present book, are not identical (i.e., the self-concept is individuals' reflection on the self; Baumeister, 1997) – often are used as if they *are* identical (see Ewen, 1998). However, among all of the major theories within the humanistic/existential school of personality psychology, Rogers's version of self-actualisation theory may have exerted the greatest influence on quantitative research regarding self-esteem (undoubtedly due to Rogers's leading role as a "guardian of the self"; Morf & Mischel, 2012, p. 23). In Box 4.1, we review the Rosenberg Self-Esteem Scale (variously labelled as the SES or the RSES; Rosenberg, 1965), which was inspired partly by Rogers's version of self-actualisation theory (Funder & Fast, 2010).

EXISTENTIAL THEORIES OF PERSONALITY

JEAN-PAUL SARTRE'S VERSION OF EXISTENTIAL PHILOSOPHY

Looming large over humanistic psychology in general is Aristotelian philosophy (e.g., *The Ethics of Aristotle: The Nicomachean Ethics*; Thomson, 1955), which defined the human *mind* as a set of psychological attributes that includes *nutritive* (i.e., appetite-orientated), *sensitive* (i.e., emotion-orientated), and *rational* (i.e., reason-

BOX 4.1 ROSENBERG'S (1965) SELF-ESTEEM SCALE

In their chapter on modes or metaphors of self-perception, Robins and John (1997) contended that the *Egoist* metaphor (exemplified by the self-enhancement motive, as we noted in Chapter 2) is evident in certain proto-humanist personality theories, especially James's (1890/2010) self-theory and G. W. Allport's (1937/1951) psychology of the individual; certain humanist personality theories, especially Rogers's (1959) version of self-actualisation theory; and Rosenberg's (1965) empirical research on self-esteem. Although the Egoist metaphor might lead one to assume that self-enhancement *per se* is maladaptive (e.g., unhealthy whether expressed via high self-esteem or via high narcissism; Baumeister, 1998), it is worth distinguishing between genuinely high self-esteem and the inflated view of self that is properly termed as *narcissism* (which we covered in Chapter 2 of the present book). The Rosenberg Self-Esteem Scale (SES, also known as the RSES), developed by Morris Rosenberg in 1965, has emerged as the most widely used measure of individuals' realistically high (versus low) levels of self-esteem within personality and social psychology (G. MacDonald & M. R. Leary, 2012).

Funder and Fast (2010) identified a direct conceptual link between Rogers's (1951, 1961) concept of unconditional positive regard (which therapists ideally should display toward clients; Walsh, Teo, & Baydala, 2014) and Rosenberg's (1965) construct of self-esteem as measured by the Self-Esteem Scale. Possibly the best-documented result regarding the impact of self-esteem on other personality constructs is the tendency for self-esteem to act as a significant negative predictor of depression (Blascovich & Tomaka, 1991). In addition, self-esteem is a significant positive predictor of life satisfaction and a significant negative predictor of anxiety (Rosenberg, 1989). All of these results can be explained by Rogers's version of self-actualisation theory, which identifies a variety of adaptive functions of the self (Morf & Mischel, 2012).

Of course, self-esteem is not a panacea for all that ails individuals (Baumeister, 1998). Nevertheless, the Self-Esteem Scale (Rosenberg, 1965) measures self-esteem in a manner that allows researchers to propose and test a large assortment of hypotheses regarding the effects of self-esteem on other personality variables (Blascovich & Tomaka, 1991). In fact, G. MacDonald and M. R. Leary (2012) credited the Rosenberg Self-Esteem Scale with fuelling the enormous rise in studies of self-esteem that occurred within personality and social psychology during the 1960s and 1970s.

orientated) "*souls*" (Garcia-Valdecasas, 2005). Despite the historical importance of Aristotelian philosophy to humanistic psychology (Moss, 2015), philosopher Jean-Paul Sartre (1943/1956) rejected Aristotle's basic premise that human beings possess "souls" at birth (or ever; Quzilbash, 1998). Instead, Sartre developed a version of *existential philosophy* that depicts individuals' *existence* (i.e., the ongoing process by which individuals make something of themselves) as necessarily preceding and giving rise to individuals' *essence* (i.e., that which individuals have made of themselves at any given point in time; L. Hoffman, S. Stewart, Warren, & Meek, 2015).

In general, Sartre (1943/1956) cast his version of existential philosophy as orientated toward human consciousness (Dolezal, 2012). However, Sartre (1953/1996) eventually attempted to combine elements of his theory with Sigmund Freud's (1900/1965) version of psychoanalytic theory to produce *existential psychoanalysis* (emphasising unconscious aspects of individuals' existence via the content of psychobiographies; Churchill & Wertz, 2015). According to Sartre's existential psychoanalysis, an important task of self-development is the excavation of personal material out of the unconscious and into consciousness (Gilliam, 2017). As it turns out, the existential psychoanalytic therapies of Medard Boss (1963) and R. D. Laing (1960), among others, were influenced by the psychoanalytic component of Sartre's existential philosophy (A. Jones, 2001).

Sartre's (1943/1956) version of existential philosophy has been criticised for logical inconsistencies concerning existence and essence (e.g., Sartre considers the philosophical and theological construct of human nature to be part of individuals' essence, yet human nature surely must exist at the time of individuals' birth; Dolezal, 2012). However, if Sartre's theory is applied narrowly to psychological constructs such as self and identity (e.g., the individual self exists at birth and subsequently gives rise to identity development; see Gilliam, 2017), then Sartre's version of existential philosophy – or, perhaps more correctly, the component of Sartre's theory that is known as *existential phenomenology* (emphasising individuals' subjective, conscious experience of themselves as existing in the world; Churchill & Wertz, 2015) – may qualify as logically consistent after all (especially if one acknowledges the role of other persons in co-creating individuals' identities over time; L. Hoffman, Stewart, Warren, & Meek, 2015). To sum it up, Sartre's version of existential philosophy – like Aristotle's philosophy (as we will learn later in the present chapter, when we examine the positive psychology movement) – offers important insight into individuals' responsibility for their own character development (Qizilbash, 1998).

SIMONE DE BEAUVOIR'S VERSION OF EXISTENTIAL PHILOSOPHY

From the standpoint of Simone de Beauvoir's (1947, 1949/2009) version of *existential philosophy*, although human beings in general possess the *capacity* for expression of their will (and, hence, seek freedom as well as morality), not all groups of individuals are in an equally advantaged position to *act* on the basis of their will (Hekman, 2015). Unlike Sartre's (1943/1956, 1953/1996) version of existential philosophy, de Beauvoir's version highlights the additional societal-level as well as individual-level difficulties that women (compared to men) must overcome in order to express free will (Tantam, 2015). Nevertheless, de Beauvoir's version of existential philosophy reflects the joint influence of Sigmund Freud's (1900/1965) version of psychoanalytic theory and Sartre's version of existential philosophy (particularly Sartre's [1953/1996] existential psychoanalysis; Adkins, 2013).

Like Sartre, de Beauvoir was not a trained psychotherapist (Tantam, 2015). However, unlike Sartre, de Beauvoir served as an unofficial counsellor for many female students. Moreover, de Beauvoir's (1947, 1949/2009) version of existential philosophy has been credited with helping psychotherapists offer practical advice to those women whose (frequently male) partners expect them to serve as relationship managers (e.g., Barker 2010). Finally, lest we give the impression that de Beauvoir's version of existential philosophy is relevant only to women's social-psychological functioning, de Beauvoir's theory has been cited for its insight into the roots of *narcissistic personality disorder* among men as well as women (e.g., even individuals who possess unusually high levels of self-love need relationship partners who are willing to affirm individuals' emotions; Gildersleeve, 2015).

A key criticism of de Beauvoir's (1947, 1949/2009) version of existential philosophy is the lack of a clear explanation regarding ways that individual women can exercise their free will (e.g., Hekman, 2015). Nonetheless, de Beauvoir's theory does suggest that groups of women (as well as some men) should band together to seek societal change that, in turn, would enable individual women to express their will and seek freedom and morality (Hekman, 2015). Perhaps the most obvious evidence concerning the lingering impact of de Beauvoir's version of existential philosophy (outside, if not necessarily within, the male-dominated school of humanistic/existential psychology during the mid-twentieth century; Tantam, 2015) is the acknowledgement by feminist Betty Friedan that de Beauvoir's *The Second Sex* (1953/2009) influenced Friedan's own classic, *The Feminine Mystique* (1963).

FRANTZ FANON'S VERSION OF EXISTENTIAL PSYCHOLOGY

According to Frantz Fanon's (1952/1967, 1961/1963) version of *existential psychology*, the existence (and, consequently, the essence) of victims of colonialism is fundamentally different from the existence (and essence) of perpetrators of colonialism throughout the world (Omar, 2009). Like de Beauvoir's (1947, 1949/2009) version of existential philosophy – and unlike Sartre's (1943/1956, 1953/1996) version of existential philosophy – Fanon's version of existential psychology directly addresses the dehumanising effects of slavery on enslaved persons and slave masters alike (as well as the descendants of slaves and masters; Adkins, 2013). However, unlike either de Beauvoir's or Sartre's versions of existential philosophy, Fanon's version of existential psychology focused on ethnicity (and especially race) as the primary construct for viewing the role of society in promoting or hindering individuals' expression of free will (Bernasconi, 2000). Despite the differences between Fanon's version of existential psychology and the existential philosophies of de Beauvoir and Sartre, Fanon's construct of the "White gaze" (literally and figuratively, a means by which persons of European descent may objectify persons of African descent; Zeiler, 2013) was derived from Sartre's construct of "the Look" (a means by which any individual may objectify another person; see Pearce, 2011).

After World War II, Fanon was trained as a psychiatrist (Clarke, 2000). Given that Fanon was well-versed in the methods of psychoanalysis (e.g., free association, probing clients' unconscious via examination of the content of dreams), Fanon's (1952/ 1967, 1961/1963) version of existential psychology deals primarily with the *interpersonal anxiety* that victims of colonialism experience on a daily basis (e.g., African-descent persons' negative affective or emotional reaction to the "White gaze"; see Maldonado-Torres, 2017). Thus, Fanon's version of existential psychology offers a unique, practitioner-based twist on the existential psychoanalysis that both Sartre (1943/1956, 1953/1996) and de Beauvoir (1947, 1949/2009) had advocated (Adkins, 2013).

Fanon's (1952/1967, 1961/1963) version of existential psychology – particularly as presented in *Black Skin, White Masks* (1952) – has been criticised as sexist, due to its objectification of women (Adkins, 2013). By the same token, in *The Wretched of the Earth* (1961/1963), Fanon's personal experience as a freedom fighter in Algeria sensitised Fanon to the negative effects of colonialism on men and women alike (Omar, 2009). All in all, Fanon's version of existential psychology has been credited with influencing the development of Black/African psychology as an interdisciplinary field, within and beyond the United States (Jamison, 2010).

ROLLO MAY'S VERSION OF EXISTENTIAL PSYCHOLOGY

In Rollo May's (1953, 1969) version of *existential psychology*, the dread that accompanies human beings' awareness of their own mortality – that is, their *existential anxiety* – emerges as a central construct (E. Craig, 2008). Perhaps to a greater extent than does any other theory within the humanistic/existential school, May's version of existential psychology challenges individuals to directly confront (if not conquer) their existential anxiety over the short term, because such confrontation is essential to individuals' success in achieving and maintaining well-being over the long term (Kiser, 2007). Nevertheless, May's version of existential psychology clearly owes an intellectual debt to Sartre's (1943/1956) version of existential philosophy (Churchill & Wertz, 2015).

Following Sartre's (1943/1956, 1953/1996) lead, May's (1953, 1969) version of existential psychology casts *love* – which May famously defined as "*a delight in the presence of the other person and an affirming of [the other person's] value and development as much as one's own [value and development]* " (1953, p. 206, emphasis in original) – as an emotion that is sufficiently powerful to enable individuals to face their existential anxiety in an authentic manner (Kiser, 2007). As a trained clinician, May applied his version of existential psychology to clients' dual concerns with (1) being versus nonbeing (manifested in clients' existential anxiety toward the spectre of death) and (2) being versus becoming (manifested in clients' love toward significant others; Medina, 2008). Subsequently, Pitchford (2009) – having been influenced by May's best-selling classic, *Love and Will* (1969) – reported the successful treatment of a former soldier who had suffered from post-traumatic stress disorder (PTSD), via a direct appeal to the client's love for his former comrades (alongside the client's love for himself).

May's (1953, 1969) version of existential psychology has been criticised for failing to stimulate quantitative research in humanistic or existential psychology (a critique that has been directed toward the existential psychology theories of Binswanger, 1963; and Boss, 1963; see C. S. Hall & Lindzey, 1970). However, May's "kinds of love" (i.e., *sex*, or lustful love; *eros*, or passionate love; *philia*, or friendship love; and *agape*, or selfless love) – described most explicitly in May's *Love and Will* (1969) – directly influenced Lee's (1976) qualitative research on "colours of love" (described earlier in the present chapter), which subsequently influenced C. Hendrick and S. S. Hendrick's (1986; C. Hendrick, S. S. Hendrick, Foote, & Clapion-Foote, 1984; C. Hendrick, S. S. Hendrick, & Dicke, 1998) aforementioned quantitative research on love styles (Gaines, 2016/2018). Overall, May's version of existential psychology arguably stands as the best-known theory of personality within the existential tradition (Ewen, 1998).

POSITIVE PSYCHOLOGY: A PREFERRED ALTERNATIVE TO HUMANISTIC/EXISTENTIAL PSYCHOLOGY(?)

In the preceding section, we noted that May's (1953, 1969) version of existential psychology elaborated upon love as a basis for individuals' ability to come to terms with a search for meaning in their all-too-finite lives. In some of his later work, May (1981/1999) distinguished between *happiness* (an emotion that is relatively static, associated with contentment) and *joy* (an emotion that is relatively dynamic, associated with excitement) as building blocks for romantic love (Bradford, 2015). May was concerned that, over time, individuals in romantic relationships may put considerable effort into holding onto happiness but do not put comparable effort into maintaining joy – a situation that might help explain why the current "happiness craze" in the biological and social sciences has been embraced more wholeheartedly within the modern-day positive psychology movement (following Seligman & Csikszentmihalyi, 2000) than it has been embraced within the older humanistic/existential school of personality psychology (see K. J. Schneider, 2015).

To some extent, the positive psychology movement is covering the same conceptual ground regarding happiness and other constructs (e.g., the self, positive aspects of human nature) that the humanistic/existential school already has covered, although positive psychologists do not consistently give due credit to their humanistic/existential predecessors (Montuori & Purser, 2015). In fact, some of the comments from positive psychologists (e.g., Seligman & Csikszentmihalyi, 2000) toward the contributions of humanistic and existential psychologists have been overtly dismissive (K. J. Schneider, 2011b). Nonetheless, the positive psychology movement may ultimately serve to complement, rather than denigrate or supplant, the humanistic/existential tradition. In the present section, we shall review those perspectives from the positive psychology movement (i.e., Diener, Oishi, & Lucas, 2003; Ryan & Deci, 2001; Ryff & Singer, 2008) that show exceptional promise regarding integration with the humanistic/existential school of personality psychology.

ED DIENER'S CONSTRUCT OF SUBJECTIVE WELL-BEING

Ed Diener and colleagues (e.g., Diener, Oishi, & Lucas, 2003) define *subjective well-being* as individuals' cognitive (i.e., thought-based) and affective (i.e., feeling-based) evaluation of their lives – basically, individuals' positive versus negative attitude toward their lives (see S. C. White, Gaines, & Jha, 2012). Diener and colleagues contend that the cognitive component of subjective well-being is *life satisfaction* (measured via the Satisfaction With Life Scale, or SWLS; Diener, Emmons, Larsen, & Griffin, 1985); whereas the affective components of subjective well-being are *positive moods* and *negative moods* (measured via the Positive and Negative Affect Schedule, or PANAS; D. Watson, Clark, & Tellegen, 1988). Thus, according to Diener and colleagues, high subjective well-being represents a combination of high levels of life satisfaction, high levels of positive moods, and low levels of negative moods (e.g., D. G. Myers & Diener, 1995).

One of the most noteworthy sets of findings from Diener and colleagues' programme of research on subjective well-being (e.g., D. G. Myers & Diener, 1995) is that (1) on average, individuals in economically rich nations report significantly higher levels of subjective well-being than do individuals in economically not-rich nations; yet (2) within the economically richest nation on Earth (i.e., the United States), the positive effect of income on individuals' subjective well-being is statistically significant but practically negligible (see Peterson & Seligman, 2004). Actually, within the US, it appears that the impact of income on subjective well-being is best understood as *curvilinear* (i.e., highest levels of subjective well-being among individuals within the \$100,000 to \$250,000 bracket, lower scores of subjective well-being among individuals whose incomes either fall below or fall above that range; D. G. Myers & Diener, 2018), rather than linear. All things considered, Diener's conceptualisation and measurement of subjective well-being have largely defined the literature on well-being within the positive psychology movement (see S. C. White, Gaines, & Jha, 2012).

CAROL RYFF'S CONSTRUCT OF PSYCHOLOGICAL WELL-BEING

Drawing partly upon Marie Jahoda's (1958) *theory of positive mental health* (a conceptual precursor to the contemporary positive psychology movement, focusing on the presence of mental wellness, not just the absence of mental illness; Peterson & Seligman, 2004), Carol Ryff and colleagues (e.g., Ryff & Singer, 1998a, 1998b) define *psychological well-being* as individuals' achievement of fulfilment and self-realisation in their lives (see S. C. White, Gaines, & Jha, 2012). Ryff and colleagues (e.g., Ryff, 1989; Ryff & Keyes,

1995) have identified six dimensions of psychological well-being on conceptual and empirical grounds (i.e., *self-acceptance*, *positive relations with others*, *autonomy*, *environmental mastery*, *purpose in life*, and *personal growth*). In Ryff's view, psychological well-being reflects a combination of high levels of all six dimensions (possibly exemplifying individuals' fundamental values and ideals; e.g., Ryff, 1995).

A major problem with Ryff's (1989; Ryff & Keyes, 1995) psychological well-being survey is the absence of published empirical support for the internal consistency of her six scales, as assessed via Cronbach's alpha (a problem that also characterised Jahoda's 1958 prototypical measures of processes that promote positive mental health; see Peterson & Seligman, 2004). In fact, Ryff and colleagues have tended to publish descriptions of hypothetical low-scorers and high-scorers on the six dimensions, rather than the actual items that comprise the scales. Although Ryff and colleagues (e.g., Ryff & Singer, 1998a, 1998b) have offered a spirited defence of their conceptualisation and measurement of psychological well-being, the long-term success or failure of their survey will depend heavily upon empirical demonstrations of the internal consistency of the six scales (see Nunnally & Bernstein, 1994, concerning the importance of Cronbach's alpha as an index of reliability in psychometric analyses of scales). In the meantime, Ryff's construct of psychological well-being has emerged as the primary counterpoint to Diener's (e.g., Diener, Emmons, Larsen, & Griffin, 1985) construct of subjective well-being (S. C. White, Gaines, & Jha, 2012) – though Diener and colleagues (i.e., Diener et al., 2010) have developed alternative measures of well-being, in response to Ryff and colleagues' critiques (see Box 4.2 concerning Diener et al.'s newer measures of flourishing, positive emotions, and negative emotions).

RICHARD RYAN AND EDWARD DECI'S CONSTRUCT OF SUBJECTIVE VITALITY

Finally, within their *self-determination theory* (e.g., Ryan & Deci, 2001), Richard Ryan and Edward Deci (e.g., Deci & Ryan, 2000; Ryan & Deci, 2000b) define *subjective vitality* as individuals' sense that they are *functioning* in an optimal manner, not just *experiencing* their lives in an optimal manner (S. C. White, Gaines, & Jha,

BOX 4.2 DIENER ET AL.'S (2010) FLOURISHING, POSITIVE EMOTION, AND NEGATIVE EMOTION SCALES

In an edition of *Psychological Inquiry* that was constructed around a target article by Ryff and Singer (1998b) on "The Contours of Positive Human Health", Diener, Sapyta, and Suh (1998, rebuttal) and Ryff and Singer (1998a, rejoinder) clashed verbally over the adequacy of subjective well-being (emphasising an hedonic or optimal-experience perspective; Diener, Emmons, Larsen, & Griffin, 1985) versus psychological well-being (emphasising an eudaimonic or optimal-functioning perspective; Ryff, 1989; Ryff & Keyes, 1995) as mental health constructs. Ryan and Deci (2001) tactfully described the clash as "an engaging and instructive debate" (p. 146). Although Ryan and Deci implied that Ryff and Singer (1998b) had struck the first verbal blow, a careful reading of that target article reveals that Ryff and Singer (1998b) had *omitted* (i.e., failed to cite) Diener and colleagues' prior work on subjective well-being. In response to that omission, Diener, Sapyta and Suh (1998) not only promoted their construct of subjective well-being but also claimed that their construct was a better reflection of the content of everyday persons' daily lives than was Ryff and colleagues' construct of psychological well-being. Subsequently, Ryff and Singer (1998a) directly challenged Diener's hedonic construct by pointing to the ostensibly superior real-world utility of their eudaimonic construct. At any rate, Diener and Ryff clearly opposed each other's views concerning the conceptual operationalisation of well-being (although the differences may have been overstated; see Lucas & Diener, 2015).

Diener et al. (2010) have attempted to reconcile their hedonic perspective with Ryff's (1989; Ryff & Singer, 1998b) eudemonic perspective on well-being, which Diener et al. labelled as "humanistic" (an overly restrictive label, considering that Ryff drew on several theories across the psychodynamic, humanistic/existential, and trait schools of personality; e.g., Ryff & Singer, 2008). Diener et al. developed the Flourishing Scale as a measure of psychological well-being (consistent with Ryff and colleagues' eudaimonic view of well-being), as well as the Scale of Positive and Negative Experience as a measure of the affective component of subjective well-being (consistent with Diener and colleagues' hedonic view of well-being). Diener et al. found that flourishing was significantly and positively correlated with all six of Ryff's (1989; Ryff & Singer, 1995) psychological well-being dimensions (Diener et al. did not say whether positive or negative feelings were significantly correlated with Ryff's dimensions). In retrospect, perhaps the Diener-Ryff debate has been "engaging and instructive" after all (!).

2012). Consistent with self-determination theory, Ryan and Frederick (1997) developed short-term and long-term versions of a scale that measures individuals' subjective vitality (Peterson & Seligman, 2004). According to Ryan and Deci, individuals' subjective vitality is high when three particular needs – specifically, *autonomy*, *competence*, and *relatedness* – have been fulfilled; whereas individuals' subjective vitality is low when those needs have been blocked or thwarted (e.g., Ryan & Deci, 2000a).

Results of studies by Ryan, Deci, and colleagues (e.g., Reis, Sheldon, Gable, Roscoe, & Ryan, 2000) indicate that individuals' fulfilment of all three human needs (i.e., autonomy, competence, and relatedness) are significant positive predictors of subjective vitality (Peterson & Seligman, 2004). Ryan and Deci (2001) interpret the results of their studies concerning human needs and subjective vitality as affirming the same *eudaimonic* view of well-being (i.e., emphasis on optimal functioning) that Ryff and colleagues (e.g., Ryff & Singer, 1998a, 1998b) have endorsed, as distinct from the *hedonic* view of well-being (i.e., emphasis on optimal experience) that Diener and colleagues (e.g., Diener, Oishi, & Lucas, 2003) have endorsed. Summing it up, Ryan and Deci's construct of subjective vitality shows promise as one of the most theoretically driven and empirically verifiable constructs within the literature on well-being (see S. C. White, Gaines, & Jha, 2012).

CRITIQUE OF HUMANISTIC AND EXISTENTIAL PERSPECTIVES

From the first edition (C. S. Hall & Lindzey, 1957) through the third edition (C. S. Hall & Lindzey, 1978) of their classic book, *Theories of Personality*, Calvin S. Hall and Gardner Lindzey covered humanistic and existential personality theories across three separate chapters (two chapters on humanistic theories, one chapter on existential theories). However, in *Introduction to Theories of Personality*, C. S. Hall and Lindzey (C. S. Hall, Lindzey, Loehlin, & Manosevitz, 1985) reduced the number of chapters to two (one chapter apiece on humanistic and existential theories, respectively). Afterward, in the fourth edition of *Theories of Personality*, C. S. Hall and Lindzey (C. S. Hall, Lindzey, & Campbell, 1998) offered a single chapter on humanistic theories (and no chapters on existential theories). Given the diminished coverage that C. S. Hall and Lindzey gave to humanistic and existential theories over the course of the late twentieth century, one might reasonably conclude that the influence of humanistic and existential theories within personality psychology is in the midst of an irreversible decline (see E. Taylor, 2010).

In spite of the decreased coverage that C. S. Hall and Lindzey (1957; 1970, 1978; C. S. Hall, Lindzey, & Campbell, 1998; C. S. Hall, Lindzey, Loehlin, & Manosevitz, 1985) have afforded to the humanistic/existential school over the years, it may be premature for personality psychologists to give up studying humanistic and existential perspectives. Looking backward, one can find precursors to the humanistic/existential school in various theories that we have considered so far, including William James's (1890/ 2010) self-theory, Gordon Allport's (1937) psychology of the individual, and Henry Murray's (1938) personology, among other sources (for details, see E. Taylor, 2010). Looking forward, one can detect the influence of the humanistic/existential school on later cognitive theories, most notably George Kelly's (1955) psychology of personal constructs (which arguably could be classified as a humanistic theory; Benjafield, 2008). All in all, the humanistic/ existential school has established itself firmly as a "third force" in challenging the onetime dominance of psychodynamic and behaviourist theories within and outside personality psychology (E. Taylor, 2000).

PRELUDE TO CHAPTER 5

During the latter half of the twentieth century, the *trait* school (which, unlike the humanistic/existential school, emphasises individuals' striving for accuracy – rather than positivity – in gathering information about themselves; see Robins & John, 1997) gradually attained the status of a fourth major perspective in personality psychology (Funder, 2001). The trait school (which is based on the belief that individuals are fully aware of those aspects of their personalities that are most relevant to their everyday behaviour; Digman, 1990) currently is the most influential perspective within personality psychology and has been championed primarily by academicians (in contrast to the practitioners who largely have promoted the humanistic and existentialist perspectives; see McAdams, 1997). Representative theories within the trait school include (in order of appearance) G. W. Allport's (1961/1963) trait theory; the factor-analytic trait theories of Cattell (1946), H. J. Eysenck (1947), Costa and McCrae (1985), J. P. Guilford (1975), and Ashton and Lee (2001); Sandra Bem's (1981) gender schema theory; Spence's (1993) multifactorial gender identity theory; and Wiggins's (1991) interpersonal circumplex theory. In Chapter 5, we cover these theories and accompanying research in detail.

CURRENT AND EMERGING
SCHOOLS OF THOUGHT

5

TRAIT PERSPECTIVES ON PERSONALITY

In Chapter 1, we learned about Gordon Allport's (1937/1951, 1961/1963) psychology of the individual, including G. W. Allport's pioneering version of *trait theory*. Legend has it that G. W. Allport developed trait theory largely as the result of an uncomfortable encounter that he experienced with Sigmund Freud, who apparently responded to G. W. Allport's recounting of an incident that he had just witnessed on a train ride (in which a little boy and the boy's mother seemed to be excessively concerned with keeping dirt off the boy's clothing) with the none-too-rhetorical question, "And was that little boy you?" (Ewen, 1998). From that day onward, G. W. Allport allegedly had little use for Freud's "depth psychology", opting instead for a direct approach to learning about the core aspects of individuals' personalities: Just ask individuals what they are like (C. S. Hall & Lindzey, 1957).

In principle, G. W. Allport and Odbert's (1936) exhaustive reading of an unabridged English-language dictionary yielded a list of approximately 18,000 trait terms, which could be narrowed to "only" 4,500 or so terms after synonyms and antonyms are taken into account (Ewen, 1998). However, in practice, G. W. Allport (1928) developed a survey to measure only one trait – specifically, "ascendance/submission", which corresponds roughly to *dominance* (i.e., individuals' tendency to behave in a manner that is intended to benefit themselves; Wiggins, 1979). In retrospect, G. W. Allport chose his construct well; every trait survey that we will review in the present chapter includes either "pure" dominance or, arguably, a blend of dominance with another trait (typically *nurturance*, or individuals' tendency to behave in a manner that is intended to benefit persons other than, or in addition to, themselves; see Gaines, 2016/2018).

In the present chapter, we will consider trait perspectives on personality, in the tradition of G. W. Allport (1937/1951, 1961/1963). As we will see, trait perspectives were subjected to withering criticism during the 1960s – most notably from Walter Mischel (1968), who contended that a particular trait usually explains no more than 9–10% of variance in behaviour across individuals (Snyder & Ickes, 1985). By the same token, we will learn about various strategies that trait theorists have pursued in order to address (and, in some instances, to overtly refute) challenges from Mischel and other critics concerning the traditional (i.e., *dispositional*) approach to personality and social behaviour (Ickes, Snyder, & Garcia, 1997; Snyder & Cantor, 1998).

BASIC ASSUMPTIONS UNDERLYING TRAIT PERSPECTIVES

According to trait perspectives on personality, one can regard *traits* (essentially, individuals' answer to the question, "How would you describe yourself"; Gaines, 2016/2018) as stable, consciously experienced aspects of personality that tend to be reflected in cross-situational consistency in individuals' behaviour across time (although the concepts of stability, consistency, and length of time as applied to trait-behaviour covariance are not absolute; Snyder & Ickes, 1985). Compared to motives (which, as we learned in Chapters 2 and 4, are emphasised in psychodynamic and humanistic/existential perspectives), traits presumably are more accessible to consciousness and are more likely to be manifested consistently across a variety of situations (McClelland, 1985/1987). Nevertheless, both motives and traits appear to be relatively stable, at least throughout individuals' adult years (McAdams, 1997).

G. W. Allport defined traits as "neuropsychic structure[s] having the capacity to render many stimuli functionally equivalent, and to initiate and guide equivalent (meaningfully consistent) forms of aptitude and expressive behaviour" (1961/1963, p. 347). Does the term "neuropsychic structure" imply that G. W. Allport viewed traits as biologically given (i.e., inherited) within individuals? Not necessarily: In G. W. Allport's view, the building blocks of traits are *habits* (i.e., repeated sequences of behaviour that eventually may characterise individuals over time; e.g., G. W. Allport, 1927), rather than genes. Unlike genes, habits tend to be learned (see F. H. Allport & G. W. Allport, 1921). However, the relative influence of "nature versus nurture" on the development of individuals' traits *en utero* and across the life span has been debated throughout the history of personality psychology (Deary, 2009).

Broadly speaking, those trait perspectives that have been concerned with identifying all of the major traits along which individuals differ (e.g., the factor-analytic trait theories of Cattell, 1946; H. J. Eysenck, 1947; J. P. Guilford, 1975; Costa & McCrae, 1985) have been especially receptive to appeals toward *nature* as a primary influence on trait development (but see the factor-analytic trait theory of Ashton & K. Lee, 2001, for a notable exception); whereas those trait perspectives that have been concerned with identifying a limited set of salient traits along which individuals differ (e.g., the gender schema theory of Sandra Bem, 1981; the multifactorial gender identity theory of Spence, 1993; and the interpersonal circumplex theory of Wiggins, 1991) have been especially receptive to appeals toward *nurture* as a primary influence on trait development (see Gaines, 2016/2018). Given the lack of solid genetic evidence outside the realm of modern-day psychiatry (where, for example, specific chromosomes have been repeatedly implicated in the development of the "abnormal" trait of *schizophrenia*, which formerly was known as "madness"; see Walker, Kestler, Bollini, & Hochman, 2004; but see also Wahlsten, 1999, in Chapter 7 of the present book, regarding a re-evaluation of results concerning schizophrenia), we do not attempt to resolve the thorny issue of nature versus nurture (following Deary, 2009). Instead, we will keep this issue in mind as we review major theories and relevant studies among trait perspectives on personality.

THEORIES PROPOSING COMPREHENSIVE LISTS OF TRAITS

RAYMOND CATTELL'S VERSION OF FACTOR-ANALYTIC TRAIT THEORY

As we noted earlier in the present chapter, G. W. Allport and Odbert (1936) tried valiantly to reduce their 18,000-term trait taxonomy to a more manageable size. Unfortunately, their remaining list of roughly 4,500 trait terms was still too unwieldy for empirical or conceptual purposes (e.g., conducting research, achieving parsimony; Wiggins & Trapnell, 1997). Thus, Raymond Cattell (1946) took it upon himself to apply the relatively new technique of *factor analysis* (a psychometric analysis that examines correlations among scores on measured variables within a particular sample, with the intention of uncovering a smaller number of latent or unmeasured variables that presumably explain individual differences in the scores; Nunnally & Bernstein, 1994) to data from an already-reduced taxonomy of 160 trait terms (Ewen, 1998). Cattell's resulting trait perspective is known as a version of *factor-analytic trait theory* (or factor theory, for short; C. S. Hall & Lindzey, 1957).

On the basis of results from factor analyses, Cattell (1950) eventually condensed G. W. Allport and Odbert's (1936) trait taxonomy to 16 terms (perhaps rising to 23 terms, if data from clinical samples were included alongside data from more commonly used, nonclinical samples; C. S. Hall & Lindzey, 1957). Although Cattell was fond of creating his own, somewhat idiosyncratic terminology, Ewen (1998) noted that Cattell's list of traits could be interpreted as *intellect, warmth, emotional stability, dominance, liveliness, rule-consciousness, social boldness, sensitivity, vigilance, abstractedness, privateness, apprehension, openness to change, self-reliance, perfectionism*, and *tension*. From the outset, Cattell's inclusion of "intellect" or intelligence (which usually is regarded as individuals' presumed cognitive ability; C. S. Hall & Lindzey, 1957) as a trait was controversial. Even more controversially, Cattell assumed that approximately half of the variance in "intellect" and (other) traits across individuals was a function of heredity – an assumption that was commonplace throughout World War II-era differential psychology but was undermined largely by the revelation that Cyril Burt (one of the earliest and best-known proponents of the

50%–heritability dictum concerning psychological attributes; e.g., Burt, 1966) had fabricated individual–differences data (Fairchild, Yee, Wyatt, & Weizmann, 1995; Yee, Fairchild, Weizmann, & Wyatt, 1993). Nevertheless, Cattell succeeded in creating a taxonomy (as well as a survey, the Sixteen Personality Factor Questionnaire, or 16PF; Cattell, 1970) that was empirically and conceptually viable as a means toward measuring individual differences in all of the major traits (Digman, 1990).

Notwithstanding the controversial aspects of Cattell's (1946) factor-analytic trait theory, some of Cattell's psychometric choices are questionable. For example, with regard to *construct validity* (i.e., the extent to which a survey actually measures the construct[s] that the survey was designed to measure; Nunnally & Bernstein, 1994), Cattell's use of a particular type of factor analysis that tends to produce a large number of interrelated latent variables (i.e., *oblique factor analysis*) probably led him to overestimate the minimum number of traits that should be identified (Digman, 1990). In addition, Cattell himself (e.g., Cattell, 1973) raised the possibility that the subscales underlying the 16PF lacked *internal consistency* (i.e., lack of measurement error; Nunnally & Bernstein, 1994) as measured by Cronbach's alpha reliability coefficient (although Cattell might have been unduly critical of his own survey in that regard; see Saville & Blinkhorn, 1981). Then again, G. W. Allport (1961/1963) – whose taxonomy (G. W. Allport & Odbert, 1936) had served as the inspiration for Cattell's 16PF – credited Cattell with helping to bring the statistical analysis of trait data into the then fledgling computer era (see also Digman, 1990).

HANS EYSENCK'S VERSION OF FACTOR-ANALYTIC TRAIT THEORY

Just as Cattell (1946) had argued that G. W. Allport and Odbert's (1936) list of 4,500 traits was too large for practical purposes, so too did Hans J. Eysenck (1947) contend that Cattell's own list of 16 traits was too unwieldy (Ewen, 1998). Like Cattell, H. J. Eysenck believed that factor analysis was the optimal means toward identifying a minimum number of major traits – hence, the labelling of Eysenck's trait as another version of *factor-analytic trait theory*. However, unlike Cattell (who drew upon the trait theory of

G. W. Allport, 1937/1951), H. J. Eysenck was influenced primarily by behaviourist theories (i.e., the classical conditioning theory of Pavlov, 1927; and the drive reduction theory of; Hull, 1943) that suggested as few as two traits that needed to be measured – namely, *extraversion* (i.e., outgoingness) and *neuroticism* (i.e., emotional instability), respectively (C. S. Hall & Lindzey, 1957).

Using the psychometric technique of *orthogonal factor analysis* (which tends to identify a relatively small number of latent variables that are independent of each other; Nunnally & Bernstein, 1994), H. J. Eysenck and S. B. G. Eysenck (1968) eventually obtained evidence from their 57-item Eysenck Personality Inventory (EPI) that yielded evidence for extraversion and neuroticism as the two major traits (Ewen, 1998). In addition to reducing Cattell's (1946) trait list considerably, H. J. Eysenck and S. B. G. Eysenck omitted "intellect" or intelligence from Cattell's list – a change that was consistent with the view that intelligence really constituted part of the subject matter for the emerging field of cognitive psychology, rather than personality psychology (Ewen, 1998). However, like Cattell, H. J. Eysenck and S. B. G. Eysenck agreed with Cattell that the major traits were likely to be 50% heritable (C. S. Hall & Lindzey, 1970).

Even if we set aside H. J. Eysenck and S. B. G. Eysenck's (1968) controversial assertions regarding the heritability of extraversion and neuroticism, one might challenge the empirical evidence for the biological systems (i.e., limbic system and ascending reticular activation system, in that order) that, according to H. J. Eysenck (1967), gave rise to the respective traits (although Gray, 1981, offered plausible alternatives to the biological systems that H. J. Eysenck had proposed; Pickering, Cooper, Smillie, & Corr, 2013). Also, despite H. J. Eysenck and S. B. G. Eysenck's (1975) assertion that their newer, 100-item Eysenck Personality Questionnaire (EPI) included a third scale that measured *psychoticism* (i.e., severe psychological impairment), H. J. Eysenck did not offer any detailed description of a specific biological system that might have been responsible for individual differences in that trait (and "psychoticism" actually seems to represent a combination of low levels of the "Big Five" traits of friendliness and conscientiousness, as noted by Digman, 1990; see the next subsection of the present chapter regarding the "Big Five"). Nevertheless, H. J. Eysenck's success in extracting extraversion and neuroticism as major traits foreshadowed findings of all subsequent studies on comprehensive lists of traits (Ewen, 1998).

PAUL COSTA AND ROBERT MCCRAE'S VERSION OF FACTOR-ANALYTIC TRAIT THEORY

By the 1970s, several independent teams of researchers (e.g., Banks, 1948; Borgatta, 1964; D. W. Fiske, 1949; Smith, 1967; Tupes & Christal, 1961) had concluded that Cattell's (1946) 16PF Questionnaire – which, as the name implies, supposedly measured 16 traits (if one counts "intellect") – actually measured no more than five major traits (Digman, 1990). The five resulting traits – which Paul Costa and Robert McCrae (1985) subsequently labelled as *openness to experience* (i.e., broad-mindedness; formerly known as Cattell's "intellect" factor), *conscientiousness* (i.e., reliability), *extraversion* (i.e., outgoingness), *agreeableness* (i.e., friendliness), and *neuroticism* (i.e., emotional instability) – included, yet were extended beyond, H. J. Eysenck's (1947) "Big Two" traits of extraversion and neuroticism (Wiggins & Pincus, 1992). Costa and McCrae's version of *factor-analytic trait theory* (i.e., the "enduring dispositional view of the Big Five", according to Wiggins & Trapnell, 1997, p. 745) proposes that those particular five traits consistently emerge for a reason: Human beings want to know where potential comrades or adversaries stand on those particular traits (and we humans are aware that other persons want to know where we stand on those particular traits; see Funder & Fast, 2010).

Like H. J. Eysenck and S. B. G. Eysenck (1968), Costa and McCrae (1985) used orthogonal factor analysis to extract latent variables (thus optimising the likelihood of extracting truly independent dimensions; Digman, 1990). However, unlike H. J. Eysenck or S. B. G. Eysenck, Costa and McCrae essentially performed second-order factor analyses (e.g., taking an initial, lower-order set of factors and then conducting another, higher-order factor analysis) on the scales from the Neuroticism-Extraversion-Openness Personality Inventory, Revised Version (NEO-PI-R; conscientiousness and agreeableness emerged as two unexpected dimensions; Wiggins & Trapnell, 1997). In any event, Costa and McCrae developed a version of factor-analytic trait theory that provided an acceptable middle ground between Cattell's (1946) insistence on a minimum of 16 traits and H. J. Eysenck's (1947) insistence on a minimum of two traits (Ewen, 1998).

Costa and McCrae (e.g., McCrae & Costa, 1986) did not originally claim that the "Big Five" traits (which can be memorised via the acronym, *OCEAN*) were largely inherited (Cervone, 2005). However, with the passage of time, Costa and McCrae (e.g., McCrae, 2009; McCrae & Costa, 1989) increasingly have made such a claim – a problematic stance, given that the evidence at hand does not identify *which* particular genes supposedly are linked to individual differences in scores on the "Big Five" traits (Deary, 2009). Nevertheless, unlike Cattell (1946) or H. J. Eysenck (1947), Costa and McCrae have *not* asserted that individuals' trait scores are linked to the same genes that are implicated in individuals' racial group membership (e.g., McCrae & Costa, 1997). Overall, Costa and McCrae's version of factor-analytic trait theory has emerged as the dominant view among trait perspectives on personality (Ewen, 1998). Given that the NEO-PI-R (Costa & McCrae, 1985, 1989, 1992) is only available commercially, we shall comment at greater length upon a freely available measure of the "Big Five" traits (i.e., the Big Five Inventory, or BFI; John, Donahue, & Kentle, 1991) in Box 5.1.

JOY PAUL GUILFORD'S VERSION OF FACTOR-ANALYTIC TRAIT THEORY

The rise of the "Big Five" trait perspective in personality (especially as proposed and measured by Costa & McCrae, 1985) brought renewed attention to Joy Paul Guilford's (1975) earlier version of *factor-analytic trait theory*, which could be interpreted as generating research findings in support of four of the "Big Five" traits (i.e., conscientiousness, extraversion, agreeableness, and neuroticism; Digman, 1990). It turns out that J. P. Guilford had developed one of the earliest factor-analytic approaches to studying traits (specifically, when examining the trait of extraversion; J. P. Guilford & R. B. Guilford, 1934). However, J. P. Guilford (1975) identified at least ten first-order traits: (1) *General activity vs.*

BOX 5.1 JOHN ET AL.'S (1991) BIG FIVE INVENTORY

The current (i.e., 240-item) version of Costa and McCrae's (1992) NEO-PI-Revised Edition is not available within the public domain. Thus, in order to gain access to the NEO-PI-R, we would need to purchase Costa and McCrae's survey. Alternatively, we could obtain freely available copies of various versions of the Big Five Inventory (BFI), which was developed by Oliver John and colleagues (e.g., John, Donahue, & Kentle, 1991; Soto & John, 2014). Like the NEO-PI in its multiple forms, all versions of the BFI were designed to measure the "Big Five" traits of openness to experience, conscientiousness, extraversion, agreeableness, and neuroticism (Cervone, 2005).

The original, 44-item BFI (John, Donahue, & Kentle, 1991) was published commercially in English but subsequently was published within the public domain by Benet-Martinez and John (1998), in Spanish as well as English versions (see Kwan & Herrmann, 2015). Afterward, the 60-item Next Big Five Inventory (BFI-2; Soto & John, 2014) was published within the public domain, in English (Ashton, K. Lee, & Visser, 2019). Unlike the original BFI (which retained the same labels for the "Big Five" traits as Costa & McCrae, 1985; 1989, 1992 had used in their versions of the NEO-PI), the BFI-2 relabelled neuroticism as *negative emotionality* and openness to experience as *open-mindedness*. Nevertheless, the original and revised versions of the BFI apparently yield comparable levels of construct validity (as established via orthogonal factor analyses) and internal consistency (as established via reliability analysis; see Nunnally & Bernstein, 1994).

Whether measured by versions of the BFI (John, Donahue, & Kentle, 1991; Soto & John, 2017) or by versions of the NEO-PI (Costa & McCrae, 1985, 1989, 1992), two of the "Big Five" traits consistently have been linked to individuals' behaviour within the context of close relationships (see Campbell & Simpson, 2013; Simpson & Campbell, 2013). Specifically, extraversion tends to promote individuals' relationship-maintaining behaviour; whereas neuroticism tends to undermine individuals' relationship-maintaining behaviour (for a review, see McNulty, 2013). The other "Big Five" traits are not consistently reflected in individuals' relationship-maintaining behaviour, although agreeableness occasionally has emerged as a significant positive predictor (see Gaines, 2016/ 2018). Overall, more research is needed concerning the *predictive ability* (i.e., ability to explain individual differences in behaviour;

Nunnally & Bernstein, 1994) of the "Big Five" traits (for a broader critique of predictive ability within personality psychology, see Funder, 2001).

slowness and lacking in energy; (2) *restraint and seriousness vs. rhathymia and impulsiveness*; (3) *ascendance and social boldness vs. submissiveness and timidity*; (4) *sociability and social interest vs. seclusiveness and shyness*; (5) *emotional stability and optimism vs. instability and depression*; (6) *objectivity vs. subjectivity and hypersensitivity*; (7) *friendliness and agreeableness vs. hostility and belligerence*; (8) *thoughtfulness or reflectiveness vs. unreflectiveness*; (9) *good personal relations and cooperativeness vs. criticalness and intolerance*; and (10) *masculinity of interests and emotions vs. femininity*. Amelang and Borkenau (1982) suggested re-interpreting and re-analysing J. P. Guilford's data in such a way that the equivalents of conscientiousness, extraversion, agreeableness, and neuroticism could be extracted as higher-level dimensions via orthogonal factor analyses (cf. Digman, 1990).

J. P. Guilford and Wayne S. Zimmerman (1949) developed the Guilford-Zimmerman Temperament Survey to measure the ten aforementioned, lower-order traits that eventually would become the core dimensions in Guilford's (1975) version of factor-analytic trait theory (Digman, 1990). The term "temperament" in the Guilford-Zimmerman Temperament Survey reflects the belief that certain biologically hardwired precursors to traits are present at birth, manifested in individual differences in behaviour from infancy onward (see Shiner, 2015) – a belief that also is reflected in the term "temperamental traits", as promoted by Cattell (1965); see also Rutter and Silberg (2002). Putting aside the question of temperamental precursors to traits, Goldberg (1981) – who apparently coined the term "Big Five" prior to Costa and McCrae's (1985, 1989, 1992) popularisation of the term (Digman, 1990) – concluded that J. P. Guilford and Zimmerman had not measured more than five traits (and, as we have seen, four factors were extracted by Amelang & Borkenau, 1982). Thus, as a measure of ten distinct traits, the Guilford-Zimmerman Temperament Survey is questionable in terms of construct validity (for a discussion of the extent to which acceptance of J. P. Guilford's ten factors is based upon the persuasiveness of theoretical arguments rather than scientific data, see

C. S. Hall & Lindzey, 1978). As for internal consistency, independent reviewers rarely (if ever) comment upon the reliability of the scales that underlie the Guilford-Zimmerman Temperament Survey (as assessed via Cronbach's alpha; e.g., Schuerger, Zarrella, & Hotz, 1989).

Unlike the other factor-analytic trait theories and relevant surveys that we have covered so far, one will not find any acknowledgement of J. P. Guilford's (1975) version of factor-analytic trait theory or the Guilford-Zimmerman Temperament Survey (J. P. Guilford & Zimmerman, 1949) in Ozer and Reise's (1994) review of the literature on personality assessment (which, in turn was designed to complement the emphasis on personality structure in an earlier review by Wiggins & Pincus, 1992). Similarly, one will not find any mention of J. P. Guilford's factor theory and trait survey within the fifth edition of Ewen's *An Introduction to Theories of Personality* (1998). Nevertheless, in the third edition of *Theories of Personality*, C. S. Hall and Lindzey (1978) regard the influence of J. P. Guilford's theory and survey upon the field of personality psychology as comparable to the influence of H. J. Eysenck's factor theory (e.g., H. J. Eysenck, 1947) and trait survey (e.g., H. J. Eysenck & S. B. G. Eysenck, 1968). Perhaps J. P. Guilford's contributions to personality psychology are best summarised as (1) pioneering the use of factor analysis to identify a manageable set of major traits, (2) developing a coherent theory to account for those theories, and (3) creating a trait survey that has stood the test of time – a set of accomplishments that, at a minimum, support the inclusion of J. P. Guilford's theory and survey in historical overviews of trait perspectives in personality (Digman, 1990).

MICHAEL ASHTON AND KIBEOM LEE'S VERSION OF FACTOR-ANALYTIC TRAIT THEORY

So far, we have regarded the "Big Five" trait approach (especially as reflected in the factor-analytic trait theory and survey of McCrae & Costa, 1985, 1989, 1992) as invariant across cultural groups (currently the consensus view within personality psychology; e.g., Caspi, Roberts & Shiner, 2005). However, in 2000, A. Timothy Church concluded that – if one broadens one's conceptual and methodological focus from participants in European-language (typically, but not always, English-language) nations to participants in Asian-language nations – then a trait that

Church labelled as "Chinese tradition" is conspicuously missing from ostensibly comprehensive surveys (Kwan & Herrmann, 2015). In turn, drawing partly upon the results of studies by Church and colleagues (e.g., Church, Katigbak, & Reyes, 1998; Church, Reyes, Katigbak, & Grimm, 1997; see also Church & Lonner, 1998) and the results of their own studies (e.g., Ashton, 1998; Ashton, Jackson, Helmes, & Panounen, 1998; Ashton, K. Lee & Son, 2000; Ashton, Panounen, Helmes, & Jackson, 1998), among other sources, Michael Ashton and Kibeom Lee (2001) proposed that the often-omitted trait of "Chinese tradition" is best interpreted as *honesty/humility* (Gaughan, Miller, & Lynam, 2012). In the process of incorporating honesty/humility into their version of *factor-analytic trait theory*, Ashton and K. Lee proposed a six-factor model with the acronym of HEXACO (i.e., *H*onesty/humility, *E*motionality/neuroticism, e*X*traversion, *A*greeableness, *C*onscientiousness, and *O*penness to experience; Hough, Oswald, & Ock, 2015).

K. Lee and Ashton (2004) developed the original, 192-item HEXACO Personality Inventory (HEXACO-PI) to measure the six dimensions within their (Ashton & Lee, 2001) version of factor-analytic trait theory (see DeYoung, 2015). Subsequently, K. Lee and Ashton (2006) published a 200-item version of their survey, labelled as the HEXACO Personality Inventory-Revised Version (HEXACO-PI -R; Gaughan, Miller, & Lynam, 2012). Both the HEXACO-PI and HEXACO-PI-R yield acceptable levels of construct validity (as assessed via orthogonal factor analyses) and internal consistency (as assessed via reliability analyses; see Nunnally & Bernstein, 1994). Moreover, results of a direct comparison between the psychometric properties of the HEXACO-PI-R (K. Lee & Ashton, 2004) and the most recent version of the NEO-PI-R (Costa & McCrae, 1992) indicate that the two surveys are similarly high in construct validity and internal consistency, with the six HEXACO traits combining to explain significantly more variance in individuals' levels of psychopathology than do the "Big Five" traits (primarily because of the inclusion of honesty/humility within the HEXACO-PI-R; Gaughan, Miller, & Lynam, 2012).

Certain problems have arisen regarding comparisons between the content of the six HEXACO traits (as measured by K. Lee & Ashton, 2004, 2006) and the content of the "Big Five" traits (as measured by Costa & McCrae, 1985, 1989, 1992). For example, K. Lee and

Ashton's emotionality trait is limited to internally directed negative emotions (whereas Costa and McCrae's neuroticism trait included externally as well as internally directed negative emotions); and K. Lee and Ashton's honesty/humility trait overlaps substantially with their own agreeableness trait (whereas Costa and McCrae likely would subsume honesty/humility within their agreeableness trait; Gaughan, Miller, & Lynam, 2012). However, it is worth noting that Costa and McCrae's own "Big Five" traits are not as empirically distinct from each other as their version of factor-analytic trait theory would suggest (see Funder, 2001). In any event, Ashton and K. Lee's factor theory and survey have emerged as viable alternatives to Costa and McCrae's earlier factor theory and survey (Paunonen & Hong, 2015).

THEORIES PROPOSING LIMITED SETS OF SALIENT TRAITS

SANDRA BEM'S GENDER SCHEMA THEORY

In a review of the literature on gender and personality, Anne Constantinople (1973) concluded that then-existing measures of gender-related personality traits (most notably Terman & Miles, 1936) tended to constrain individuals to score *either* as "masculine" (i.e., possessing psychological attributes that stereotypically are associated with males in a particular society) *or* as "feminine" (i.e., possessing psychological attributes that stereotypically are associated with females in a given society), possibly leading to an exaggeration of gender differences in those traits. Subsequently (though not specifically mentioning Constantinople's review), Sandra Bem (1974) published the appropriately-named Bem Sex Role Inventory (BSRI), which contained separate scales measuring "masculinity" (20 items) and "femininity" (20 items). Finally, having shown that some (but not most) men and women are "androgynous" (i.e., possess "masculine" as well as "feminine" personality characteristics), S. Bem (1981) proposed a *gender schema theory* that promoted the ideal of "androgyny" (reflecting individuals' refusal to create mental constructions of themselves and the world in rigid, "masculine" versus "feminine" terms) as an index of mental well-being (Lenney, 1991).

In terms of psychometric analyses, S. Bem (1974) reported that the internal consistency of the masculinity and femininity scales was satisfactory (i.e., Cronbach's alphas consistently > .70; see Nunnally & Bernstein, 1994). However, S. Bem did *not* report results of factor analyses, which would have allowed readers to evaluate the construct validity of the masculinity and femininity scales. As it turns out, results of orthogonal factor analyses by subsequent researchers revealed that (1) the term "masculine" does *not* fit with the rest of the items (e.g., "acts as a leader", "self-sufficient") within the so-called "masculinity" scale; and (2) the term "feminine" does *not* fit with the rest of the items (e.g., "affectionate", "gentle") within the so-called "femininity" scale (R. Brown, 1986). Thus, some critics (most notably Spence, 1985) have concluded that – despite S. Bem's (e.g., S. Bem, 1985) assertions to the contrary – the BSRI does not measure general "sex role orientations" but, rather, measures the specific, gender-related traits of *instrumentality* (essentially, dominance as defined earlier in the present chapter) and *expressivity* (basically, nurturance as defined in the present chapter; see Wiggins, 1991).

Perhaps the most controversial assertion within S. Bem's (1981) gender schema theory is the claim that individuals' *psychological* "androgyny" (i.e., simultaneous possession of instrumental and expressive traits) covaries with individuals' *sexual* "androgyny" (i.e., *bisexuality*, or attraction toward both men and women as potential sexual partners; Spence & Helmreich, 1978). The available evidence does not support S. Bem's assumption that individuals' personality traits and sexual orientation are empirically linked (R. Brown, 1986). Nevertheless, S. Bem's gender schema theory and BRSI have emerged as the most influential theory and gender-related trait survey, respectively, in the post-1960s literature on gender and personality (Lenney, 1991).

JANET SPENCE'S MULTIFACTORIAL GENDER IDENTITY THEORY

During the same year that S. Bem (1974) published the aforementioned BSRI, Janet Spence and colleagues (Spence, Helmreich, & Stapp, 1974) released their own survey – namely, the 24-item

Personal Attributes Questionnaire (PAQ) — that was designed to measure "masculinity" and "femininity" as separate dimensions (Lenney, 1991). Like S. Bem, Spence et al. concluded that some men and some women are psychologically "androgynous" (i.e., score relatively high in "masculine" and "feminine" traits). However, unlike S. Bem, Spence and colleagues never assumed that the PAQ (or the BSRI, for that matter) measured individuals' sexual orientation (R. Brown, 1986). Indeed (as noted in Chapter 1 of the present book), Spence et al. eventually developed surveys that not only measured gender-related traits (e.g., Spence, Helmreich, & Holahan, 1979) but also gender-related attitudes (e.g., Spence, Helmreich, & Stapp, 1973) and achievement-related motives that have been linked empirically to gender (e.g., Helmreich & Spence, 1978) — an eclectic approach that led to the development of Spence's (1993) *multifactorial gender identity theory* (Frable, 1997).

Having reflected upon the content of S. Bem's (1974) BSRI and their own PAQ (Spence, Helmreich, & Stapp, 1974), Spence and Helmreich (1978) concluded that they (and S. Bem) had primarily (and, in the case of the PAQ, exclusively) measured socially desirable or positive aspects of "masculinity" and "femininity". Afterward, Spence and colleagues (Spence, Helmreich, & Holahan, 1979) developed the 40-item Extended Personal Attributes Questionnaire (EPAQ) to measure negative as well as positive aspects of "masculinity" and "femininity". Finally, Spence and colleagues (Helmreich, Spence, & Wilhelm, 1981) published results regarding the psychometric properties of the original PAQ and the EPAQ. Not only did oblique factor analyses identify positive and negative aspects of "masculinity" and "femininity" as distinct dimensions; but — with the notable exception of negative "femininity" in the EPAQ (i.e., Cronbach's alphas below .50) — the internal consistency of the PAQ and EPAQ scales proved to be satisfactory (i.e., Cronbach's alphas near or above .70; Nunnally & Bernstein, 1994).

Spence's (1993) multifactorial gender identity theory and two versions of the PAQ (Spence, Helmreich, & Holahan, 1979; Spence, Helmreich, & Stapp, 1974) have not enjoyed quite the same popularity that S. Bem's (1981) gender schema theory and BSRI (Bem, 1974) have enjoyed within the literature on gender and personality (see Wood & Eagly, 2010). However, both Spence and S. Bem have made major contributions to the literature, consistently obtaining modest-but-significant gender differences on scores on the separate dimensions of "masculinity" (with men scoring higher than women) and "femininity" (with women scoring higher than men; Helgeson, 2015). Moreover, Spence and colleagues (e.g., Spence, Deaux, & Helmreich, 1985) have led the way toward replacing the overloaded trait terms of "masculinity" and "femininity" with the more limited (and arguably more accurate) trait terms of instrumentality and expressivity (R. Brown, 1986). All in all, Spence's multifactorial gender identity theory and relevant research clearly are reflected in Deaux and LaFrance's (1998) conclusion that – where personality is concerned – gender is "part of the 'air [that] we breathe'" (p. 788).

JERRY WIGGINS'S INTERPERSONAL CIRCUMPLEX THEORY

In Chapter 2 of the present book, we learned that Harry Stack Sullivan's (1953) interpersonal theory (a "social-psychological" theory of personality; C. S. Hall & Lindzey, 1957) emphasised the importance of target persons' behaviour toward significant others (with therapists potentially qualifying as clients' "significant others"; see Sullivan, 1954) as the data that ideally serve as bases for social perceivers' attributions concerning target persons' personality characteristics (Ewen, 1998). Subsequently, based on his interpretation of Sullivan's interpersonal theory and his own analysis of clinical data via the Kaiser Foundation, Timothy Leary (1957) concluded that *dominance* and *nurturance* (described earlier in the present chapter) are the two major interpersonal traits along which individuals differ (Millon, 1996). In turn, building upon T. Leary's circumplex model of interpersonal traits, Maurice Lorr and Douglas McNair (1965) obtained reports from clinicians regarding clients' behaviour, extracting T. Leary's constructs of dominance and nurturance as interpersonal traits. Finally, Jerry Wiggins and Ana Holzmuller (1978) collected self-reported data from non-clinical samples and (like T. Leary, 1957; as well as Lorr & McNair, 1963) identified dominance and nurturance as the two major interpersonal traits that differ across individuals. Wiggins (1991) ultimately developed a wide-ranging *interpersonal circumplex theory* that identifies *agency* as an intrapersonally directed aspect of the human condition (including, but not limited to, the trait of dominance) and *communion* as an interpersonally directed aspect of the human condition (including, but not limited to, the trait of nurturance; Gaines, 2016/2018).

In an effort to measure interpersonal traits in all of their complexity, Wiggins (1979) developed the 128-item Interpersonal Adjective Scales (IAS), which included eight lower-order traits (i.e., *assured-dominant, arrogant-calculating, cold-quarrelsome, aloof-introverted, unassured-submissive, unassuming-ingenuous, warm-agreeable,* and *gregarious-extraverted*) with intercorrelations that allowed researchers to plot those traits in a circular or circumplex order around the underlying, higher-order traits of dominance (the Y axis) and nurturance (the X axis; Millon, 1996). Afterward, Wiggins and colleagues (Wiggins, Trapnell, & Phillips, 1988) published the 64-item Revised Interpersonal Adjective Scales (IAS-R), which preserved the statistical properties of the original IAS (i.e., starting at the 12 o'clock position and working one's way anticlockwise through the set of lower-order traits that are listed above, at approximately 45-degree angles, one begins with the assured-dominant trait and ends with the gregarious-extraverted trait; Gaines, 2016/2018). Using an independent or orthogonal version of principal components analyses (which are similar, though not identical to, factor analyses; Tabachnick & Fidell, 2007), Wiggins et al. consistently obtained support for dominance and nurturance as underlying dimensions (Fabrigar, Visser, & Browne, 1997). Although some critics (e.g., Gaines et al., 1997b) have questioned the precision by which the IAS and IAS-R measure interpersonal traits within a two-dimensional grid, the consensus view (e.g., Gurtman & Pincus, 2000) is that the IAS and IAS-R provide optimal measures of interpersonal traits (Acton & Revelle, 2002).

The most persistent criticism of the original and revised versions of the original and revised versions of the IAS (Wiggins, 1979; Wiggins, Trapnell, & Phillips, 1988) may be that – despite high levels of construct validity (at least when using scores on the eight lower-order traits to extract dominance and nurturance as higher-order dimensions via principal components analyses) and high levels of internal consistency (as assessed via Cronbach's alpha; e.g., Wiggins, 1995; Wiggins, Steiger, & Gaelick, 1981) –

Wiggins and colleagues have relied too heavily upon obscure synonyms and antonyms (e.g., "unbold", "ironhearted") in order to generate nearly-perfect circumplex patterns of lower-order trait correlations (e.g., Benjamin, 2011). In an effort to resolve the linguistic problems that underlie the IAS and IAS-R, Patrick M. Markey and Charlotte N. Markey (2009) have developed the everyday-language International Personality Item Pool-Interpersonal Circumplex (IPIP-IPC) survey (which is profiled in Box 5.2). Notwithstanding empirical issues concerning Wiggins et al.'s measurement of interpersonal traits, Wiggins's (1991) interpersonal circumplex theory has gained prominence due to the ease with which it allows researchers to incorporate the gender-related traits of positive "masculinity" (i.e., high end of the dominance axis), positive "femininity" (high end of the nurturance axis), negative "femininity" (low end of the dominance axis), and negative "masculinity" (low end of the nurturance axis) – as well as the "Big Five" traits of extraversion (combination of high dominance and high nurturance) and agreeableness (combination of low dominance and high nurturance) – within one circular model of interpersonal traits (Helgeson, 2015).

CRITIQUE OF TRAIT PERSPECTIVES

Given the current pre-eminence of trait perspectives within personality psychology (Funder & Fast, 2010), one might be surprised to learn that the practical (if not statistical) significance of trait measurement was a point of contention during the late 1960s, particularly by Walter Mischel (1968). However, Mischel helped to instigate a crisis throughout personality psychology by asserting that traits did not explain nearly as much variance in individuals' behaviour as trait theories (going as far back as Allport, 1937/1951, 1961/1963) would suggest (for an analogous critique concerning attitudes as predictors of behaviour within social psychology, see Wicker, 1969). Although some trait theorists may find it tempting to cast Mischel as the "bad guy" in contrast to Allport as the "good guy" in the debate over the practical value of traits (Wiggins & Pincus, 1992), Mischel did have a point regarding the possibility that personality psychologists generally had placed excessive emphasis on construct validity, as opposed to predictive validity (Snyder & Ickes, 1985).

BOX 5.2   P. M. MARKEY AND C. N. MARKEY'S (2009) INTERNATIONAL PERSONALITY ITEM POOL-INTERPERSONAL CIRCUMPLEX INVENTORY

Notwithstanding its widespread popularity (Locke, 2011), the IAS (Wiggins, 1979; Wiggins, Trapnell, & Phillips, 1988) has been criticised for its use of terms that are so infrequently used that Wiggins and colleagues have found it necessary to make English-language dictionaries available to their participants (see Benjamin, 2011). Influenced by Wiggins's (1991) interpersonal circumplex theory, Patrick M. Markey and Charlotte N. Markey (2009) published the 32-item International Personality Item Pool-Interpersonal Circumplex (IPIP-IPC). However, unlike Wiggins and colleagues (who drew largely upon the 4,500-word, dictionary-driven taxonomy of Allport & Odbert when constructing the IAS; e.g., Wiggins, 1979), P. M. Markey and C. N. Markey used commonly used words and phrases from the general IPIP, as developed by Goldberg (1999).

Relying primarily (though not exclusively) upon orthogonal versions of principal components analyses of scores from the eight lower-order traits of assured-dominant, arrogant-calculating, cold-quarrelsome, aloof-introverted, unassured-submissive, unassuming-ingenuous, warm-agreeable, and gregarious-extraverted, P. M. Markey and C. N. Markey concluded that the IPIP-IPC possessed satisfactory construct validity as a measure of the higher-order traits of dominance and nurturance. However, internal consistency across the eight subscales within the IPIP-IPC varied dramatically, with Cronbach's alphas ranging from highs of nearly .80 (highly impressive, especially for 4-item subscales) to lows of .50 (not impressive, even for subscales with only four items; see Cortina, 1993). Thus, the measurement error for certain subscales of the IPIP-IPC is potentially problematic (see Nunnally & Bernstein, 1994).

In a direct comparison of the IPIC-IPC (P. M. Markey & C. N. Markey, 2009) and the IAS-R (Wiggins, Trapnell, & Phillips, 1988), DeYoung and colleagues (DeYoung, Weisberg, Quilty, & Peterson, 2013, Study 3) concluded that the two surveys possess adequate construct validity. However, it is not clear whether either survey possesses *predictive* validity, with regard to individuals' relationship behaviour (see Gaines, 2016/2018). The most relevant evidence comes from the literature on gender-related traits, whereby nurturance/positive "femininity" (typically as measured by the BSRI of S. Bem, 1974; or the PAQ of Spence, Helmreich, & Stapp, 1974) tends to promote individuals' relationship-maintaining behaviour; whereas dominance/positive "masculinity" (again, typically as measured by the BSRI or PAQ) is not consistently related to individuals' relationship-maintaining behaviour (Ickes, 1985). Clearly, more research is needed regarding the IPIP-IPC as well as the IAS-R when it comes to prediction of interpersonal behaviour.

According to Ickes, Snyder and Garcia (1997), constructive responses on the part of personality psychologists regarding challenges to the traditional, *"dispositional" approach* to personality and social behaviour (exemplified by the trait theory of Allport, 1937/1951, 1961/1963) include the development of a *statistical version of an interactionist approach* (whereby greater attention was paid to specifying *which* traits, behaviours, persons, and situations would be more versus less likely to yield trait-behaviour covariance that was practically as well as statistically significant) as well as a *dynamic version of an interactionist approach* (whereby greater attention was paid to individuals' relative freedom to choose the situations within which their traits and behaviour are examined; see also Funder, 1991). Furthermore, according to Snyder and Cantor (1998), personality psychologists increasingly have articulated a *functionalist approach* to personality and social behaviour (whereby features of persons and features of situations are conceptualised as influences on intrapersonal, social, relational, and group agendas; see Gaines, 2016/2018). Overall, personality psychologists have succeeded in defending trait perspectives from conceptual and empirical challenges by Mischel (1968) and other critics (for a review, see Zuroff, 1986).

PRELUDE TO CHAPTER 6

By the end of the twentieth century, a fifth major school of thought had emerged within personality psychology – namely, the *cognitive* school (which emphasises individuals' information-processing and other higher-order thought processes as influences on behaviour; Butt, 2004). Initially, Funder (2001) referred to this school of thought as *social-cognitive* – an overt nod to the legacy of the social learning theories of Rotter (1954) and the team of

Bandura and Walters (1963) that we reviewed in Chapter 3 of the present book (see also Gaines, 2016/2018). However, Funder and Fast (2010) labelled the school simply as "cognitive" – a term that is sufficiently inclusive to accommodate contributions from cognitive psychology (see Gobet, in preparation), as distinct from social psychology (Frings, in preparation). Representative theories within the cognitive school include (in order of appearance) Kelly's (1955) personal construct theory, Mischel's (1973) version of social-cognitive theory, Bandura's (1986) recasting of his earlier social learning theory (Bandura & Walters, 1963) as a separate version of social-cognitive theory, Higgins's (1987) self-discrepancy theory, and Baldwin's (1992) relational schema theory. In Chapter 6, we shall examine cognitive theories of personality in greater detail.

6

COGNITIVE PERSPECTIVES ON PERSONALITY

Even as post-World War II-era personality psychologists focussed heavily upon the conceptualisation and measurement of traits (and, to a large degree, obtaining consensus on a middle ground between the sixteen-factor trait theory of Cattell, 1946; and the two-to-three-factor trait theory of Eysenck, 1952/1970), the field of cognitive psychology was emerging from the methodological shadows of experimental psychology (see Robinson & Wilkowski, 2015). By the late 1990s, several cognitive theories had gained prominence within the field of personality psychology (Fleeson, 2012). Indeed, an entire book was devoted to "the coherence of personality" (edited by Cervone & Shoda, 1999b), showcasing a variety of social-cognitive perspectives (for an overview, see Funder, 2001).

One of the earliest cognitive theories of personality was George Kelly's (1955) *personal construct theory*, which asserts that each individual's "personality" is nothing more (and nothing less) than the unique set of general theories and specific hypotheses about self and the world that he or she possesses (C. S. Hall & Lindzey, 1970). Kelly's personal construct theory exemplifies the Scientist mode or metaphor of self-perception as clearly as does any of the trait theories that we covered in Chapter 5 (see also Robins &

John, 1997). However, Kelly's personal construct theory abandons the core personality constructs that we have encountered throughout the present book (e.g., traits, motives; see also Ewen, 1998). Instead, Kelly placed the construct of *cognitive complexity* (i.e., the extent to which individuals' theories and hypotheses concerning self and the world reflect individuals' active testing, refinement, and potential rejection on an ongoing basis; Mischel, 2004) at the forefront of his personal construct theory and within the methodology of his instrument for personality assessment (i.e., the Role Repertory or REP Test; see Tiedemann, 1989).

In the present chapter, we shall review several cognitive theories of personality that implicitly build upon insights from Kelly's (1955) personal construct theory (even though Kelly's theory is not typically cited as a direct influence; see Funder, 2001). We will learn that, to the extent that cognitive perspectives on personality invoke the Scientist mode or metaphor of self-perception (as well as the Consistency Seeker mode/metaphor, which we encountered briefly in Chapter 2 of the present book), those perspectives are vulnerable to criticism on the grounds that they fail to capture "ordinary personology" (i.e., laypersons' actual attempts to understand themselves and the world that they inhabit, as distinct from personality psychologists' often-idealised version of laypersons' attempts; Gilbert, 1998). By the same token, we will learn that – in the wake of the cognitive revolution that swept through psychology as a whole (Mischel, 2004) – various post-1960's-era cognitive theories of personality contain adaptive responses to such criticism (see S. T. Fiske & S. E. Taylor, 1991).

BASIC ASSUMPTIONS UNDERLYING COGNITIVE PERSPECTIVES

According to cognitive perspectives on personality, higher-order thought processes such as the encoding, storage, retention, and retrieval of information give rise to consciousness (including *self-*consciousness) among human beings (M. Leary & Tangney, 2012). Furthermore, higher-order thought processes not only may moderate links between individuals' personality characteristics and behaviour (Robinson & Wilkowski, 2015) but also may directly or indirectly influence individuals' behaviour (in some instances, by facilitating the development of personality characteristics; Yar-koni, 2015). Although higher-order thought processes are frequently cast as functional, "rational" antidotes to individuals' experience of dysfunctional, "irrational" emotions at a particular point in time (e.g., the rational-emotive behaviour therapy and theory of Ellis, 1962), certain thought processes may prove to be dysfunctional over time (e.g., when unduly negative views about self and the world place individuals at risk for developing depression as a mood disorder; e.g., the cognitive therapy and theory of A. T. Beck, 1967).

As noted by S. T. Fiske and S. E. Taylor (1991), cognitive perspectives on personality clearly are compatible with constructs such as *values* (i.e., individuals' organised sets of beliefs – basically, individuals' answer to the question, "What do you believe in?") and *attitudes* (i.e., individuals' combination of thoughts and feelings toward a particular entity – in order words, individuals' answer to the question, "How would you evaluate that person/place/thing?"). However, cognitive perspectives also are compatible with the construct of *traits* (especially the "Big Five" trait of openness to experience; DeYoung, 2015). Finally, although cognitive perspectives may not be directly compatible with the construct of *motives* (given that individuals are not necessarily aware of the impact of motives on their own behaviour; McClelland, 1985/1987), some of the goals that enable individuals to fulfil their motives may be consciously experienced (e.g., self-image goals that serve power-related motives and compassionate goals that serve intimacy-related motives; see Crocker & Canevello, 2015).

Among cognitive perspectives on personality, one can make a broad distinction (e.g., Funder, 2001) between (1) "grand theories" that are sweeping in scope and demonstrate potential for unifying the cognitive school as a whole (e.g., the separate versions of social cognitive theory that were developed by Mischel, 1973 and Bandura, 1986); and (2) "mini-theories" that are limited in scope and never were intended to unify the cognitive school *per se* (e.g., the self-discrepancy theory of Higgins, 1987; and the relational schema theory of Baldwin, 1992). Not coincidentally, one of the "grand theories" that we will consider (i.e., the social-cognitive theory of Mischel, 1973) was influenced indirectly by Kelly's (1955) wide-ranging theory of personal constructs (although

Mischel's theory was influenced more directly by the social learning theory of Rotter, 1954; see Endler, 2000). We shall examine the contributions of "grand theories" and "mini-theories" alike to understanding the interplay between cognition and personality (consistent with Funder, 2001).

GRAND THEORIES OF COGNITION

WALTER MISCHEL'S VERSION OF SOCIAL-COGNITIVE THEORY

In Chapter 5 of the present book, we learned that Walter Mischel (1968) helped to bring about a crisis throughout personality psychology by questioning the practical significance of covariance between individuals' scores on traits and behaviour (Snyder & Ickes, 1985). As Mischel (2004) acknowledged in later years, one of the most promising responses within the field was personality psychologists' collective adoption of a statistical version of an interactionist approach to personality and social behaviour (e.g., taking into account joint effects of individual-difference and social-psychological variables on individuals' behaviour) – an approach that Mischel credited to Magnusson and Endler (1977) in particular. However, Mischel also identified an alternative approach that he had advocated as early as 1973 – specifically, the adoption of an early version of *social-cognitive theory* that acknowledged the impact of individual differences in the construal of social situations (e.g., through specific encoding and appraisal processes) on individual differences in behaviour (see Funder & Fast, 2010).

As Funder (2001) observed, Mischel and Shoda (1995) developed the *cognitive-affective personality system*, or CAPS, model as an extension of Mischel's (1973) version of social-cognitive theory. In particular, "if-then" behavioural profiles or *behavioural signatures* are key concepts in Mischel and Shoda's CAPS model (Holmes, 2002). These behavioural profiles or signatures specify what a given individual will do in each particular situation that he or she encounters (Endler, 2000). In the process of elaborating upon the CAPS model, Mischel (2004) alluded to one hypothetical example of behavioural signatures in action – specifically, considering two children who score equally high on a trait measure of aggressiveness, but who show different behaviours across different social situations (i.e., Child A might display aggressive tendencies on the playground, but not in the classroom; whereas the reverse might be true for Child B).

In a critique of Mischel's (1973) version of social cognitive theory in general and Mischel and Shoda's (1995) CAPS model in particular, Funder (2001) argued that the usefulness of Mischel's model is limited by the fact that no clear, simple system exists for classifying those situations that will yield particular if-then profiles. By the same token, Funder and Fast (2010) concluded that Mischel's (1973) version of social-cognitive theory successfully incorporates the diverse array of models and studies that reflect cognitive approaches to personality. Furthermore, as we note in Box 6.1, John Holmes (2002) used Mischel and Shoda's CAPS model as the conceptual framework for his own situation-Partner A-Partner B-interaction (SABI) model of interdependence between individuals in close relationships (see also Gaines, 2016/2018). Thus, it may be safe to say that Mischel is no longer a "villain" in personality psychology (to the extent that he ever deserved that dis-honour; McAdams, 1997).

ALBERT BANDURA'S VERSION OF SOCIAL-COGNITIVE THEORY

As we learned in Chapter 3 of the present book, Albert Bandura and Richard Walters's (1963) version of social learning theory followed the lead of Julian Rotter's (1954) earlier version of social learning theory in moving away from neo-Freudian perspectives on drives as presumed predictors of behaviour (see also C. S. Hall & Lindzey, 1970). As it happens, Bandura (1978) elaborated upon Bandura and Walters (1963) version of social learning theory, noting that factors within individuals, together with factors within the environment, were reflected in individuals' behaviour at one point in time (indeed, one can conceive of individuals' personalities, situational contexts, and behaviour influencing each other; Ewen, 1998). Subsequently, Bandura (1986) introduced his version of *social-cognitive theory* (which is concerned explicitly with humans' capacity to reflect on their own personalities, their own behaviour, and the environment that they inhabit) as an extension of Bandura and Walters's version social learning theory (Funder, 2001).

BOX 6.1 HOLMES'S (2002) SABI MODEL

Prior to the cognitive revolution within psychology, Kurt Lewin (1936) developed *field theory*, which argues that a given person's behaviour (*B*) can be understood as a joint function of the person (*P*) and the environment (*E*; for a review, see Schellenberg, 1978). Although field theory is an individual-differences theory (C. S. Hall & Lindzey, 1957), Lewin's theory served as a basis for John Thibaut and Harold Kelley's (1959; Kelley, 1979; Kelley & Thibaut, 1978) social-psychological *interdependence theory* (which contends that close relationships are defined by the extent to which partners influence each other's thoughts, feelings, and behaviour; Van Lange & Balliet, 2015). Subsequently, John Holmes (2002) combined elements of field theory and interdependence theory with elements of Mischel's (1973) version of social-cognitive theory (especially the aforementioned CAPS model of Mischel & Shoda, 1995) and Baldwin's (1992) relational schema theory (which we shall encounter later in the present chapter) to produce the SABI model (see Rusbult & Van Lange, 2003).

According to Holmes (2002), interpersonal situations vary in the degree to which they make particular aspects of individuals' personalities relevant to individuals' interactions with relationship partners (see also Holmes, 2000). Furthermore, Holmes's SABI model suggests that certain interpersonal situations may reveal the extent to which particular personality constructs are manifested in individuals' interpersonal behaviour (see Reis, Capobianco, & Tsai, 2002). Holmes's model identifies six dimensions of situations (i.e., *degree of interdependence, mutuality of interdependence, correspondence of outcomes, basis of control, temporal structure*, and *degree of uncertainty*), each of which logically calls for the expression of one or two relevant interpersonal dispositions (thus affirming the role of cognition in activating certain aspects of individuals' personality repertoire within close relationships; Rusbult & Van Lange, 2003).

Holmes's (2002) SABI model was instrumental to the development of a taxonomy of twenty interpersonal situations by Kelley, Holmes, Kerr, Reis, Rusbult, and Van Lange (2003) – an accomplishment that, so far, has not been accompanied by a corresponding taxonomy of interpersonal dispositions (Gaines, 2016/2018). However, as the field of relationship science progresses from "greening" (Berscheid, 1994) to "ripening" (Reis 2007) to "blossoming" (Campbell & Simpson, 2013), researchers increasingly seek to identify those personality constructs and interpersonal goals that are most relevant to particular relationship contexts (see Finkel, Simpson, & Eastwick, 2017). Overall, Holmes's SABI model demonstrates potential as a cognitive account of personality and behaviour in close relationships (Rusbult & Van Lange, 2003).

In his version of social-cognitive theory, Bandura (1986) explained that because of their capacity for active reflection, humans possess *agency* (i.e., individuals' ability to exert control over their personalities, behaviour, and environment; Ewen, 1998). Furthermore, Bandura identified *self-efficacy* (i.e., the belief that one can exert control over the events that affect one's life, with the caveat that individuals differ in this belief) as a key personality construct within his social-cognitive theory (Funder, 2001). Some followers of Bandura (e.g., Kihlstrom & Harackiewicz, 1990) have argued that self-efficacy is best understood as a *state* (i.e., unstable, dependent upon the situation); whereas other followers of Bandura (e.g., Schunk, 1991) have contended that self-efficacy is best understood as a *trait* (i.e., stable, independent of the situation). In any event, at least when one considers the academic domain, individuals' academic self-efficacy is a significant positive predictor of individuals' academic performance over time (Funder & Fast, 2010).

Lefcourt (1991) questioned whether Bandura's (1986) construct of self-efficacy is different from Rotter's (1966) construct of locus of control (which we covered in Chapter 3) or Rosenberg's (1965) construct of self-esteem (which we covered in Chapter 4). However, unlike locus of control, self-efficacy does not address individuals' expectations regarding success or failure (see Eccles & Wigfield, 2002). Also, unlike self-esteem, self-efficacy does not address individuals' feelings about themselves (see Brewin, 1996). Overall, the construct of self-efficacy is central to Bandura's version of social-cognitive theory, which (like Mischel, 1973 version of social-cognitive theory) provides a useful conceptual bridge between personality psychology and other areas of psychology (e.g., cognitive, social; Kihlstrom & Harackiewicz, 1990).

MINI-THEORIES OF COGNITION

E. TORY HIGGINS'S SELF-DISCREPANCY THEORY

Cognitive consistency theories (invoking the Consistency Seeker mode/metaphor to which we alluded to earlier in the present chapter) have tended to (1) ignore individuals' specific affective states for the most part (e.g., the balance theory of Heider, 1958) or (2) acknowledge the conceptual importance of specific affective states (e.g., anxiety) to individuals' consistency-seeking processes, yet fail to generate empirical research that directly assesses those affective states (e.g., the cognitive dissonance theory of Festinger, 1957; for a review, see Robins & John, 1997). In contrast to most cognitive consistency theories (and, we would add, in contrast to the other cognitive theories of personality that are highlighted in the present chapter), E. Tory Higgins's *self-discrepancy theory* places individuals' particular affective states at the forefront of a conceptual framework that lends itself readily to empirical research (Funder, 2001). Specifically, Higgins's self-discrepancy theory predicts that individuals' failure to be whom they *should* be (i.e., ought-self discrepancy) can place individuals at risk for anxiety and "agitation emotions"; whereas individuals' failure to be whom they *want* to be (i.e., ideal-self discrepancy) can place individuals at risk for depression and "dejection emotions" (Silvia & Eddington, 2012).

As Karniol and Ross (1996) pointed out, Higgins's (1987) self-discrepancy theory proposes that individuals possess (1) an *ought-self regulatory system* that directs individuals to avoid situations in which they anticipate negative outcomes, and (2) an *ideal-self regulatory system* that directs individuals to approach situations in which they anticipate positive outcomes, during the course of their daily lives. Over time, according to Higgins's theory, individuals develop and pursue goals that enable individuals to act in accordance with their regulatory systems (Cervone, 2005). Furthermore, Higgins has conducted a programme of research that documents a variety of negative versus positive cognitive, affective, and behavioural consequences of individuals' resulting avoidance-related versus approach-related activities (Funder, 2001). Higgins's self-discrepancy theory and related research represent marked departures from much of the conceptual and empirical literature on social cognition that characterised the mid-1980s (during which emotions were commonly regarded as "hot cognitions"; Markus & Zajonc, 1985).

In a critique of Higgins's (1987) self-discrepancy theory, Silvia and Eddington (2012) noted that scores on ought-self and ideal-self discrepancies are so highly correlated (sometimes exceeding +.70 in value, which would suggest that the two forms of self-discrepancy share 50% or more of their variance across individuals, especially if measurement error is taken into account; see Nunnally & Bernstein, 1994). Such high intercorrelations between the independent variables make it difficult (though not necessarily impossible) for researchers to confidently state how much variance in depression, anxiety, and other specific affective states can be explained separately by ought-self versus ideal-self discrepancies (see J. Cohen, P. Cohen, West, & Aiken, 2003). Nevertheless, Higgins's conceptual distinction between ought-self and ideal-self regulatory systems has proven to be useful within Daniel Cervone's (2004) *knowledge-and-appraisal personality architecture* (KAPA), a model of within-individual personality structures and processes that is based largely upon the assumption that individuals possess separate-yet-interrelated cognitive structures or schemas about ought, ideal, and actual selves (e.g., Shadel, Cervone, Niaura, & Abrams, 2004).

MARK BALDWIN'S RELATIONAL SCHEMA THEORY

In Chapter 2 of the present book, we learned that Bowlby's (1969/1997, 1973/1998a, 1980/1998b) attachment theory made a broad distinction between secure and insecure forms of attachment – a distinction that is reflected in Bartholomew and Horowitz (1991) measurement of one secure attachment style and three insecure attachment styles (i.e., preoccupied/anxious-ambivalent, fearful-avoidant, and dismissing-avoidant). However, Bartholomew and Horowitz's research also reflects Bowlby's concept of *internal working models of self and other* (i.e., individuals' internal representation of themselves, as well as individuals' internal representation of their significant others in general, in relation to each other; Bartholomew, 1990). Drawing partly upon Bowlby's attachment theory, Mark Baldwin (1992) proposed a *relational schema theory* in which (1) Bowlby's internal working model of self was reconceptualised as a *self-schema*; (2) Bowlby's internal working model of other was reconceptualised as a partner-specific *other-schema*; and (3) a script for anticipated sequences of interaction between self and partner was added and conceptualised as an *event schema* (Berscheid, 1994).

According to Baldwin (1992), the cognitive structures of self-schema, other-schema, and event schema are incorporated into an overarching cognitive structure or relational schema for each close relationship in which a particular individual is involved (Holmes, 2000). To the extent that relational schemas reflect individuals' inferences concerning the causes of their own behaviour, relational schemas can be interpreted as individual-difference variables (Funder, 2001). However, to the extent that relational schemas reflect individuals' inferences regarding the causes of particular significant others' behaviour, relational schemas also can be interpreted as social-psychological variables (Berscheid, 1994). Finally, to the extent that both partners in a given relationship bring their separate relational schemas to bear upon their behaviour toward each other, the potential for conflict can be considerable – an interpersonal scenario that can provide important challenges for clinical and counselling psychologists who seek to reduce (if not eliminate) conflict among distressed couples (Fincham & Beach, 1999).

Just as Charles Cooley's (1902) version of self-theory has been criticised for fragmenting William James's (1890/2010) construct of the self beyond recognition (i.e., by championing a "looking-glass self" that adds a new vantage point for every new member who joins the target person's audience; Swann & Bosson, 2010), so too has Baldwin's (1992) relational schema theory been criticised for fragmenting Allport's (1937/1951, 1961/1963) construct of personality beyond recognition (see Funder, 2001). Nevertheless, John Holmes has pointed out areas of compatibility between Baldwin's relational schema theory and the aforementioned CAPS model of Mischel and Shoda (1995), as well as areas of compatibility between Baldwin's relational schema theory and Holmes's own SABI model (Holmes, 2002). All in all, Baldwin's relational schema theory serves as a consciously orientated counterpoint to

Bowlby's (1969, 1973, 1980) attachment theory (the latter of which relies heavily upon nonconscious, if not overtly *un*conscious, personality processes; Bugental & Johnston, 2000).

CRITIQUE OF COGNITIVE PERSPECTIVES

In a review of the literature on social cognition, S. T. Fiske and S. E. Taylor (1991) criticised the Scientist mode or metaphor of self-perception (exemplified by the personal construct theory of Kelly, 1955 in the present chapter) and the Consistency Seeker mode or metaphor of self-perception (exemplified by the self-discrepancy theory of Higgins, 1987 in the present chapter) as failing to adequately account for the information-processing steps that mediate between everyday persons' perceptions and responses to social stimuli (which include other persons as well as themselves; Gilbert, 1998). On the one hand, everyday persons routinely make mistakes in person perception, especially under conditions in which they experience information overload (Robinson & Wilkowski, 2015) – a fact that led to the emergence of the Cognitive Miser variation on the Scientist metaphor (see Robins & John, 1997). On the other hand, everyday persons can reduce mistakes in person perception to the extent that they choose among various social-psychological strategies on the basis of goals (and, perhaps, underlying motives; Bargh, Gollwitzer, & Oettingen, 2010) – a fact that led to the emergence of the Motivated Tactician variation on the Cognitive Consistency metaphor.

To what extent do cognitive perspectives on personality retain outdated versions of Scientist and Consistency Seeker modes or metaphors of self- and other-perception? According to Cervone (1999), Kelly's (1955) classic theory of personal constructs acknowledges potential errors in person perception (e.g., cognitive simplicity can lead individuals to adopt inaccurate stereotypes; Epting & Paris, 2006), thus hinting that Kelly's theory is compatible with the Cognitive Miser metaphor. In addition, according to Cervone and Shoda (1999), updated versions of Mischel's (1999) version of social-cognitive theory, Bandura's (1999) version of social-cognitive theory, Higgins's (1999) self-discrepancy theory, and Baldwin's (1999) relational schema theory all acknowledge the potential impact of goals and motives on person perception (e.g., goals can direct individuals to perceive relationship partners and themselves as possessing more desirable characteristics than objectively can be documented, thus helping to preserve relationships in the process; Bargh, Gollwitzer, & Oettingen, 2010), thus suggesting that these contemporary cognitive perspectives on personality are compatible with the Motivated Tactician metaphor. In summary, the cognitive theories of personality that we have covered in the present chapter do not appear to be outdated after all (Funder & Fast, 2010).

PRELUDE TO CHAPTER 7

The end of the 1990s marked the emergence of a sixth major school of thought within personality psychology – namely, the *biological* school (which emphasises "organic" influences on individuals' behaviour; Funder & Fast, 2010). To some extent, one can trace the origins of the biological school to the trait perspective in personality (Funder, 2001). Moreover, we have already encountered one prominent personality theory that is largely biological in orientation (see Chapter 5 of the present book) – namely, H. J. Eysenck's (1947) version of factor-analytic trait theory (which, at its core, is a physiological theory of arousability; Geen, 1997). However, given that psychophysiologists have noted a lack of empirical support for (and, to some extent, significant results in the opposite direction to) key predictions from H. J. Eysenck's theory (Haslam, Smillie, & Song, 2017), we will not highlight that theory in Chapter 7 of the present book. Instead, for our purposes, representative theories within the biological school include (in order of appearance) Darwin's (1859) theory of natural selection; Galton's (1869) theory of eugenics; J. A. Gray's (1970) reinforcement sensitivity theory; Cloninger's (1987) version of neurotransmitter theory; Depue's (1995) version of neurotransmitter theory; A. H. Buss and Plomin (1975) temperament theory of personality development; Trivers's (1972) theory of parental investment; and D. M. Buss and Schmitt (1993) sexual strategy theory.

7

BIOLOGICAL PERSPECTIVES ON PERSONALITY

Throughout the present book, we have encountered several passing references to Charles Darwin's (1859) theory of natural selection. At this point in the present chapter, we shall add a few details about Darwin's theory of natural selection as a forerunner to modern-day theories and research within the biological school of personality (consistent with Haslam, Smillie, & Song, 2017). According to Darwin's theory, to the extent that organisms within any species possess biological (and, at least among humans and [other] great apes, cognitive) characteristics that enable them to survive long enough to reproduce within a particular environment, the descendants of those organisms will tend to possess characteristics that are comparable – yet not necessarily identical – to the organisms in question (see Gross, 2010). Although Darwin (e.g., Darwin, 1871) developed his theory around the time that Alfred Russell Wallace (e.g., Wallace, 1869) developed his own theory of natural selection (which Wallace initially labelled as a theory of organisms' "struggle for existence"; Benton, 2010), Darwin's version emerged as the default theory of natural selection (Walsh, Teo, & Baydala, 2014). Indeed, no chapter on biological perspectives on personality would be complete without a nod to Darwin's seminal contributions (Gangestad, 2012).

Sir Francis Galton (1869)'s theory of *eugenics* (which proposed that governments should decide who was or was not "fit" to reproduce, based on individuals' measured physical and/or mental characteristics; Fancher, 2009) was influenced by Darwin's (1859) theory of natural selection (perhaps not surprisingly, given that Galton and Darwin were half-cousins; Prager, 2011). However, Galton's eugenics arguably should be labelled as a theory of *artificial* selection, due to Galton's belief that powerful human beings (rather than nature) should be the ultimate arbiters of individuals' "fitness" for propagating *Homo sapiens* (Fancher, 2009). Many contemporary psychologists may be unaware that Galton developed a variety of statistical tools (e.g., prototypes of correlation and regression analyses) in order to test contentious ideas about race and psychological characteristics (e.g., Galton believed – falsely – that individuals' race somehow determines individuals' skull size, which in turn supposedly determines individuals' intelligence; see Howitt & Owusu-Bempah, 1994). In any event, Galton's attempts to quantify individual differences in psychological characteristics (e.g., Galton, 1869) helped to lay the groundwork for methodology in differential psychology (including personality psychology; see Riegel, 1972).

In the present chapter, we will examine several biologically orientated personality theories that bear the marks of Darwin's (1859) theory of natural selection and – to a lesser extent – Galton's (1869) theory of eugenics. We shall learn that, according to biological theories of personality, individual differences are largely – if not primarily – heritable (a controversial assumption, especially when one considers that seemingly robust results concerning genetic markers for "abnormal" personality traits such as schizophrenia have been exposed as "false positives"; Wahlsten, 1999). In addition, we shall learn that behaviour geneticists in particular have claimed heritability coefficients approaching 50% for the Big Five traits of openness to experience, conscientiousness, extraversion, agreeableness, and neuroticism (as identified by McCrae & Costa, 2008; see also Chapter 5 of the present book), while defining "environment" so narrowly that *culture* (i.e., the human-made part of the environment; Herskovits, 1955) is excluded from consideration in studies of the Big Five traits (South, Reichborn-Kjennerud, Eaton, & Krueger, 2015); whereas cultural psychologists have commented on variability in the number and content of major personality traits across nations (i.e., the Big Five model is less "universal" than many biologic-ally orientated psychologists had assumed; Kwan & Herrmann, 2015). Finally, we will learn about attempts by evolutionary psychologists to reconcile evolutionary and cultural perspectives on personality (D. M. Buss & Kenrick, 1998).

BASIC ASSUMPTIONS UNDERLYING BIOLOGICAL PERSPECTIVES

In order to appreciate the importance of biological perspectives to contemporary personality psychology, one needs to understand the importance of the *scientific revolution* (i.e., the gradual shift from faith-based to data-based assumptions about the workings of nature, including the workings of humanity, from the 1400s to the 1700s; Walsh, Teo, & Baydala, 2014) as the disciplines of biol-ogy and psychology emerged from the shadows of "natural phil-osophy" during the 1800s. In an epochal declaration that helped to give rise to the scientific revolution, Nicolaus Copernicus pro-posed that the Earth revolved around the Sun (and not vice versa) – thus articulating an early version of *heliocentric theory* (Mila-vec, 2006). Three centuries later, Alfred Russell Wallace (1869) and Charles Darwin (1859) surmised independently that – just as humankind's home planet had been proven to occupy a nondescript position within the cosmological order – so too had humankind itself been shown to occupy an unexceptional role within the biological order (see Lerwill, 2009). Both Wallace and Darwin contended that humans' bodily evolution obeyed the laws of nature; whereas Darwin departed from Wallace by arguing that humans' *cognitive* evolution similarly followed laws of nature (rather than laws of divinity; Gross, 2010).

In his theory of natural selection, Darwin (1859) struggled to account for the development of human consciousness (C. U. M. Smith, 2010). Not only are humans aware of the phys-ical and social environments that they inhabit, from post-infancy childhood onward; but humans also are aware of their own aware-ness concerning their physical and social environments (a major tenet of self-theory as conceived by James, 1890/2010). One hall-mark of biological theories of personality, undoubtedly owing to their Darwinian roots, is a de-emphasis on humans' uniquely high levels of consciousness, in favour of an emphasis on nonconscious internal influences on individuals' behaviour (though we hasten to add that automated "nonconscious" processes are not necessarily synonymous with the motive-laden "unconscious" processes that were depicted in numerous psychodynamic theories of personality that we encountered in Chapter 2 of the present book). In any event, biological perspectives on personality are compatible with theoretical and empirical developments within the modern-day field of animal psychology (see Gosling & Harley, 2009).

One can distinguish broadly between two classes of biologically orientated personality theories: (1) *Anatomical and physiological theories* that focus on the impact of person-level brain structure and function on personality characteristics across individuals (e.g., the reinforcement sensitivity theory of J. A. Gray, 1970; and the neurotransmitter theory of; Depue, 1995); and (2) *behaviour genetics and evolutionary psychology theories* that focus on species-level heritability of differences and similarities in personality characteristics across individuals (e.g., the temperament theory of personality development by A. H. Buss & Plomin, 1975; and the sexual strategy theory of D. M. Buss & Schmitt, 1993). Within these broad groupings (following Haslam, Smillie, & Song, 2017), one can make further distinctions (a) *between* anatomical and physiological theories (see Cervone, 2005) and (b) between behaviour genetics and evolutionary psychology theories (Funder, 2001). Thus, we shall review examples of anatomical, physiological, behaviour genetics, and evolutionary psychology theories in turn (following Funder & Fast, 2010).

ANATOMICAL AND PHYSIOLOGICAL THEORIES

JEFFREY GRAY'S REINFORCEMENT SENSITIVITY THEORY

One of the more curious theories from pre-Scientific Revolution Era medicine was *humourism* (i.e., the belief that imbalances among the proportions of individuals' bodily fluids give rise to various mental and physical disorders; J. F. Brennan, 2003). Dating as far back as ancient Greece (if not earlier), practitioners of humourism pointed to an internal balance among (1) "*black bile*" (which, in excessive amounts, leads to a melancholic or depressive temperament); (2) "*yellow bile*" (which, in excessive amounts, leads to a choleric of quick-tempered temperament); (3) *phlegm* (which, in excessive amounts, leads to a "phlegmatic" or calm-yet-sluggish temperament); and (4) *blood* (which, in excessive amounts, leads to a sanguine or cheerful temperament) as essential to individuals' physical and mental health (Walsh, Teo, & Baydala, 2014). One might be surprised to learn that echoes of humourism reverberate through Pavlov's (1927) reflexology (which we covered in Chapter 3, though we did not refer to humourism in that chapter), via Pavlov's typology of individuals' nervous systems: (1) *Weak* (analogous to melancholic temperament); (2) *strong, yet unbalanced* (analogous to choleric temperament); (3) *strong and balanced, yet slow* (analogous to phlegmatic temperament); and (4) *strong, balanced, and mobile* (analogous to sanguine temperament; Haslam, Smillie, & Song, 2017). Furthermore (and especially relevant to the present chapter), one can detect traces of humourism in H. J. Eysenck's (1967) version of factor-analytic trait theory, in the form of Eysenck's typology of personality traits: (1) *Neurotic introversion* (analogous to melancholic temperament); (2) *neurotic extraversion* (analogous to choleric temperament); *stable introversion* (analogous to phlegmatic temperament); and (4) *stable extraversion* (analogous to sanguine temperament; Sheehy, 2004).

In his *reinforcement sensitivity theory*, Jeffrey A. Gray (1970) – a former student of H. J. Eysenck – literally overhauled Eysenck's (1967) version of factor-analytic trait theory from top-bottom to bottom-up (Corr, 2009). Rather than begin with *a priori* hypotheses concerning the existence of particular traits (i.e., neuroticism and extraversion) and then develop *a posteriori* hypotheses concerning the brain structures that might give rise to those traits, J. A. Gray (1972, 1981) began by postulating three brain structures (i.e., the *Fight/Flight/Freeze System*, or FFFS, that is associated with individuals' specific emotion of fear; the *Behavioural Inhibition System*, or BIS, that is associated with individuals' generalized emotion of anxiety; and the *Behavioural Approach System*, or BAS, that is associated with individuals' motivation toward fulfilling their desires) that are most likely to be implicated in personality traits (Haslam, Smillie, & Song, 2017). Having identified specific brain structures, J. A. Gray (e.g., J. A. Gray & McNaughton, 2000) settled on *punishment sensitivity* (reflecting the chronic activation of individuals' FFFS and/or BIS) and *reward sensitivity* (reflecting the chronic activation of individuals' BAS) as the resulting traits, which in principle can be measured by existing inventories of *anxiety* and *impulsivity*, respectively (although, in practice, anxiety is not empirically separable from neuroticism; and impulsivity is not empirically separable from extraversion; DeYoung & J. R. Gray, 2009). Notwithstanding critiques about the oversimplified nature of theories of arousability, such as J. A. Gray's reinforcement stimulus theory (as well as the version of factor-analytic theory by H. J. Eysenck, 1967; see Geen, 1997), J. A. Gray's theory arguably has breathed new life into an area of research that had been in decline (partly due to the inconsistency of results from previous studies that had been driven by H. J. Eysenck's theory; see Sheehy, 2004). Moreover, J. A. Gray's theory (alongside H. J. Eysenck's theory) helped to pave the way for Marvin Zuckerman's (1971) model and research concerning sensation-seeking as a trait, which we shall review in Box 7.1.

RICHARD DEPUE'S VERSION OF NEUROTRANSMITTER THEORY

In the wake of J. A. Gray's (1970), 1972, 1981) reinforcement stimulus theory, C. Robert Cloninger (1987) developed a version of *neurotransmitter theory* that essentially retained two of the brain structures (i.e., the BIS and the BAS) from Gray's theory, dropped the third brain structure (i.e., the FFFS) from Gray's theory, and added a new brain structure (i.e., the *Reward Dependence System*, or RDS; Haslam, Smillie, & Song, 2017). According to Cloninger's theory, (1) the BIS promotes the production of *serotonin* (involved in emotion regulation) as a neurotransmitter, which in turn promotes the chronic expression of *harm avoidance* as a temperament; (2) the BAS promotes the production of *dopamine* (involved in the experience of reward) as a neurotransmitter, which consequently promotes the chronic expression of *novelty seeking* as a temperament; and (3) the RDS promotes the production of *norepinephrine* (also known as *noradrenaline*, involved in the "fight or flight" response) as a neurotransmitter, which subsequently promotes the chronic expression of *reward dependence* as a temperament (Yarkoni, 2015). However, not only is the predicted one-to-one correspondence between neurotransmitters and

BOX 7.1 ZUCKERMAN'S (1971) SENSATION-SEEKING MODEL

As we noted in Chapter 1 of the present book, despite the considerable influence that social situations can exert upon individuals' behaviour, not all individuals behave the same way in the same situation (see also Funder & Fast, 2010). A case in point involves research on individuals' responses to sensory deprivation: Not all persons are equally likely to pursue physical or psychological stimulation in a particular situation (Zuckerman, 1969). After reviewing results from previous sensory deprivation studies, Marvin Zuckerman (1971) developed the trait construct of *sensation-seeking* (Geen, 1997). Both the name and the content of Zuckerman's sensation-seeking trait are similar (though not identical) to C. Robert Cloninger's (1987) *novelty-seeking* temperament (e.g., Zuckerman & Cloninger, 1996), the latter of which we will cover shortly in the present chapter.

As measured by the Sensation-Seeking Scale (SSS; Zuckerman, S. B. G. Eysenck, & H. J. Eysenck, 1978), sensation-seeking comprises four interrelated dimensions: (1) *thrill/adventure-seeking*, (2) *experience-seeking*, (3) *boredom susceptibility*, and (4) *disinhibition* (Geen, 1997). The thrill/adventure-seeking and disinhibition dimensions have been studied most intensively, with scores on those two dimensions correlating significantly and positively with individuals' skin conductance responses to sensory stimuli (e.g., Feji, Orlebeke, Gazendam, & Van Zuilen, 1985; T. N. Robinson & Zahn, 1983). Some researchers have obtained similar results with total scores on sensation-seeking (e.g., Neary & Zuckerman, 1976; but see also Ridgeway & Hare, 1981, for nonsignificant results regarding total scores on sensation-seeking).

Zuckerman (1984, 1990) proposed an elaborate model concerning the biological origins and functions of sensation-seeking that is beyond the scope of the present book (see also DeYoung & Gray, 2009). Suffice it to say that – within limits – Zuckerman viewed sensation-seeking as an adaptive trait that presumably enabled humans' ancestors to explore a wide variety of often-challenging environments (with the effect – though not necessarily the intent – of dispersing members of the species across the globe and, thus, maximizing access to food and other resources; see Geen, 1997). Zuckerman's model of sensation-seeking (like the factor-analytic trait theory of H. J. Eysenck, 1967; and the reinforcement sensitivity theory of J. A. Gray, 1970) has been criticised as unduly simplistic in its depiction of arousal (with some of Zuckerman's own results failing to support the hypothesis that chronic under-arousal leads to sensation-seeking; e.g., Carroll, Zuckerman, & Vogel, 1982). However, some independent results (e.g., individuals who score high on sensation-seeking tend to possess low levels of *cortisol*, a key "fight-or-flight" hormone; e.g., Beaton et al., 2006) indicate that Zuckerman's original predictions may have been correct after all (see Funder & Fast, 2010).

temperaments unsupported by evidence; but Cloninger, Svrakic, and Przybeck's (1993) own Temperament and Character Inventory (TCI) apparently measures the Big Five traits of openness to experience, conscientiousness, extraversion, agreeableness, and neuroticism – *not* the three temperaments of harm avoidance, novelty seeking, or reward dependence (or, for that matter, the additional temperament of *persistence*; let alone the "character dimensions" of *self-directedness, cooperativeness*, or *self-transcendence*; DeYoung & Gray, 2009).

Following the publication of Cloninger's (1987) version of neurotransmitter theory, Richard Depue (1995) offered his own version of *neurotransmitter theory* that deals primarily with the traits of "*agentic extraversion*" (akin to the Big Five trait of extraversion), *affiliation* (akin to agreeableness), and *constraint* (akin to conscientiousness; Haslam, Smillie, & Song, 2017). Depue generally has used the Multidimensional Personality Questionnaire (MPQ; Tellegen, 1982) in measuring the three traits in question (S. T. Smith & Guller, 2015). At the heart of Depue's theory is the premise (e.g., Depue & Collins, 1999) that individual differences regarding activities of the *mesolimbic dopamine pathway* (which promotes reward-seeking behaviour) are reflected in individual differences regarding the expression of agentic extraversion – a premise that has received substantial empirical support (Yarkoni, 2015). Depue's theory is not nearly as detailed regarding links between specific neurotransmitters and the other traits that he has measured (although serotonin has been associated with constraint; Carver, 2015). Nevertheless, Depue's version of neurotransmitter theory has emerged as the best-known alternative to Cloninger's version (DeYoung & Gray, 2009).

BEHAVIOUR GENETICS AND EVOLUTIONARY PSYCHOLOGY THEORIES

ARNOLD BUSS AND ROBERT PLOMIN'S TEMPERAMENT THEORY OF PERSONALITY DEVELOPMENT

At the time that he published his theory of natural selection, Darwin (1859) was not aware that an unassuming monk, Gregor Johann Mendel, already had begun a programme of then-unpublished botanical research that eventually would serve as the cornerstone of modern-day genetics (Walsh, Teo, & Baydala, 2014). Although Darwin had referred to hypothetical "*pangens*" (the term that would be recast as *genes*) as "factors" that somehow must be passed from parents to offspring, it was Mendel's work that would provide the definitive account of biological inheritance (Gangestad, 2012). Indeed, Mendel's results helped to reinforce the empirical foundation underlying Darwin's theory (J. F. Brennan, 2003).

Following the establishment of genetics within the discipline of biology, several biologically orientated psychologists contributed to the development of *behaviour genetics* – a misnomer, since "behaviour geneticists" typically are not trained in genetics (Cervone, 2005) and tend to study personality characteristics, not behaviour (Funder, 2001). At any rate, one of the best-known theories within behaviour genetics is Arnold H. Buss and Robert Plomin's (1984) *temperament theory of personality development* (Rowe, 1997). According to A. H. Buss and Plomin, *temperament* refers to individual differences in stable traits that are observable from birth onward (although one could argue that "temperament" might be defined more precisely as individual differences in unstable *emotions* at birth that, if experienced repeatedly over time, may serve as the bases for the development of individual differences in stable traits; e.g., Goldsmith, A. H. Buss, Plomin, Rothbart, Thomas, Chess, Hinde, & McCall, 1987). A. H. Buss and Plomin (1975) originally proposed four temperaments (i.e., *emotionality, activity, sociability*, and *impulsivity*) but subsequently dropped impulsivity after concluding (on the basis of scores that mothers gave to identical versus fraternal twins on the Emotionality, Activity, Sociability, and Impulsivity [EASI] Temperament Inventory; A. H. Buss, Plomin, & Willerman, 1973) that twins' heritability estimates across all temperaments except impulsivity exceeded 50% (although some behaviour geneticists have advocated re-inclusion of impulsivity, on the grounds that A. H. Buss and Plomin's criteria for inclusion were overly restrictive; e.g., Shiner, K. A. Buss, McClowry, Putman, Saudino, & Zentner, 2012). Like other theories within behaviour genetics, A. H. Buss and Plomin's theory has not been supported by any evidence concerning actual genes or combinations of genes that ostensibly are reflected in temperaments (see Haslam, Smillie, & Song, 2017). Perhaps the fairest way to evaluate A. H. Buss and Plomin's theory would be to conclude that – as long as one acknowledges that the impact of actual genes, gene x gene interactions, and gene x "environment" interactions likely will be no more than a fraction of the aforementioned 50% heritability estimate (see Munafo, 2009) – the temperament theory of personality development remains viable (Shiner, 2015).

DAVID BUSS AND DAVID SCHMITT'S SEXUAL STRATEGY THEORY

So far, we have commented extensively upon Darwin's (1859) original theory of natural selection – a logical starting point for any discussion of evolutionary influences on the personality characteristics that distinguish humans from members of other species (D. M. Buss, 1997). However, in *The Descent of Man, and Selection in Relation to Sex*, Darwin (1871) delved more deeply into *sexual selection* among humans – a topic that addresses within-sex and between-sex differences in personality (D. M. Buss & Kenrick, 1998). According to Darwin's theory, to the extent that individuals survive long enough to reproduce, those individuals are likely to have benefited from a millennia-long set of adaptive characteristics that enable them to compete successfully against members of the same sex, en route to mating with members of the opposite sex, while contending with various environmental pressures (see Figueredo, Gladden, Vasquez, Wolf, & D. N. Jones, 2009). A century later, Darwin's ideas about sexual selection inspired Robert Trivers (1972) to develop his *theory of parental investment*, which holds that men and women seek different, albeit complementary, personality and social characteristics from potential mates (e.g., men are more likely to value fidelity in their partners than are women; whereas women are more likely to value upward mobility in their partners than are men; D. M. Buss & Penke, 2015).

In general, *evolutionary psychology* applies Darwin's (1859, 1871) theory of natural selection to human behaviour (Gangestad, 2012). One of the most influential of the evolutionary psychology approaches to personality has been D. M. Buss and Schmitt (1993) *sexual strategy theory*, which draws upon Darwin's theory (as well as the theory of parental investment by Trivers, 1972) in asserting that differing concerns regarding paternity versus maternity lead men and women to pursue different (yet complementary) strategies for short-term and long-term mating (Hazan & Diamond, 2000). D. M. Buss (son of A. H. Buss, whose temperament theory of personality development we reviewed earlier in the present chapter; i.e., A. H. Buss & Plomin, 1975, 1984) and Schmitt have amassed an impressive amount of evidence (e.g., D. H. Buss's, 1989b study across 37 nations and more than 10,000 participants) in support of their theory (see Funder, 2001). However, D. H. Buss and Schmitt's theory has been criticised for invoking outdated stereotypes about "typical" men's and women's personality characteristics (see Funder & Fast, 2010). To their credit, D. M. Buss and Schmitt (2011) have demonstrated their willingness to debate their theory with feminist critics (e.g., Pedersen, Putcha-Bhagavatula, & Miller, 2011; Smiler, 2011), although Tate (2013) subsequently pointed out that D. M. Buss and Schmitt had placed the burden of proof upon their critics to disconfirm sexual strategy theory. All things considered, D. M. Buss and Schmitt (1993) theory shows promise as an evolutionary theory of personality, particularly within the field of relationship science (see Kenrick, Neuberg, & A. E. White, 2013).

CRITIQUE OF BIOLOGICAL PERSPECTIVES

In a chapter on the future of personality psychology, Veronica Benet-Martinez and colleagues (Benet-Martinez et al., 2015) not only expressed optimism regarding increased attention toward generic "environmental" influences on personality but also pointed toward the need for more research regarding specific *cultural* influences on personality. When one considers the default stance of many behaviour geneticists within the biological school of personality (e.g., South, Reichborn-Kjennerud, Eaton, & Krueger, 2015) concerning "environmental" influences on the Big Five traits (McCrae & Costa, 2008), Benet-Martinez et al.'s cautious optimism is understandable: "Genes" and "environment" are presumed to jointly influence personality; yet actual "genes" or combinations of genes tend not to be identified, and the "environment" – which includes "shared" aspects (e.g., siblings' having been raised in the same home) and "nonshared" aspects (e.g., siblings' belonging to different peer groups) – tends not to include measures of cultural variables (Kwan & Herrmann, 2015). Especially when one takes the non-infrequent lack of generalisability concerning trait dimensions across nations, claims about the heritability of Big Five traits may be greatly overstated (see also D. M. Buss & Penke, 2015).

Within the biological school of personality, some evolutionary psychologists (e.g., D. M. Buss & Kenrick, 1998) have suggested ways to reconcile evolutionary and cultural perspectives on personality. For example, A. P. Fiske and colleagues (1998) expanded Markus and Kitayama (1991) *self-construal model* (which originally was limited to the constructs of *independent self-construal*, or individuals' mental representation of themselves as separate from significant others, popularly associated with persons from Western nations; and *interdependent self-construal*, or individuals' mental representation of themselves as bound together with significant others, popularly associated with persons from Eastern nations) into a full-fledged theory of antecedents (i.e., collective reality, sociopsychological processes, and individual reality) and consequences (i.e., actions) of self-construals and other psychological tendencies (see Matsumoto, 1999). Given that A. T. Fiske et al. incorporate "universal" as well as cross-culturally variant influences on psychological tendencies into their theory, such a perspective – combined with measures of actual genetic variance – could provide the reconciliation that some evolutionary psychologists (alongside some cultural psychologists) have sought.

PRELUDE TO CHAPTER 8

Having surveyed each of the major schools of thought regarding personality, we are struck by many personality psychologists' lack of attention to individuals' *intentionality* – a concept that is associated primarily with the humanistic/existential school (see Chapter 4 of the present book). In order to understand why human beings behave as they do, one must account for human beings' exceptional capacity for setting goals for themselves *and* for acting upon those goals (Funder & Fast, 2010). Even within the biological school – which, at times, can be so deterministic in proclaiming genetic influences on behaviour that it runs the risk of rendering key hypotheses immune to *disconfirmability* (a fundamental requirement for scientific theories, within and outside personality psychology; Funder, 2001) – one can find acknowledgements of humans' uniqueness concerning (1) a keen sense of selfhood (e.g., A. H. Buss, 1997b) that makes intentionality possible, and (2) an enhanced ability to benefit from past experience (e.g., D. M. Buss, 1997b) that enables humans to modify behaviour as needed to achieve sought-after goals in the future (for details regarding humans' agenda-setting capabilities and behavioural outcomes, see Snyder & Cantor, 1998). In Chapter 8, we shall revisit the concept of intentionality as we offer a road map for future theorising and research that incorporates the self more fully than has been the case throughout much of post-Cognitive Revolution-era personality psychology (see Cervone, 2005).

CONCLUSION

8

CONCLUDING THOUGHTS ON PERSONALITY PSYCHOLOGY

In Chapter 1 of the present book, we learned that the self (which comprises all of the personality constructs that we have covered, as well as many additional personality constructs that space restrictions have prevented us from covering) is characterised partly by an awareness of its own awareness (i.e., *reflexive consciousness*) and partly by its ongoing existence within a social context (i.e., *interpersonal being*; see Baumeister, 1997). However, as Baumeister (1998) noted, the self is also characterised partly by its decision-making and behaviour-initiating capacities (i.e., *executive function*) – a set of capacities that personality psychologists within the humanistic/existential school have labelled as *intentionality* (which we associated primarily with the humanistic psychology of Buhler, 1968, in Chapter 4). Although Baumeister suggested that existentialist philosophers such as Sartre (1943/1956) had overestimated the extent to which individuals' executive function is engaged on a daily basis, one could counter that – outside the humanistic/existential school – personality psychologists have tended to *under*estimate individuals' attempts to act in a manner that reflects their intentionality (see Ewen, 1998).

Wegner and Bargh (1998) contended that individuals' displays of intentionality reflect an underlying need for control – a construct that

Baumeister (1998) viewed as the motive that underlies individuals' self-regulatory behaviour (see Swann & Bosson, 2010). The construct of self-regulation has been especially influential within the cognitive school of personality psychology, as exemplified by its prominence within Higgins's (1987) self-discrepancy theory (which we covered in Chapter 5 of the present book). Nevertheless, one might reasonably wonder whether cognitive constructs such as self-regulation fully capture individuals' day-to-day experience of intentionality (see Kuhl, Quirin, & Koole, 2015). For example, some of Baumeister's writings (e.g., an allusion to "the self lost and found" at the beginning of a chapter on the self-concept, self-esteem, and identity; Baumeister, 1997, p. 681) hint toward individuals' desire to discover their selves – a desire that existential psychologists such as May (author of *Man's Search for Himself* [1953]) would view as more fundamental to understanding the human condition than is a need for control *per se* (Strohl, 1998).

In this concluding chapter, we shall elaborate upon intentionality (especially as articulated by May, 1969) as we attempt to weave together diverse conceptual strands across the major schools of personality. By design, the present chapter is more integrative and forward-looking than were the previous chapters (following Benet-Martinez et al., 2015), even as we continue to acknowledge the distinctive contributions of theorists and researchers within the major schools of thought (consistent with Funder & Fast, 2010). Along the way, we will examine personality characteristics that may reflect intentionality gone awry – namely, the "Dark Triad" of narcissism, Machiavellianism, and psychopathy (Paulhus & K. Williams, 2002). Finally, we return to G. W. Allport's (1937/ 1951, 1961/1963) psychology of the individual as we revisit the intellectual boundaries of personality psychology (following McAdams & Manczak, 2015).

INTENTIONALITY: A QUINTESSENTIALLY EXISTENTIALIST CONSTRUCT

In *Love and Will*, May (1969) devoted two chapters to the construct of intentionality. First, May offered an academic conceptualisation of intentionality, transforming Rene Descartes' famous dictum of "I think, therefore I am" into "I conceive – I can – I will – I am" (p.

243). Second, May commented on the clinical implications of intentionality, noting that Descartes's dictum prioritises human cognition over human affect – an ironic prioritisation on Descartes's part, given that Descartes developed an entire theory regarding emotions as "*passions of the soul*" that ostensibly direct the "*rational soul*" or mind toward particular objects, energising individuals to approach or avoid those objects (Greenberg, 2007). In any event, we shall cover May's academic and clinical observations concerning intentionality, in that order.

According to Damasio (1994), Descartes introduced the *mind-body problem* (i.e., the question of how a supposedly immortal "rational soul" or mind manages to co-exist, let alone interact, with a mortal body) into natural philosophy and, consequently, into modern psychology. One might question the assumption (articulated by Damasio, 2001, among others) that Descartes had incorrectly depicted thinking as an activity that was separate from the body (e.g., see Kirkeboen, 2001). Nevertheless, from the standpoint of the existentialist perspective (e.g., May, Angel, & Ellenberger, 1958), Descartes's mind-body dualism does not adequately capture humans' lived experience (Buxton, 2005). May (1969) in particular challenged the premise of Descartes's mind-body problem by emphasising core aspects of humans' intentionality (e.g., consciousness as experienced *toward* something or someone, not as occurring in a social-psychological vacuum; action as reflecting individuals' active decision-making processes, not as passively responding to emotional states; see Eliason, Grafton, Samide, G. Williams, & Lepore, 2010).

One need not embrace May's (1969) conceptualisation of intentionality (or, more generally, May's theory of existential psychology) in order to appreciate May's practical contributions to psychotherapy (e.g., see A. H. Craig, 1995). However, Eliason and colleagues (2010) hinted that May's view of therapists as co-creators of genuine relationships with clients (rather than dispassionate dispensers of advice to clients) reflects May's belief in intentionality as a human capacity that transcends social roles (a belief that also is reflected in the neo-Freudian interpersonal theory of Sullivan, 1953; see Shahar, 2011). Interestingly, Milton (1993) argued that May's advocacy of authenticity among therapists and clients alike (within the context of therapist-client relationships) was compatible with Descartes's prioritisation of consciousness over the unconscious (a stance that would place May at odds with the orthodox, unconscious-oriented psychoanalysis of S. Freud, 1900/1965). Thus, perhaps May's intentionality construct as applied to therapy settings is not inherently anti-Cartesian after all (see also Rowan, 2000).

ON THE IMPORTANCE OF INTENTIONALITY, WITHIN AND (POSSIBLY) BEYOND THE HUMANISTIC/EXISTENTIAL SCHOOL

Considering the status of *Love and Will* (1969) as a bestseller, May receives surprisingly little credit for promoting the construct of intentionality (for an exception, see DeCarvalho, 1990). Nevertheless, the attention that May and colleagues (e.g., May, Angel, & Ellenberger, 1958) have paid to intentionality attests to the importance of the construct (see Berke & S. Schneider, 2006). All in all, May's commentary on intentionality has helped earn him a place alongside Maslow (1954) and Rogers (1961) as the "Big Three" humanistic/existential psychologists (Ewen, 1998). Moreover, notwithstanding Buhler's (1968) contributions to personality psychologists' understanding of intentionality (as summarised in Chapter 4 of the present book), May's (1953) positioning of intentionality as a precursor to love makes May's existential psychology especially relevant to theories and research within the field of relationship science (see DeCarvalho, 1992).

Although much of Dan McAdams's early research on motives regarding power and intimacy (e.g., McAdams, 1980; McAdams & Bryant, 1987; McAdams & Powers, 1981) reflects the influence of Murray's (1938) personology within the psychodynamic school (McClelland, 1985/1987), McAdams's more recent research on life stories (e.g., McAdams et al., 2008; McAdams, Diamond, de St. Aubin, & Mansfield, 1997; McAdams, Reynolds, Lewis, Patten, & Bowman, 2001) overtly draws upon May's (1969) version of existential psychology, especially May's conceptualisation of intentionality (for a review, see McAdams, 2010). According to McAdams and colleagues, part of individuals' quest to answer the question of "Who am I?" involves individual's ongoing construction of *narrative identity* (an autobiographical, though not necessarily recorded, account of individuals' lives that reflects key events that helped shape individuals' past, present, and possible future selves; McAdams & Manczak, 2015), starting from the years of late adolescence and early adulthood. McAdams's research on life stories is unusual in its combination of intensive, qualitative data collection from each individual (i.e., the *idiographic* approach, pioneered by G. W. Allport, 1965) with quantification of the data across large numbers of individuals (i.e., the *nomothetic* approach, likewise pioneered by G. W. Allport, 1928). Although McAdams's past and present research methods tend to be associated with the trait school (founded by G. W. Allport, 1937/1951, 1961/1963), McAdams treats Allport's psychology of the individual (which, after all, addresses the entire person; e.g., McAdams, 1997) as compatible with May's version of existential psychology.

In principle, May's (1969) conceptualisation of intentionality *could* be (but is not) explored in research on a variety of relevant constructs beyond the humanistic/existential school of personality. For example, within the psychodynamic school, Bowlby's (1969/ 1997, 1973/1998a, 1980/1998b) attachment theory led to thousands of studies on attachment styles (following the lead of Hazan & Shaver, 1987; Bartholomew & Horowitz, 1991) that presumably reflect *internal working models* or mental representations of (1) self in relation to significant others and (2) significant others in relation to the self, from infancy onward (and long before individuals' consciousness is well-developed; Bartholomew, 1990); yet *caregiver styles* (i.e., individual differences in proximity versus distance, sensitivity versus insensitivity, cooperation versus control, and compulsive caregiving; Kunce & Shaver, 1994) – which likewise reflect internal working models but are manifested primarily during adolescence and adulthood, when consciousness is highly developed and individuals presumably have developed attitudes toward (1) self in relation to significant others and (2) significant others in relation to self (e.g., Griffin & Bartholomew, 1994) – are vastly understudied by comparison (see B. C. Feeney & Woodhouse, 2016). Also, within the (neo)behaviourist school, Rotter (1966) is known mostly for his research on locus of control, which reflects individual differences in reinforcement-based expectations about the successes versus failures of their actions (see Chapter 3 of the present book); yet Rotter's (1967) work on *interpersonal trust* (i.e., differences among individuals' reinforcement-based expectations that they can rely upon other persons and groups, whether the persons in question are significant others or not) has been relatively neglected, even though both constructs reflect Rotter's (1954) version of social learning theory (see Wrightsman, 1991). In addition, within the trait school, Spence and colleagues are known to a considerable extent for their research on positive masculinity and positive femininity (J. T. Spence, Helmreich, & Stapp, 1974) and, to a lesser extent, negative masculinity and one aspect of negative femininity that is known as *negative communion* (J. T. Spence, Helmreich, & Holahan, 1979; see Chapter 5 of the present book); yet trait theorists (ironically, including Spence and colleagues) have ignored a second aspect of negative femininity that J. T. Spence, Helmreich, and Holahan (1979) identified as *verbal passive-aggressiveness* (akin to introversion, but *not* assumed to be determined by genes), despite the fact that all five gender-related traits can be understood within J. T. Spence's (1993) multifactorial gender identity theory (see Deaux & Lafrance, 1998). Finally, as we will see in Box 8.1, the "Dark Triad" of narcissism, Machiavellianism, and psychopathy (Paulhus & K. Williams, 2002) might reveal important ways that individuals' intentionality can go awry in terms of personality development.

INTENTIONALITY AND BEYOND: A MATTER OF WILL

One construct that May (1969) regarded as intimately connected to intentionality is *will*, or "*the capacity to organize one's self* so that movement in a certain direction or toward a certain goal may take place" (p. 218, emphasis in original). At times, May described intentionality and will as if they were interchangeable constructs (see also May, 1950/1996). However, one can distinguish between (1) will as involving the *development* of the self (an active process that is predominantly internal); and (2) intentionality as involving the *engagement* of the self with the physical and social environment (a similarly active process that is external as well as internal; see Moss, 2015). Perhaps the clearest distinction between intentionality and will can be found in May's *The Discovery of Being* (1983/1994): "The acorn becomes an oak regardless of any choice, but

BOX 8.1 PAULHUS AND K. WILLIAMS'S (2002) "DARK TRIAD" MODEL

In an elaboration of *personality systems interactions theory* (which postulates that the self, reason, intuitive behaviour control, and object recognition system all contribute to the structure of individuals' personalities; Kuhl, 2000), Julius Kuhl and colleagues (Kuhl, Quirin, & Koole, 2015) contended that individuals can achieve intentionality via the development of an *integrated self* as a combined cognitive and neuropsychological system (although such development is not entirely conscious; see Farmer & Maister, 2017). According to Kuhn et al., intentionality ideally is facilitated by the development of situation-specific goals that are consistent with individuals' generic (i.e., cross-situational) goals – a process that can be derailed when individuals experience high levels of stress (Kuhl & Quirin, 2011). Kuhl and colleagues surmised that effective responses to stress involve *self-activation* (i.e., a process by which individuals draw upon their long-term life stories to ward off short-term threats to their self-esteem; Koole & Kuhl, 2003).

Kuhl, Quirin, and Koole (2015) did not mention Delroy Paulhus and Kevin Williams's (2002) *Dark Triad* or socially undesirable, covarying personality characteristics of *narcissism* (an inflated attitude toward the self, measured via the Narcissistic Personality Inventory, or NPI; Raskin & Terry, 1988), *Machiavellianism* (a manipulative attitude toward other persons, measured via the Machiavellianism, or Mach, Scale; Christie & Geis, 1970), and *psychopathy* (an antisocial behavioural trait, measured via the Psychopathic Personality Inventory, or PPI; Lilienfeld & Andrews, 1996) in their article on the integrated self. However, our review of Kuhl et al.'s functional characteristics of the integrated self suggests that the dimensions of the Dark Triad can be understood within the context of Kuhl's (2000) personality systems interactions theory: (1) Narcissism reflects a low level of *extended self-development* (i.e., integrative competence); (2) Machiavellianism reflects a low level of *extended trust* (i.e., self-positivity and inner security); and (3) psychopathy reflects a low level of *extended resilience* (i.e., turning vulnerabilities into strengths). Our interpretation of the Dark Triad is consistent with the findings that (1) narcissism is significantly and negatively associated with *accommodation* (i.e., refraining from reciprocating relationships partners' anger or criticism over the short term, instead responding with behaviours that are intended to maintain relationships over the long term; Rusbult, Verette, Whitney, Slovik, & Lipkus, 1991) among women and men (W. K. Campbell & Foster, 2002; but see also Brewer et al., 2018, concerning null effects for women in a separate study); (2) Machiavellianism is significantly and negatively associated with accommodation among women (Brewer et al., 2018; data were not collected from men); and (3) psychopathy is significantly and negatively associated with accommodation among women (Brewer et al., 2018; data were not collected from men).

Kuhl, Quirin, and Koole's (2015) functional characteristics of the integrated self do not offer the only conceptual means toward interpreting the negative interpersonal consequences of the Dark Triad. For example, returning to Robins and John (1997) modes of metaphors of self-perception that we have explored throughout the present book, (1) we have already identified narcissism with the *Egoist* metaphor (concerned with obtaining positive information about the self); (2) Machiavellianism can be associated with the *Politician* metaphor (which we had not covered up to this point, concerned with making positive impressions on other persons); and (3) on a more speculative note, psychopathy might be associated with the Cognitive Miser variation on the *Scientist* metaphor (concerned with collecting information about themselves that fits individuals' attributional biases and errors; see S. T. Fiske & S. E. Taylor, 1991). At any rate, the Dark Triad may comprise one of the most consequential sets of characteristics within personality psychology.

man cannot realize his being except as he wills it in his encounters" (p. 77). Thus, in May's version of existential psychology, will is a prerequisite for intentionality (keeping in mind that will is more purely conscious, whereas intentionality is partly conscious and partly unconscious; Ewen, 1998).

May's (1969) conceptualisation of will as a precursor to intentionality can help us appreciate the richness of Snyder and Cantor's (1998) *functionalist approach* to personality and social behaviour (which we encountered briefly in Chapter 5). First, let us suppose that various features of persons (e.g., personality characteristics) and various features of situations initially lead individuals to formulate a series of agendas (at the intrapersonal, social, relational, and group levels), all of which individuals may pursue in order to achieve desired behavioural outcomes (again, at the intrapersonal, social, relational, and group levels) – a process that May (1950/1996) might summarise as *willing*. Next, let us suppose that individuals' personality characteristics subsequently lead them to identify and choose those situations that are more versus less likely to enable them to achieve their agendas via desired behavioural outcomes – a process that May (1969) might summarise as *intending*. Thus, to the extent that individuals' entry into (or, alternatively, exit from) certain situations serves as a means toward the end of achieving goals via interpersonal behaviour, one can ascertain that willing and intending have occurred (although we do not rule out the possibility that some individuals may seek situations that will propel them toward *change* in their selves; Ickes, Snyder, & Garcia, 1997; Snyder & Ickes, 1985).

May (1969) and Snyder and Cantor (1998) acknowledged the influence of William James's (1890/2010) self-theory on their respective depictions of self as manifested strategically in interpersonal behaviour. As it happens, James offered considerable insight into will (although James's observations on will have been neglected throughout most of the history of personality psychology; May, 1983/1994). In a panoramic chapter that spanned more than 100 pages of *The Principles of Psychology* (1890/2010, Vol. 2), James engaged in *introspection* (a systematic, trained version of self-observation, historically associated with the content psychology of Wundt, 1874/1910; see Zehr, 2000) regarding his own consciousness. James concluded that *attention* is a key attribute of will, orientating individuals toward a specific object (e.g., person, place, or thing) and enabling individuals to adopt a course of action versus inaction toward that object. Although May criticised James for failing to discuss intentionality by name, a close reading of *Principles of Psychology* reveals that James distinguished between deliberations and actions – a distinction that, one could argue, is consistent with May's own distinction between will and intentionality. In any event, James's self-theory allows us to draw meaningful parallels between the existential psychology of May (1969) and the functionalist approach of Snyder and Cantor (1998).

BACK TO THE SELF AND PERSONALITY

As our extended discussion of concepts from May's *Love and Will* (1969) indicates, May had a great deal to say about aspects of the self. Furthermore, in *Man's Search for Himself*, May (1953) offered one of the most profound, yet concise, definitions of self that one will find within personality psychology: "The self is the organizing function within the individual and the function by means of which one human being can relate to another [human being]" (p. 79). Nevertheless, as Ewen (1998) noted, May's version of existential psychology does not make any direct contributions to the ever-expanding catalogues of personality traits, motives, values, attitudes, emotions, and moods (although May's "kinds of love" are reflected indirectly in the "love styles" of C. Hendrick and S. S. Hendrick [1986], as we learned in Chapter 4 of the present book). Perhaps May's de-emphasis of the Me or self-as-object (within which personality constructs presumably reside, according to the self-theory of James, 1890/2010) is responsible for the lack of such direct contributions (e.g., May, 1983/1994).

According to DeRobertis (2015), May's (1991) version of existential psychology and G. W. Allport's (1954/1979) psychology of the individual share an interest in individuals' life stories (which helps explain the ease with which McAdams (1997, 2010) navigates between the two theories). However, May and Allport do not appear to have been substantively influenced by each other's work (notwithstanding the fact that May and Allport were among the A-list attendees at the Old Saybrook Conference in 1964, which gave enormous impetus to the formal development of the humanistic/existential school within personality psychology; DeCarvalho, 1992). Moreover, unlike May's existential psychology, G. W. Allport's psychology of the individual readily incorporates major personality constructs — such as traits, values, and attitudes — within the self (or, at least, within the *proprium*; see Chapter 1 of the present book). Thus, as we approach the end of the present book, we return to G. W. Allport's perspective on the self and personality (including, but not limited to, trait theory; C. S. Hall & Lindzey, 1970).

According to G. W. Allport (1955), the proprium in general seeks expression on a consistent basis, even though certain societal agents (e.g., family members, educational institutions, religious institutions, mass media) may try to keep such expression in check (Langle & Kriz, 2015). Moreover, all of the personality dimensions that are housed within the proprium are candidates for expression as individuals engage in the daily task of affirming their personhood in a society that may be indifferent (if not overtly hostile) to such pursuits (Polkinghorne, 2015). Although May (1983/1994) criticised Allport for devoting too much attention to issues of "being versus becoming" (and, conversely, too little attention to "being versus nonbeing"), one is struck by the similarity between May's and Allport's respective emphases on individuals' conscious self-strivings (see also DeCarvalho, 1991). Given the level of self-affirmation that one finds within May's (1953, 1969) existential psychology as well as G. W. Allport's (1937/1951, 1961/1963) psychology of the individual, one can understand why some historians of psychology (e.g., J. F. Brennan, 2003) place G. W. Allport alongside May as founders of the "third force" movement.

A FINAL WORD

In their chapter on the future of personality psychology, Benet-Martinez et al. (2015) offered an eclectic set of recommendations and aspirations concerning conceptual and empirical trends in the field. For the sake of brevity, we shall limit our own "wish list" for the future of personality psychology to a single (albeit multifaceted) request: Building upon the promise of Wiggins's (1991) interpersonal circumplex theory (which we reviewed in Chapter 5 of the present book), apply a laser-like focus to those dimensions of personality that are especially likely to be reflected in individuals' behaviour toward significant others (following Gaines, 2016/2018). For example, within the context of heterosexual romantic relationships, the interpersonal trait of nurturance (see Wiggins, 1979) generally emerges as a significant positive predictor of individuals' giving of interpersonal resources (i.e., affection and respect; U. G. Foa & E. B. Foa, 1974) toward their partners (see Gaines, 1996); but will future researchers obtain similar results for the interpersonal value of *altruism* (equivalent to the *communal value*; Trapnell & Paulhus, 2012), the interpersonal attitude of *positivity toward significant others in relation to self* (frequently labelled as *positive working model of other*; Griffin & Bartholomew, 1994), or the interpersonal motive of *intimacy* (also known as the *need for tenderness*; Sullivan, 1953)? Such research could simultaneously assess the *construct validity* (i.e., the extent to which scales measure the dimensions that they were designed to measure) and *predictive validity* (i.e., the extent to which scores on psychological dimensions are reflected in scores on outcome measures, such as behaviour; Carmines & Zeller, 1979).

Although G. W. Allport (1937/1951, 1961/1963) was not a relationship scientist, his psychology of the individual encompasses many constructs across personality and social psychology (Snyder & Ickes, 1985) – a quality that lends Allport's theory to the study of close relationships (Snyder & Cantor, 1998). In addition, although the present book is not primarily a monograph about personality and close relationship processes (see Gaines, 2016/2018, for such a book), we have seen that much of the literature in personality psychology is relevant to understanding individuals' behaviour in close relationships. In closing, perhaps the most exciting frontiers for personality psychology will be the expanding domains of theorising and research concerning the role of personality in individuals' choosing the situations in their lives (see Ickes, Snyder, & Garcia, 1997), within and outside the context of close relationships.

REFERENCES

Acton, G. S., & Revelle, W. (2002). Interpersonal personality measures show circumplex structure based on new psychometric criteria. *Journal of Personality Assessment, 79*, 456–481.

Adair, J. G., Paivio, A., & Ritchie, P. (1996). Psychology in Canada. *Annual Review of Psychology, 47*, 341–371.

Adams, W. W. (2010). Nature's participatory psyche: A study of consciousness in the shared Earth community. *The Humanistic Psychologist, 38*, 15–39.

Adkins, A. V. (2013). Black/feminist futures: Reading Beauvoir in Black Skin, White Masks. *The South African Quarterly, 112*, 697–723.

Adler, A. (1925). *The practice and theory of individual psychology*. London: Routledge.

Adler, A. (1932). The meaning of life. *Individual Psychology and Social Problems, 5*, 9–23.

Adler, A. (1935). What is neurosis? *International Journal of Individual Psychology, 1*, 9–17.

Adler, A. (1957). *Understanding human nature*. New York: Greenberg. (Original work published 1927).

Adorno, T. W., Frenkel-Brunswik, E., Levinson, D. J., & Sanford, R. N. (1950). *The authoritarian personality*. New York: Harper.

Afek, O. (2018, July 19). Reflections on Kohut's theory of self psychology and pathological narcissism – Limitations and concerns. *Psychoanalytic Psychology*. Advance online publication. 10.1037/pap0000201

Ainsworth, M. D. S. (1963). The development of infant-mother interaction among the Ganda. In B. M. Foss (Ed.). *Determinants of infant behavior* (pp. 67–104). New York: Wiley.

Ainsworth, M. D. S. (1967). *Infancy in Uganda: Infant care and the growth of love*. Baltimore: Johns Hopkins University Press.

Ainsworth, M. D. S., Blehar, M. C., Waters, E., & Wall, S. (1978). *Patterns of attachment: A psychological study of the Strange Situation*. Hillsdale, NJ: Erlbaum.

Ainsworth, M. D. S., & Bowlby, J. (1992). An ethological approach to personality development. *American Psychologist, 46*, 333–341.

Allport, F. H., & Allport, G. W. (1921). Personality traits: Their classificiation and measurement. *Journal of Abnormal and Social Psychology, 16*, 6–40.

Allport, G. W. (1927). Concepts of trait and personality. *Psychological Bulletin, 24*, 284–293.

Allport, G. W. (1928). A test for ascendance–submission. *Journal of Abnormal and Social Psychology, 23*, 118–136.

Allport, G. W. (1950). *The individual and his religion: A psychological interpretation*. Oxford: Macmillan.

Allport, G. W. (1951). *Personality: A psychological interpretation*. New York: Holt. (Original work published 1937).

Allport, G. W. (1955). *Becoming: Basic considerations for a psychology of personality*. New Haven, CT: Yale University Press.

Allport, G. W. (1963). *Pattern and growth in personality*. London: Holt, Rinehart and Winston. (Originally published in 1961).

Allport, G. W. (1965). *Letters from Jenny*. New York: Harcourt, Brace and World.

Allport, G. W. (1979). *The nature of prejudice*. Reading, MA: Addison-Wesley. (Original work published 1954).

Allport, G. W. (1985). The historical background of social psychology. In G. Lindzey & E. Aronson (Eds.), *Handbook of social psychology* (3rd ed., Vol. 1, pp. 1–107). New York: Random House. (Original work published 1968).

Allport, G. W., & Odbert, H. S. (1936). Trait-names: A psycho-lexical study. *Psychological Monographs, 47* (Whole No. 211), i-171.

Allport, G. W., Vernon, P. E., & Lindzey, G. (1960). *Study of values: Manual and test booklet* (3rd ed.). Boston, MA: Houghton Mifflin.

Altemeyer, B. (1981). *Right-wing authoritarianism*. Winnipeg: University of Manitoba Press.

Altemeyer, B. (1988). *Enemies of freedom: Understanding right-wing authoritarianism*. San Francisco, CA: Jossey-Bass.

Altemeyer, B. (1994). *Right-wing authoritarianism and economic philosophy among North American legislators*. London, ON: Department of Economics, University of Western Ontario.

Altemeyer, B. (1996). *The authoritarian specter*. Cambridge, MA: Harvard University Press.

Altemeyer, B. (1998). The other "authoritarian personality". In M. P. Zanna (Ed.), *Advances in experimental social psychology* (Vol. 30, pp. 47–92). San Diego, CA: Academic Press.

Amelang, M., & Borkenau, P. (1982). Uber die faktorielle Struktur und externe validitat einiger fragebogen-skalen zur erfassung von dimensionen der extraversion und emotionalen stabilitat. *Zeitschrift Für Differentielle Und Diagnostische Psychologie*, *3*, 119–146.

Ansbacher, H. L. (1978). The development of Adler's concept of social interest: A critical study. *Journal of Individual Psychology*, *34*, 118–152.

Ansbacher, H. L. (1988). Dreikurs's four goals of children's disturbing behavior and Adler's social interest-activity typology. *Individual Psychology: the Journal of Adlerian Theory, Research & Practice*, *44*, 282–289.

Arlow, J. A. (2002). Transference as defense. *Journal of the American Psychoanalytic Association*, *50*, 1139–1150.

Ashton, M. C. (1998). Personality and job performance: The importance of narrow traits. *Journal of Organizational Behavior*, *19*, 289–303.

Ashton, M. C., Jackson, D. N., Helmes, E., & Paunonen, S. V. (1998). Joint factor analysis of the personality research form and the Jackson personality inventory: comparisons with the Big Five. *Journal of Research in Personality*, *32*, 243–250.

Ashton, M. C., & Lee, K. (2001). A theoretical basis for the major dimensions of personality. *European Journal of Personality*, *15*, 327–353.

Ashton, M. C., Lee, K., & Son, C. (2000). Honesty as the sixth factor of personality: Correlations with Machiavellianism, primary psychopathy, and social adroitness. *European Journal of Personality*, *14*, 359–368.

Ashton, M. C., Lee, K., & Visser, B. A. (2019). Where's the H? Relations between BFI-2 and HEXACO-60 scales. *Personality and Individual Differences*, *137*, 71–75.

Ashton, M. C., Paunonen, S. V., Helmes, E., & Jackson, D. N. (1998). Kin altruism, reciprocal altruism, and the Big Five personality factors. *Evolution and Human Behaviour*, *19*, 243–255.

Atalay, M. (2007). Psychology of crisis: An overall account of the psychology of Erikson. *Ekev Academic Review*, *11*, 15–34.

Augustine, A. A., & Larsen, R. J. (2015). Personality, affect, and affect regulation. In M. Mikulincer & P. R. Shaver (Eds.), *APA handbook of personality and social psychology* (Vol. 4: Personality processes and individual differences, pp. 147–165). Washington, DC: American Psychological Association.

Azim, H. F. A., & Piper, W. E. (1991). The quality of object relations scale. *Bulletin of the Menninger Clinic*, *55*, 323–343.

Bachar, E., Canetti, L., Galilee-Weisstub, E., Kaplan-DeNour, A., & Shalev, A. Y. (1998). Childhood versus adolescence transitional object attachment and its relations to mental health, and parental bonding. *Child Psychiatry and Human Development*, *28* 149–167.

Baldwin, M. W. (1992). Relational schemas and the processing of social information. *Psychological Bulletin*, *112*, 461–484.

Baldwin, M. W. (1999). Relational schemas: Research into social-cognitive aspects of interpersonal experience. In D. Cervone & Y. Shoda (Eds.), *The coherence of personality: Social-cognitive bases of consistency, variability, and organization* (pp. 127–154). New York: Guilford Press.

Bandura, A. (1978). The self-system in reciprocal determinism. *American Psychologist, 33*, 344–358.

Bandura, A. (1986). *Social foundations of thought and action: A social cognitive theory.* Cambridge: Cambridge University Press.

Bandura, A. (1999). Social cognitive theory of personality. In D. Cervone & Y. Shoda (Eds.), *The coherence of personality: Social-cognitive bases of consistency, variability, and organization* (pp. 185–241). New York: Guilford Press.

Bandura, A., Ross, D., & Ross, S. A. (1961). Transmission of aggression through the imitation of aggressive models. *Journal of Abnormal and Social Psychology, 63*, 575–582.

Bandura, A., & Walters, R. (1963). *Social learning and personality development.* New York: Holt, Rinehart and Winston.

Banks, C. (1948). Primary personality factors in women: A reanalysis, 1948. *British Journal of Psychology, 1*, 204–218.

Bargh, J. A., Gollwitzer, P. M., & Oettingen, G. (2010). Motivation. In S. T. Fiske, D. T. Gilbert, & G. Lindzey (Eds.), *Handbook of social psychology* (5th ed., Vol. 1, pp. 268–316). New York: Wiley.

Barker, M. (2010). Self-care and relationship conflict. *Sexual and Relationship Therapy, 25*, 37–47.

Bartholomew, K. (1990). Avoidance of intimacy: An attachment perspective. *Journal of Social and Personal Relationships, 7*, 147–178.

Bartholomew, K. (1994). The assessment of individual differences in adult attachment. *Psychological Inquiry, 5*, 23–27.

Bartholomew, K., & Horowitz, L. M. (1991). Attachment styles among young adults: Atest of a four-category model. *Journal of Personality and Social Psychology, 61*, 226–244.

Baumeister, R. F. (1997). Identity, self-concept, and self-esteem: The self lost and found. In R. Hogan, J. Johnson, & S. Briggs (Eds.), *Handbook of personality psychology* (pp. 681–710). San Diego, CA: Academic Press.

Baumeister, R. F. (1998). The self. In D. T. Gilbert, S. T. Fiske, & G. Lindzey (Eds.), *Handbook of social psychology* (4th ed., Vol. 1, pp. 680–740). New York: McGraw-Hill.

Baumeister, R. F., Dale, K., & Sommer, K. L. (1998). Freudian defense mechanisms and empirical findings in modern social psychology: Reaction formation, projection, displacement, undoing, isolation, sublimation, and denial. *Journal of Personality, 66*, 1081–1124.

Beaton, E. A., Schmidt, L. A., Ashbaugh, A. R., Santesso, D. L., Antony, M. M., McCabe, R. E., Seaglowitz, D. J., & Schulkin, J. (2006). Low salivary cortisol levels among socially anxious young adults: Preliminary evidence from a selected and a non-selected sample. *Personality and Individual Differences, 41,* 1217–1228.

Beck, A. T. (1967). *The diagnosis and management of depression.* Philadelphia, PA: University of Pennsylvania Press.

Beck, H. P., Levinson, S., & Irons, G. (2009). Finding little Albert: A journey to John B. Watson's infant laboratory. *American Psychologist, 64,* 605–614.

Bem, D. J. (1965). An experimental analysis of self-persuasion. *Journal of Experimental Social Psychology, 1,* 199–218.

Bem, D. J. (1967). Self-perception: An alternative interpretation of cognitive dissonance phenomena. *Psychological Review, 74,* 183–200.

Bem, D. J. (1972). Self-perception theory. In L. Berkowitz (Ed.), *Advances in Experimental Social Psychology* (Vol. 6, pp. 1–62). New York: Academic Press.

Bem, S. L. (1974). The measurement of psychological androgyny. *Journal of Consulting and Clinical Psychology, 42,* 155–162.

Bem, S. L. (1981). Gender schema theory: A cognitive account of sex typing. *Psychological Review, 88,* 354–364.

Bem, S. L. (1985). Androgyny and gender schema theory: A conceptual and empirical integration. In T. B. Sonderegger (Ed.), *Nebraska symposium on motivation 1984: Psychology and gender* (pp. 76–103). Lincoln, NE: University of Nebraska Press.

Bem, S. L. (1994). *The lenses of gender: Transforming the debate on sexual inequality.* New Haven, CT: Yale University Press.

Benet-Martínez, V., & John, O. P. (1998). Los Cinco Grandes across cultures and ethnic groups: Multitrait method analyses of the Big Five in Spanish and English. *Journal of Personality and Social Psychology, 75,* 729–750.

Benet-Martínez, V., Donnellan, M. B., Fleeson, W., Fraley, R. C., Gosling, S. D., King, L. A., Robins, R. W., & Funder, D. C. (2015). In M. Mikulincer & P. R. Shaver (Eds.), *APA handbook of personality and social psychology* (Vol. 4: Personality processes and individual differences, pp. 665–689). Washington, DC: American Psychological Association.

Benjafield, J. G. (2008). George Kelly: Cognitive psychologist, humanistic psychologist, or something else entirely? *History of Psychology, 11,* 239–262.

Benjamin, L. B. (2011). Structural analysis of social behavior (SASB). In L. M. Horowitz & S. Strack (Eds.), *Handbook of interpersonal psychology: Theory, research, assessment, and therapeutic implications* (pp. 325–342). Hoboken, NJ: John Wiley & Sons, Inc.

Benton, T. (2010). Race, sex and the "earthly paradise": Wallace versus Darwin on human evolution and prospects. *Sociological Review, 57,* 23–46.

Berke, J. H., & Schneider, S. (2006). The self and the soul. *Mental Health, Religion & Culture, 9,* 333–354.

Bernasconi, R. (2000). Almost always more than philosophy proper. *Research in Phenomenology, 30,* 1–11.

Berscheid, E. (1985). Interpersonal attraction. In G. Lindzey & E. Aronson (Eds.), *The handbook of social psychology* (3rd ed., Vol. 2, pp. 413–484). New York: Random House.

Berscheid, E. (1994). Interpersonal relationships. *Annual Review of Psychology*, *45*, 79–129.

Berscheid, E. (1999). The greening of relationship science. *American Psychologist*, *54*, 260–266.

Binswanger, L. (1963). *Being-in-the-world: Selected papers of Ludwig Binswanger*. New York: Basic Books.

Bitter, J. R., Robertson, P. E., Healey, A. C., & Cole, L. K. J. (2009). Reclaiming a profeminist orientation in Adlerian therapy. *Journal of Individual Psychology*, *65*, 13–33.

Blair, I. V., Dasgupta, N., & Glaser, J. (2015). Implicit attitudes. In M. Mikulincer & P. R. Shaver (Eds.), *APA handbook of personality and social psychology* (Vol. 1: Attitudes and social cognition, pp. 665–691). Washington, DC: American Psychological Association.

Blais, M. A., Norman, D. K., Quintar, D., & Herzog, D. B. (1995). The effect of administration method: A comparison of the Rapaport and Exner Rorschachsystems. *Journal of Clinical Psychology*, *51*, 100–107.

Blascovich, J., & Tomaka, J. (1991). Measures of self-esteem. In J. Robinson, P. Shaver, & L. Wrightsman (Eds.), *Measures of personality and social psychological attitudes* (pp. 161–194). New York: Academic Press.

Blaser, R. E., & Bellizzi, C. (2014). The comparative study of learning from 1994–2013. *International Journal of Comparative Psychology*, *27*, 31–49.

Blatt, S. J., & Auerbach, J. S. (2000). Psychoanalytic models of the mind and their contributions to personality research. *European Journal of Personality*, *14*, 429–447.

Boag, S. (2006). Freudian repression, the common view, and pathological science. *Review of General Psychology*, *10*, 74–86.

Borgatta, E. F. (1964). The structure of personality characteristics. *Behavioral Science*, *12*, 8–17.

Boss, M. (1963). *Psychoanalysis and Daseinsanalysis*. New York: Basic Books.

Bowlby, J. (1953). *Child care and the growth of love*. London: Penguin.

Bowlby, J. (1997). *Attachment and loss* (Vol. 1: Attachment). London: Pimlico. (Original work published 1969).

Bowlby, J. (1998a). *Attachment and loss* (Vol. 2: Separation: Anxiety and anger). London: Pimlico. (Original work published 1973).

Bowlby, J. (1998b). *Attachment and loss* (Vol. 3: Loss: Sadness and depression). London: Pimlico. (Original work published 1980).

Bradford, G. K. (2015). Romantic love as a path: Tensions between erotic desire and security needs. In K. J. Schneider, J. F. Pierson, & J. F. T. Bugental (Eds.), *The handbook of humanistic psychology: Theory, research, and practice* (2nd ed., pp. 653–680). Los Angeles, CA: Sage.

Brennan, J. F. (2003). *History and systems of psychology* (6th ed.). Upper Saddle River, NJ: Prentice Hall.

Brennan, K. A., Clark, C. L., & Shaver, P. R. (1998). Self-report measurement of adult romantic attachment: An integrative overview. In J. A. Simpson & W. S. Rholes (Eds.), *Attachment theory and close relationships* (pp. 46–76). New York: Guilford Press.

Bretherton, I. (1992). The origins of attachment theory: John Bowlby and Mary Ainsworth. *Developmental Psychology, 28,* 759–775.

Breuer, J., & Freud, S. (1895/1995). Studies on hysteria. In J. Strachey (Ed.), *The standard edition of the complete psychological works of Sigmund Freud.* (Vol. 2, xxxii, pp. 1–335). London: Hogarth Press.

Brewer, G., Bennett, C., Davidson, L., Ireen, I., Phipps, A.-J., Stewart-Wilkes, D., & Wilson, B. (2018). Dark triad traits and romantic relationship attachment, accommodation, and control. *Personality and Individual Differences, 120,* 202–208.

Brewer, M. B., & Brown, R. J. (1998). Intergroup relations. In D. T. Gilbert, S. T. Fiske, & G. Lindzey (Eds.), *Handbook of social psychology* (4th ed., pp. 554–594). New York: McGraw-Hill.

Brewin, C. R. (1996). Theoretical foundations of cognitive-behavior therapy for anxiety and depression. *Annual Review of Psychology, 47,* 33–57.

Brookfield, S. (2002). Overcoming alienation as the practice of adult education: The contribution of Erich Fromm to a critical theory of adult learning and education. *Adult Education Quarterly, 52,* 96–111.

Brown, R. (1965). *Social psychology.* New York: Free Press.

Brown, R. (1986). *Social psychology* (2nd ed.). New York: Free Press.

Bugental, D. B., & Johnston, C. (2000). Parental and child cognitions in the context of the family. *Annual Review of Psychology, 51,* 315–344.

Buhler, C. (1968). The general structure of the human life cycle. In C. Buhler & F. Massarik (Eds.), *The course of human life: A study of goals in the humanistic perspective* (pp. 12–26). New York: Springer.

Buhler, C., & Allen, M. (1972). *Introduction to humanistic psychology.* Monterey, CA: Brooks/Cole Publishing Co.

Burt, D. L. (1966). The genetic determination of differences in intelligence: A study of monozygotic twins reared together and apart. *British Journal of Psychology, 57,* 137–153.

Buss, A. H. (1989a). Personality as traits. *American Psychologist, 44,* 1348–1378.

Buss, A. H. (1997a). Evolutionary perspectives on personality traits. In R. Hogan, J. Johnson, & S. Briggs (Eds.), *Handbook of personality psychology* (pp. 345–366). San Diego, CA: Academic Press.

Buss, A. H., & Plomin, R. (1975). *A temperament theory of personality development.* New York: Wiley.

Buss, A. H., & Plomin, R. (1984). *Temperament: Early developing personality traits.* Hillsdale, NJ: Erlbaum.

Buss, A. H., Plomin, R., & Willerman, L. (1973). The inheritance of personality traits. *Journal of Personality, 41,* 513–524.

Buss, D. M. (1989). Sex differences in human mate preferences: Evolutionary hypotheses tested in 37 cultures. *Behavioral and Brain Sciences, 12,* 1–14.

Buss, D. M. (1997). Evolutionary foundations of personality. In R. Hogan, J. Johnson, & S. Briggs (Eds.), *Handbook of personality psychology* (pp. 317–344). San Diego, CA: Academic Press.

Buss, D. M., & Kenrick, D. T. (1998). Evolutionary social psychology. In D. T. Gilbert, S. T. Fiske, & G. Lindzey (Eds.), *The handbook of social psychology* (4th ed., Vol. 2, pp. 982–1026). New York: McGraw-Hill.

Buss, D. M., & Penke, L. (2015). Evolutionary personality psychology. In M. Mikulincer & P. R. Shaver (Eds.), *APA handbook of personality and social psychology* (Vol. 4: Personality Processes and Individual Differences, pp. 3–29). Washington, DC: American Psychological Association.

Buss, D. M., & Schmitt, D. P. (1993). Sexual strategies theory: An evolutionary perspective on human mating. *Psychological Review, 100,* 204–232.

Buss, D. M., & Schmitt, D. P. (2011). Evolutionary psychology and feminism. *Sex Roles, 64,* 768–787.

Butt, T. (2004). *Understanding people.* London: Palgrave Macmillan.

Buxton, A. (2005). Conceptualisation and existential therapy. *Existential Analysis, 16,* 131–143.

Calkins, M. W. (1917). The case of self against soul. *Psychological Review, 24,* 278–300.

Campbell, W. K., & Campbell, S. M. (2009). On the self-regulatory dynamics created by the particular benefits and costs of narcissism: A contextual reinforcement model and examination of leadership. *Self and Identity, 8,* 214–232.

Campbell, W. K., & Foster, C. A. (2002). Narcissism and commitment in romantic relationships: An investment model analysis. *Personality and Social Psychology Bulletin, 28,* 484–495.

Campbell, L., & Simpson, J. A. (2013). The blossoming of relationship science. In J. A. Simpson & L. Campbell (Eds.), *The Oxford handbook of close relationships* (pp. 3–10). Oxford: Oxford University Press.

Capps, D. (2012). Erikson's schedule of human strengths and the childhood origins of the resourceful self. *Pastoral Psychology, 61,* 269–283.

Carlin, N. (2010). The paranoia of everyday life: Some personal, psychological, and pastoral thoughts. *Pastoral Psychology, 59,* 679–695.

Carmines, E. G., & Zeller, R. A. (1979). *Reliability and validity assessment.* Newbury Park, CA: Sage.

Carroll, E. N., Zuckerman, M., & Vogel, W. H. (1982). A test of the optimal level of arousal theory of sensation seeking. *Journal of Personality and Social Psychology, 42,* 572–575.

Carton, J. S., & Nowicki, S. (1994). Antecedents of individual differences in locus of control of reinforcement: A critical review. *Genetic, Social, and General Psychology Monographs, 120,* 31–81.

Carver, C. S. (2015). Behavioral approach, behavioural avoidance, and behavioural inhibition. In M. Mikulincer & P. R. Shaver (Eds.), *APA handbook of personality and social psychology* (Vol. 4: Personality Processes and Individual Differences, pp. 307–327). Washington, DC: American Psychological Association.

Caspi, A., Roberts, B. W., & Shiner, R. L. (2005). Personality development: Stability and change. *Annual Review of Psychology, 56,* 453–484.

Castagna, P. J., Davis, T. E., III, & Lilly, M. E. (2017). The behavioral avoidance task with anxious youth: A review of procedures, properties, and criticisms. *Clinical Child & Family Psychology Review, 20,* 162–184.

Cattell, R. B. (1946). *Development and measurement of personality.* New York: World Book Co.

Cattell, R. B. (1950). *Personality: A systematic, theoretical, and factual study.* New York: McGraw-Hill.

Cattell, R. B. (1965). Factor analysis: An introduction to essentials I: The purpose and underlying models. *Biometrics, 21,* 190–215.

Cattell, R. B. (1970). *Personality and social psychology: Collected papers of Raymond B. Cattell.* San Diego, CA: Knapp.

Cattell, R. B. (1973). *Personality and mood by questionnaire.* San Francisco, CA: Jossey-Bass.

Celani, D. P. (2001). Working with Fairbairn's ego structures. *Contemporary Psychoanalysis, 37,* 381–416.

Cervone, D. (1999). Bottom-up explanation in personality psychology: The case of cross-situational coherence. In D. Cervone & Y. Shoda (Eds.), *The coherence of personality: Social-cognitive bases of consistency, variability, and organization* (pp. 303–341). New York: Guilford Press.

Cervone, D. (2004). The architecture of personality. *Psychological Review, 111,* 183–204.

Cervone, D. (2005). Personality architecture: Within-person structures and processes. *Annual Review of Psychology, 56,* 423–452.

Cervone, D., & Shoda, Y. (1999a). Social-cognitive theories and the coherence of personality. In D. Cervone & Y. Shoda (Eds.), *The coherence of personality: Social-cognitive bases of consistency, variability, and organization* (pp. 3–33). New York: Guilford Press.

Cervone, D., & Shoda, Y., Eds. (1999b). *The coherence of personality: Social-cognitive bases of consistency, variability, and organization.* New York: Guilford Press.

Chase, C. I. (1998). A chat room – Educational psychologists but no curriculum methodologists? *Educational Psychology Review, 10,* 239–248.

Chescheir, M. W., & Schulz, K. M. (1989). The development of a capacity for concern in antisocial children: Winnicott's concept of human relatedness. *Clinical Social Work Journal, 17*, 24–39.

Chodorow, N. J. (1978). *The reproduction of mothering: Psychoanalysis and the sociology of gender*. Berkeley, CA: University of California Press.

Chodorow, N. J. (2004). The American independent tradition: Loewald, Erikson, and the (possible) rise of intersubjective ego psychology. *Psychoanalytic Dialogues, 14*, 207–232.

Chomsky, N. (1959). Review of Skinner's *Verbal behavior*. *Language, 35*, 26–58.

Christie, R. (1991). Authoritarianism and related constructs. In J. P. Robinson, P. R. Shaver, & L. S. Wrightsman (Eds.), *Measures of personality and social psychological attitudes* (pp. 501–571). San Diego, CA: Academic Press.

Christie, R., & Geis, F. (1970). *Studies in Machiavellianism*. New York: Academic Press.

Church, A. T., Katigbak, M. S., & Reyes, J. A. S. (1998). Further exploration of Filipino personality structure using the lexical approach: Do the Big-Five or Big-Seven dimensions emerge? *European Journal of Personality, 12*, 249–269.

Church, A. T., & Lonner, W. J. (1998). The cross-cultural perspective in the study of personality: Rationale and current research. *Journal of Cross-Cultural Psychology, 29*, 32–62.

Church, A. T., Reyes, J. A. S., Katigbak, M. S., & Grimm, S. D. (1997). Filipino personality structure and the Big Five model: A lexical approach. *Journal of Personality, 65*, 477–528.

Churchill, S. D., & Wertz, F. J. (2015). An introduction to phenomenological research in psychology: Historical, conceptual, and methodological foundations. In K. J. Schneider, J. F. Pierson, & J. F. T. Bugental (Eds.), *The handbook of humanistic psychology: Theory, research, and practice* (2nd ed., pp. 275–293). Los Angeles, CA: Sage.

Clarke, S. (2000). Psychoanalysis, psychoexistentialism and racism. *Psychoanalytic Studies, 2*, 343–355.

Clavijo, A. (2013). The psyche as behavior. *Revista Columbiana De Psicologia, 22*, 377–387.

Cloninger, C. R. (1987). A systematic method for clinical description and classification of personality variants. *Archives of General Psychiatry, 44*, 573–588.

Cloninger, C. R., Svrakic, D. M., & Przybeck, T. R. (1993). A psychobiological model of temperament and character. *Archives of General Psychiatry, 50*, 975–990.

Cohen, J. (2005). *How to read Freud*. London: Granta Books.

Cohen, J., Cohen, P., West, S. G., & Aiken, L. S. (2003). *Applied multiple regression/correlation analysis for the behavioral sciences* (3rd ed.). Mahwah, NJ: Erlbaum.

Cokley, K. (2007). Critical issues in the measurement of ethnic and racial identity: A referendum on the state of the field. *Journal of Counseling Psychology*, *54*, 224–234.

Constantinople, A. (1969). An Eriksonian measure of personality development in college students. *Developmental Psychology*, *1*, 357–372.

Constantinople, A. (1973). Masculinity-Femininity: An exception to a famous dictum? *Psychological Bulletin*, *80*, 389–407.

Cooley, C. H. (1902). *Human nature and the social order*. New York: Scribner's.

Coolidge, F. L., Moor, C., Yamazaki, G. F., Stewart, S. E., & Segal, D. L. (2001). On the relationship between Karen Horney's tripartite neurotic type theory and personality disorder features. *Personality and Individual Differences*, *30*, 1387–1400.

Cooper, C. R., & Denner, J. (1998). Theories linking culture and psychology: Universal and community-specific processes. *Annual Review of Psychology*, *49*, 559–584.

Corr, P. J. (2009). The reinforcement sensitivity theory of personality. In P. J. Corr & G. Matthews (Eds.), *The Cambridge handbook of personality psychology* (pp. 347–376). Cambridge, UK: Cambridge University Press.

Cortina, J. M. (1993). What is coefficient alpha? An examination of theory and applications. *Journal of Applied Psychology*, *78*, 98–104.

Cortina, M. (2015). The greatness and limitations of Erich Fromm's humanism. *Contemporary Psychoanalysis*, *51*, 388–422.

Costa, P. T., Jr., & McCrae, R. (1992). *Revised NEO Personality Inventory (NEO-PI-R) and NEO Five Factor Model (NEO-FFI) professional manual*. Odesa, FL: Psychological Assessment Center.

Costa, P. T., Jr., & McCrae, R. R. (1985). *The NEO personality inventory manual*. Odessa, FL: Psychological Assessment Resources.

Costa, P. T., Jr., & McCrae, R. R. (1989). *The NEO PI manual supplement*. Odessa, FL: Psychological Assessment Resources.

Craig, A. H. (1995). Psychology's subject. *South African Journal of Psychology*, *25*, 236–243.

Craig, E. (2008). The human and the hidden: Existential wonderings about depth, soul, and the unconscious. *The Humanistic Psychologist*, *36*, 227–282.

Crastnopol, M. (2001). Convergence and divergence in the characters of analyst and patient: Fairbairn treating Guntrip. *Psychoanalytic Psychology*, *18*, 120–136.

Crocker, J., & Canevello, A. (2015). Relationships and the self: Ecosystem and egosystem. In M. Mikulincer & P. R. Shaver (Eds.), *APA handbook of personality and social psychology* (Vol. 3: Interpersonal relations, pp. 93–116). Washington, DC: American Psychological Association.

Curlette, W. L., Kern, R. M., & Wheeler, M. (1996). Uses and interpretations of scores on the BASIS-A Inventory. *Individual Psychology*, *52*, 95–103.

Damasio, A. R. (1994). *Descartes' error: Emotion, reason, and the human brain*. New York: Putman.

Damasio, A. R. (2001). Descartes' error revisited. *Journal of the History of the Neurosciences, 10*, 192–194.

Danzer, G. (2012). Integrating ego psychology and strengths-based social work. *Journal of Theory Construction & Testing, 16*, 9–15.

Darwin, C. R. (1859). *On the origin of species by means of natural selection, or the preservation of favoured races in the struggle for life*. London: John Murray.

Darwin, C. R. (1871). *The descent of man, and selection in relation to sex*. London: John Murray.

Davis, M., Barad, M., Otto, M., & Southwick, S. (2006). Combining pharmacotherapy with cognitive behavioral therapy: Traditional and new approaches. *Journal of Traumatic Stress, 19*, 571–581.

Davis, T. (2007). The relevance of the Freudian concept of 'transference' to existential psychotherapy. *Existential Analysis, 18*, 348–357.

Davison, K., & MacGregor, M. W. (1998). A critical appraisal of self-report defense mechanism measures. *Journal of Personality, 66*, 965–992.

de Beauvoir, S. (1947). *The ethics of ambiguity*. New York: Philosophical Library.

de Beauvoir, S. (2009). *The second sex* (Vol.'s 1 & 2). New York: Knopf. (Original work published 1949).

Deary, I. J. (2009). The trait approach to personality. In P. J. Corr & G. Matthews (Eds.), *The Cambridge handbook of personality psychology* (pp. 89–109). Cambridge: Cambridge University Press.

Deaux, K., & LaFrance, M. (1998). Gender. In D. T. Gilbert, S. T. Fiske, & G. Lindzey (Eds.), *The handbook of social psychology* (4th ed., Vol. 1, pp. 788–827). Boston, MA: McGraw-Hill.

Debbane, E. (2011). Envy and its relation to destructiveness. *Canadian Journal of Psychoanalysis, 19*, 108–124.

DeCarvalho, R. J. (1990). The growth hypothesis and self-actualization: An existential alternative. *The Humanistic Psychologist, 18*, 252–258.

DeCarvalho, R. J. (1991). Gordon Allport and humanistic psychology. *Journal of Humanistic Psychology, 31*, 8–13.

DeCarvalho, R. J. (1992). The humanistic ethics of Rollo May. *Journal of Humanistic Psychology, 32*, 7–18.

Deci, E. L., & Ryan, R. M. (2000). The "what" and "why" of goal pursuits: Human needs and the self-determination of behavior. *Psychological Inquiry, 11*, 227–268.

Depue, R. A. (1995). Neurobiological factors in personality and depression. *European Journal of Personality, 9*, 413–439.

Depue, R. A., & Collins, P. F. (1999). Neurobiology of the structure of personality: Dopamine, facilitation of incentive motivation, and extraversion. *Behavioral and Brain Sciences, 22*, 491–569.

DeRobertis, E. M. (2006). Charlotte Buhler's existential-humanistic contributions to child and adolescent psychology. *Journal of Humanistic Psychology*, *46*, 48–76.

DeRobertis, E. M. (2015). Toward a humanistic-multicultural model of development. In K. J. Schneider, J. F. Pierson, & J. F. T. Bugental (Eds.), *The handbook of humanistic psychology: Theory, research, and practice* (2nd ed., pp. 227–242). Los Angeles, CA: Sage.

Dewey, J. (1909). *Moral principles in education*. New York: Houghton Mifflin.

Dewsbury, D. A. (2000). Comparative cognition in the 1930s. *Psychonomic Bulletin & Review*, *7*, 267–283.

DeYoung, C. G. (2015). Openness/intellect: A dimension of personality reflecting cognitive exploration. In M. Mikulincer & P. R. Shaver (Eds.), *APA handbook of personality and social psychology* (Vol. 4: Personality Processes and Individual Differences, pp. 369–399). Washington, DC: American Psychological Association.

DeYoung, C. G., & Gray, J. R. (2009). Personality neuroscience: Explaining individual differences in affect, behavior, and cognition. In P. J. Corr & G. Matthews (Eds.), *The Cambridge handbook of personality psychology* (pp. 323–346). Cambridge, UK: Cambridge University Press.

DeYoung, C. G., Weisberg, Y. J., Quilty, L. C., & Peterson, J. B. (2013). Unifying the aspects of the Big Five, the interpersonal circumplex, and trait affiliation. *Journal of Personality*, *81*, 465–475.

Diener, E., Emmons, R. A., Larsen, R. J., & Griffin, S. (1985). The satisfaction with life scale. *Journal of Personality Assessment*, *49*, 71–75.

Diener, E., Oishi, S., & Lucas, R. E. (2003). Personality, culture, and subjective well-being: Emotional and cognitive evaluations of life. *Annual Review of Psychology*, *54*, 403–425.

Diener, E., Sapyta, J. J., & Suh, E. (1998). Subjective well-being is essential to well-being. *Psychological Inquiry*, *9*, 33–37.

Diener, E., Wirtz, D., Tov, W., Kim-Prieto, C., Choi, D.-W., Oishi, S., & Biswas-Diener, R. (2010). New well-being measures: Short scales to assess flourishing and positive and negative feelings. *Social Indicators Research*, *97*, 143–156.

Digman, J. M. (1990). Personality structure: Emergence of the Five-Factor model. *Annual Review of Psychology*, *41*, 417–440.

Dijkic, M., & Oatley, K. (2004). Love and personal relationships: Navigating on the border between the ideal and the real. *Journal for the Theory of Social Behaviour*, *34*, 199–209.

Dixon, J., & Levine, M. (2012). Introduction. In J. Dixon & M. Levine (Eds.), *Beyond prejudice: Extending the social psychology of conflict, inequality and social change* (pp. 1–22). Cambridge: Cambridge University press.

Dixon-Gordon, K. L., Turner, B. J., & Chapman, A. L. (2011). Psychotherapy for personality disorders. *International Review of Psychiatry*, *23*, 282–302.

Dolezal, L. (2012). Reconsidering the look in Sartre's being and nothingness. *Sartre Studies International*, *18*, 9–28.

Dollard, J., Doob, L. W., Miller, N. E., Mowrer, O. H., & Robert Sears, R. R. (1939). *Frustration and aggression*. New Haven, CT: Yale University Press.

Donahoe, J. W. (1999). Edward L Thorndike: The selectionist connectionist. *Journal of the Experimental Analysis of Behavior*, *72*, 451–454.

Drescher, J. (2010). There is no there there: A discussion of "Narcissism and self-esteem among homosexual and heterosexual male students". *Journal of Sex & Marital Therapy*, *36*, 38–47.

Eccles, J. S., & Wigfield, A. (2002). Motivational beliefs, values, and goals. *Annual Review of Psychology*, *53*, 109–132.

Eibl-Eibesfeldt, I. (1977). Evolution of destructive aggression. *Aggressive Behavior*, *3*, 127–144.

Eliason, G. T., Samide, J. L., Williams, G., & Lepore, M. F. (2010). Existential theory and our search for spirituality. *Journal of Spirituality in Mental Health*, *12*, 86–111.

Elkind, D. (1999). Educational research and the science of education. *Educational Psychology Review*, *11*, 271–287.

Ellis, A. (1962). *Reason and emotion in psychotherapy*. New York: Lyle Stuart.

Endler, N. S. (2000). The interface between personality and cognition. *European Journal of Personality*, *14*, 377–389.

Enns, C. Z. (1989). Toward teaching inclusive personality theories. *Teaching of Psychology*, *16*, 111–117.

Epting, F. R., & Paris, M. E. (2006). A constructive understanding of the person: George Kelly and humanistic psychology. *Humanistic Psychologist*, *34*, 21–37.

Erikson, E. H. (1950). *Childhood and society*. New York: Norton.

Erikson, E. H. (1980). *Identity and the life cycle*. New York: Norton. (Original work published 1959).

Erikson, E. H. (1994). *Identity: Youth and crisis*. New York: Norton. (Original work published 1968).

Erikson, E. H. (1995). *Childhood and society*. London: Vintage. (Original work published 1963).

Etcheverry, P. E., Le, B., Wu, T. F., & Wei, M.. (2013). Attachment and the investment model: Predictors of relationship commitment, maintenance, and persistence. *Personal Relationships*, *20*, 546–567.

Ewen, R. B. (1998). *An introduction to theories of personality* (5th ed.). Mahwah, NJ: Erlbaum.

Exner, J. E. (1986). *The Rorschach: A comprehensive system* (Vol. 1: Basic foundations, 2nd ed.). New York: Wiley & Sons.

Eysenck, H. J. (1947). *Dimensions of personality*. New York: Methuen.

Eysenck, H. J. (1967). *The biological basis of personality*. Springfield, IL: Charles C. Thomas.

Eysenck, H. J. (1970). *The structure of human personality* (3rd ed.). London: Methuen. (Original work published 1952).

Eysenck, H. J., & Eysenck, S. B. G. (1968). *Manual for the Eysenck personality inventory*. San Diego, CA: Educational and Industrial Testing.

Eysenck, H. J., & Eysenck, S. B. G. (1975). *Manual of the Eysenck personality questionnaire*. London: Hodder and Stoughton.

Fabrigar, L. R., Visser, P. S., & Browne, M. W. (1997). Conceptual and methodological issues in testing the circumplex structure of data in personality and social psychology. *Personality and Social Psychology Review, 1*, 184–203.

Fairbairn, W. R. D., (1952). *Psychoanalytic studies of personality*. New York: Routledge.

Fairchild, H. H., Yee, A. H., Wyatt, G., & Weizmann, F. (1995). Readdressing psychology's problems with race. *American Psychologist, 50*, 46–47.

Fancher, R., & Rutherford, A. (2017). *Pioneers of psychology* (5th ed.). New York: Norton.

Fancher, R. E. (2009). Scientific cousins: The relationship between Charles Darwin and Francis Galton. *American Psychologist, 64*, 84–92.

Fanon, F. (1963). *The wretched of the earth*. New York: Grove Weidenfeld. (Original work published 1961).

Fanon, F. (1967). *Black skin, White masks*. New York: Grove Press. (Original version published 1952).

Farmer, H., & Maister, L. (2017). Putting ourselves in another's skin: Using the plasticity of self-perception to enhance empathy and decrease prejudice. *Social Justice Research, 30*, 323–354.

Feeney, B. C., & Woodhouse, S. S. (2016). Caregiving. In J. Cassidy & P. R. Shaver (Eds.), *Handbook of attachment: Theory, research and clinical applications* (3rd ed., pp. 827–851). New York: Guilford Press.

Feest, U. (2005). Operationism in psychology: What the debate is about, what the debate should be about. *Journal of the History of the Behavioral Sciences, 41*, 131–149.

Feij, J. A., Orlebeke, J. F., Gazendam, A., & Van Zuilen, R. W. (1985). Sensation seeking: Measurement and psychophysiological correlates. In J. Strelau & A. Gale (Eds.), *The biological bases of personality and behaviour* (Vol. 1: Theories, measurement techniques and development, pp. 195–210). Washington, DC: Hemisphere Press.

Festinger, L. (1957). *A theory of cognitive dissonance*. Stanford, CA: Stanford University Press.

Field, A. P., & Nightingale, Z. C. (2009). Test of time: What if Little Albert had escaped? *Clinical Child Psychology and Psychiatry, 14*, 311–319.

Figueredo, A. J., Gladden, P., Vasquez, G., Wolf, P. A. A., & Jones, D. N. (2009). Evolutionary theories of personality. In P. J. Corr & G. Matthews (Eds.), *The Cambridge handbook of personality psychology* (pp. 265274–265376). Cambridge, UK: Cambridge University Press.

Fincham, F. D., & Beach, S. R. (1999). Marital conflict: Implications for working with couples. *Annual Review of Psychology, 50*, 47–77.

Finkel, E. J., Cheung, E. O., Emery, L. F., Carswell, K. L., & Larson, G. M. (2015). The suffocation model: Why marriage in America is becoming an all-or-nothing institution. *Current Directions in Psychological Science, 24*, 238–244.

Finkel, E. J., Hui, C. M., Carswell, K. L., & Larson, G. M. (2014). The suffocation of marriage: Climbing Mount Maslow without enough oxygen. *Psychological Inquiry, 25*, 1–41.

Finkel, E. J., Larson, G. M., Carswell, K. L., & Hui, C. M. (2014). Marriage at the summit: Response to the commentaries. *Psychological Inquiry, 25*, 120–145.

Finkel, E. J., Simpson, J. A., & Eastwick, P. W. (2017). The psychology of close relationships: Fourteen core principles. *Annual Review of Psychology, 68*, 383–411.

Fisher, S. (1949). An overview of trends in research dealing with personality rigidity. *Journal of Personality, 17*, 342–351.

Fiske, A. P., Kitayama, S., Markus, H. R., & Nisbett, R. E. (1998). The cultural matrix of social psychology. In D. T. Gilbert, S. T. Fiske, & G. Lindzey (Eds.), *The handbook of social psychology* (4th ed., Vol. 2, pp. 915–981). New York: McGraw-Hill.

Fiske, D. W. (1949). Consistency of the factorial structures of personality ratings from different sources. *Journal of Abnormal and Social Psychology, 44*, 329–344.

Fiske, S. T. (1998). Prejudice, stereotyping, and discrimination. In D. T. Gilbert, S. T. Fiske, & G. Lindzey (Eds.), *Handbook of social psychology* (4th ed., pp. 357–411). New York: McGraw-Hill.

Fleeson, W. (2012). Perspectives on the person: Rapid growth and opportunities for integration. In K. Deaux & M. Snyder (Eds.), *Oxford handbook of personality and social psychology* (pp. 33–63). Oxford: Oxford University Press.

Foa, U. G., & Foa, E. B. (1974). *Societal structures of the mind*. Springfield, IL: Charles C. Thomas.

Frable, D. E. S. (1997). Gender, racial, sexual, and class identities. *Annual Review of Psychology, 48*, 139–163.

Freeman, T. (2008). Psychoanalytic concepts of fatherhood: Patriarchal paradoxes and the presence of an absent authority. *Studies in Gender and Sexuality, 9*, 113–139.

Freidan, B. (1963). *The feminine mystique*. New York: Norton.

Freud, A. (1958). Adolescence. *Psychoanalytic Study of the Child*, *13*, 255–278.

Freud, A. (1966). *The ego and the mechanisms of defense*. New York: International Universities Press. (Original work published 1936).

Freud, A. (1975). *Introduction to the technique of child analysis*. Stratford, NH: Ayer Company Publishers. (Original work published 1927).

Freud, S. (1922). *Group psychology and the analysis of the ego*. New York: Bond & Liveright.

Freud, S. (1925). Character and anal eroticism. In S. Freud, *Collected papers* (Vol. 2, pp. 167–175). London: Hogarth Press. (Original work published 1908).

Freud, S. (1927). *The ego and the id*. London: Hogarth Press. (Original work published 1923).

Freud, S. (1950). Libidinal types. In S. Freud, *Collected papers* (Vol. 5). London: Hogarth Press. (Original work published 1931).

Freud, S. (1953). On narcissism: An introduction. In J. Strachey (Ed. & Trans.), *The standard edition of the complete psychological works of Sigmund Freud* (Vol.14, pp. 69–102). London: Hogarth Press. (Original work published 1914).

Freud, S. (1961). *Beyond the pleasure principle*. New York: Norton. (Original work published 1920).

Freud, S. (1962). *Three essays on the theory of sexuality* (James Strachey, translator). New York: Basic Books. (Original work published 1905).

Freud, S. (1965). *The interpretation of dreams*. New York: Avon. (Original work published 1900).

Freud, S. (1990). *New introductory lectures on psychoanalysis*. New York: Norton. (Original work published 1933).

Fridlund, A. J., Beck, H. P., Goldie, W. D., & Irons, G. (2012). Little Albert: A neurolologically impaired child. *History of Psychology*, *15*, 302–327.

Friedman, H. (2008). Humanistic and positive psychology: The methodological and epistemological divide. *Humanistic Psychologist*, *36*, 113–126.

Frings, D. (2019). *Social psychology: The basics*. London: Routledge.

Fromm, E. (1941). *Escape from freedom*. New York: Farrar & Rinehart.

Fromm, E. (1957). *The art of loving*. London: George Allen & Unwin.

Funder, D. C. (1991). Global traits: A neo-Allportian approach to personality. *Psychological Science*, *2*, 31–39.

Funder, D. C. (2001). Personality. *Annual Review of Psychology*, *52*, 197–221.

Funder, D. C., & Fast, L. A. (2010). Personality in social psychology. In S. T. Fiske, D. T. Gilbert, & G. Lindzey (Eds.), *Handbook of social psychology* (5th ed., Vol. 1, pp. 668–697). Hoboken, NJ: John Wiley & Sons, Inc.

Gaines, S. O., Jr. (2007a). Personality and personal relationship processes: An introduction to the special issue. *Journal of Social and Personal Relationships*, *24*, 475–478.

Gaines, S. O., Jr. (2007b). Personality and personal relationship processes: Concluding thoughts. *Journal of Social and Personal Relationships*, *24*, 613–617.

Gaines, S. O., Jr. (2012). Stereotyping, prejudice and discrimination revisited: From William James to W. E. B. Du Bois. In J. Dixon & M. Levine (Eds.), *Beyond prejudice: Extending the social psychology of conflict, inequality and social change* (pp. 105–119). Cambridge, UK: Cambridge University Press.

Gaines, S. O., Jr. (2017). *Identity and interethnic marriage in the United States*. New York: Routledge.

Gaines, S. O., Jr. (2018). *Personality and close relationship processes*. Cambridge, UK: Cambridge University Press. (Original work published 2016).

Gaines, S. O., Jr., Marelich, W. D., Bledsoe, K. L., Steers, W. N., Henderson, M. C., Granrose, C. S., Barajas, L., Hicks, D., Lyde, M., Takahashi, Y., Yum, N., Rios, D. I., Garcia, B. F., Farris, K., & Page, M. S. (1997a). links between race/ethnicity and cultural values as mediated by racial/ethnic identity and moderated by gender. *Journal of Personality and Social Psychology*, *72*, 1460–1476.

Gaines, S. O., Jr. (1996). Impact of interpersonal traits and gender-role compliance on interpersonal resource exchange among dating and engaged/married couples. *Journal of Social and Personal Relationships*, *13*, 241–261.

Gaines, S. O., Jr., Marelich, W. D., Bunce, D., Robertson, T., & Wright, B. C. (2013). MEIM expansion: Racial, religious, and national aspects of sense of ethnic identity within the United Kingdom. *Identity: an International Journal of Theory and Research*, *13*, 289–317.

Gaines, S. O., Jr., Panter, A. T., Lyde, M. D., Steers, W. N., Rusbult, C. E., Cox, C. L., & Wexler, M. O. (1997b). Evaluating the circumplexity of interpersonal traits and the manifestation of interpersonal traits in interpersonal trust. *Journal of Personality and Social Psychology*, *73*, 610–623.

Gaines, S. O., Jr., & Reed, E. S. (1994). Two social psychologies of prejudice: Gordon W. Allport, W. E. B. Du Bois, and the legacy of Booker T. Washington. *Journal of Black Psychology*, *20*, 8–28.

Gaines, S. O., Jr., & Reed, E. S. (1995). Prejudice: From Allport to Du Bois. *American Psychologist*, *50*, 96–103.

Galton, F. (1869). *Hereditary genius*. London: Macmillan.

Gammelgaard, J. (2003). Ego, self and otherness. *Scandinavian Psychoanalytic Review*, *26*, 96–108.

Gangestad, S. W. (2012). Evolutionary perspectives. In K. Deaux & M. Snyder (Eds.), *The Oxford handbook of personality and social psychology* (pp. 151–181). Oxford: Oxford University Press.

Garcia-Valdecases, M. (2005). Psychology and mind in Aquinas. *History of Psychiatry*, *16*, 291–310.

Gaughan, E. T., Miller, J. D., & Lynam, D. R. (2012). Examining the utility of general models of personality in the study of psychopathy: A comparison of the HEXACO-PI-R and NEO PI-R. *Journal of Personality Disorders*, *26*, 513–523.

Geen, R. G. (1997). Psychophysiological approaches to personality. In R. Hogan, J. A. Johnson, & S. R. Briggs (Eds.), *Handbook of personality psychology* (pp. 387–414). New York: Academic Press.

Gieser, M. T. (1993). The first behavior therapist as I knew her. *Journal of Behavior Therapy and Experimental Psychiatry*, *24*, 321–324.

Gilbert, D. T. (1998). Ordinary personology. In D. T. Gilbert, S. T. Fiske, & G. Lindzey (Eds.), *The handbook of social psychology* (4th ed., Vol. 2, pp. 89–150). Boston, MA: McGraw-Hill.

Gildersleeve, M. (2015). Beauvoir and demystifying paradoxical characteristics of Narcissistic Personality Disorder. *Indian Journal of Psychological Medicine*, *37*, 251–253.

Gillett, G. (2001). Signification and the unconscious. *Philosophical Psychology*, *14*, 477–498.

Gilliam, C. (2017). The existential unconscious: Sartre and the dialectic of freedom. *Existential Analysis*, *28*, 351–360.

Gobet, F. (in preparation). *Intelligence: The basics*. London: Routledge.

Goddard, M. J. (2012). On certain similarities between mainstream psychology and the writings of B. F. Skinner. *Psychological Record*, *62*, 563–576.

Goffman, E. (1959). *The presentation of self in everyday life*. Garden City, NY: Doubleday.

Goffman, E. (1963). *Stigma: Notes on the management of spoiled identity*. Englewood Cliffs, NJ: Prentice-Hall.

Goldberg, L. (1981). Language and individual differences: The search for universals in personality lexicons. In L. Wheeler (Ed.), *Review of personality and social psychology* (pp. 141–165). Beverly Hills, CA: Sage.

Goldberg, L. R. (1999). A broad-bandwideth, public domain, personality inventory measuring the lower-level facets of several five-factor models. In I. Mervielde, I. Deary, F. DeFruyt, & F. Ostendorf (Eds.), *Personality psychology in Europe* (Vol. 7, pp. 7–28). Tilburg, The Netherlands: Tilburg University Press.

Goldsmith, H. H., Buss, A. H., Plomin, R., Rothbart, M. K., Thomas, A., Chess, S., Hinde, R. A., & McCall, R. B. (1987). What is temperament? Four approaches. *Child Development*, *58*, 505–529.

Goldstein, K. (1939). *The organism: A holistic approach to biology derived from pathological data in man*. New York: American Book Company.

Goldstein, K. (1940). *Human nature in the light of psychopathology*. Cambridge, MA: Harvard University Press.

Gore, P. M., & Rotter, J. B. (1963). A personality correlate of social action. *Journal of Personality*, *31*, 58–64.

Gosling, S. D., & Harley, B. A. (2009). Animal models of personality and cross-species comparisons. In P. Corr & G. Matthews (Eds.), *Cambridge handbook of personality psychology* (pp. 275–286). Cambridge, UK: Cambridge University Press.

Gray, J. A. (1970). The psychophysical basis of Introversion-Extraversion. *Behavior Research and Therapy, 8*, 249–266.

Gray, J. A. (1972). The psychophysiological nature of introversion-extraversion: A modification of Eysenck's theory. In V. D. Nebylitsyn & J. A. Gray (Eds.), *The biological bases of individual behaviour* (pp. 182–205). New York: Academic Press.

Gray, J. A. (1981). A critique of Eysenck's theory of personality. In H. J. Eysenck (Ed.), *A model for personality* (pp. 246–277). Berlin: Springer-Verlag.

Gray, J. A., & McNaughton, N. (2000). *The neuropsychology of anxiety: An enquiry into functions of the septo-hippocampal system*. Oxford: Oxford University Press.

Greenberg, S. (2007). Descartes on the passions: Function, representation, and motivation. *Nous, 41*, 714–734.

Greening, T. (1992). Existential challenges and responses. *The Humanistic Psychologist, 20*, 111–115.

Griffin, D., & Bartholomew, K. (1994). Models of the self and other: Fundamental dimensions underlying measures of adult attachment. *Journal of Personality and Social Psychology, 67*, 430–445.

Gross, C. (2010). Alfred Russell Wallace and the evolution of the human mind. *Neuroscientist, 16*, 496–507.

Grotstein, J. (2008). The overarching role of unconscious phantasy. *Psychoanalytic Inquiry, 28*, 190–205.

Grotstein, J. S. (1993). A reappraisal of W. R. D. Fairbairn. *Bulletin of the Menninger Clinic, 57*, 421–449.

Grusec, J. E. (1992). Social learning theory and developmental psychology: The legacies of Robert Sears and Albert Bandura. *Developmental Psychology, 28*, 776–786.

Guest, H. S. (2014). Maslow's hierarchy of needs – The sixth level. *The Psychologist, 27*, 982–983.

Guilford, J. P. (1975). Factors and factors of personality. *Psychological Bulletin, 82*, 802–814.

Guilford, J. P., & Guilford, R. B. (1934). An analysis of the factors in a typical test of introversion-extroversion. *Journal of Abnormal and Social Psychology, 28*, 377–399.

Guilford, J. P., & Zimmerman, W. S. (1949). *The Guilford- Zimmerman temperament survey: Manual*. Beverly Hills, CA: Sheridan Supply.

Guntrip, H. (1969). *Schizoid phenomena, object-relations, and the self*. New York: International Universities Press.

Gurtman, M. B., & Pincus, A. L. (2000). Interpersonal adjective scales: Confirmation of circumplex structure from multiple perspectives. *Personality and Social Psychology Bulletin*, *26*, 374–384.

Hall, C. S., & Lindzey, G. (1957). *Theories of personality*. New York: Wiley & Sons.

Hall, C. S., & Lindzey, G. (1970). *Theories of personality* (2nd ed.). New York: Wiley & Sons.

Hall, C. S., & Lindzey, G. (1978). *Theories of personality* (3rd ed.). New York: Wiley & Sons.

Hall, C. S., Lindzey, G., & Campbell, J. B. (1998). *Theories of personality* (4th ed.). New York: Wiley & Sons.

Hall, C. S., Lindzey, G., Loehlin, J. C., & Manosevitz, M. (1985). *An introduction to theories of personality*. New York: Wiley & Sons.

Hall, T. W. (2007). Psychoanalysis, attachment, and spirituality Part 1: The emergence of two relational traditions. *Journal of Psychology and Theology*, *35*, 14–28.

Hartman, D., & Zimberoff, D. (2004). Corrective emotional experience in the therapeutic process. *Journal of Heart-Centered Therapies*, *7*, 3–84.

Hartmann, H. (1939). *Ego psychology and the problem of adaptation*. New York: International Universities Press.

Hartmann, L. (2010). Invited commentary on "Narcissism, self-esteem, and sexual orientation". *Journal of Sex and Marital Therapy*, *36*, 35–37.

Haslam, N., Smillie, L., & Song, J. (2017). *An introduction to personality, individual differences and intelligence* (2nd ed.). London: Sage.

Hazan, C., & Diamond, L. M. (2000). The place of attachment in human mating. *Journal of General Psychology*, *4*, 186–204.

Hazan, C., & Shaver, P. R. (1987). Romantic love conceptualized as an attachment process. *Journal of Personality and Social Psychology*, *52*, 511–524.

Hazan, C., & Shaver, P. R. (1994a). Attachment as an organizational framework for research on close relationships. *Psychological Inquiry*, *5*, 1–22.

Hazan, C., & Shaver, P. R. (1994b). Deeper into attachment theory: Reply to commentaries. *Psychological Inquiry*, *5*, 68–79.

Hebb, D. O. (1960). The American revolution. *American Psychologist*, *15*, 735–745.

Heider, F. (1958). *The psychology of interpersonal relations*. New York: John Wiley & Sons, Inc.

Hekman, S. (2015). Simone de Beauvoir and the beginnings of the feminine subject. *Feminist Theory*, *16*, 137–151.

Helgeson, V. S. (2015). Gender and personality. In M. Mikulincer & P. R. Shaver (Eds..), *APA handbook of personality and social psychology* (Vol. 4:

Personality processes and individual differences, pp. 515–534). Washington, DC: American Psychological Association.

Helmreich, R. L., & Spence, J. T. (1978). The work and family orientation questionnaire: An objective instrument to assess components of achievement motivation and attitudes toward family and career. *JSAS Catalog of Selected Documents in Psychology*, 8, 35.

Helmreich, R. L., Spence, J. T., & Wilhelm, J. A. (1981). A psychometric analysis of the personal attributes questionnaire. *Sex Roles*, 7, 1097–1108.

Helms, J. E. (2007). Some better practices for measuring racial and ethnic identity constructs. *Journal of Counseling Psychology*, 54, 235–246.

Hendrick, C., Hendrick, S., Foote, F. H., & Slapion-Foote, M. J. (1984). Do men and women love differently? *Journal of Social and Personal Relationships*, 1, 177–195.

Hendrick, C., & Hendrick, S. S. (1986). A theory and method of love. *Journal of Personality and Social Psychology*, 50, 392–402.

Hendrick, C., Hendrick, S. S., & Dicke, A. (1998). The love attitudes scale: Short form. *Journal of Social and Personal Relationships*, 15, 147–159.

Hepworth, J. X., & West, S. G. (1988). Lynchings and the economy: A time-series reanalysis of Hovland and Sears (1940). *Journal of Personality and Social Psychology*, 55, 239–247.

Herskovits, M. J. (1955). *Cultural anthropology*. New York: Knopf.

Hewstone, M., Rubin, M., & Willis, H. (2002). Intergroup bias. *Annual Review of Psychology*, 53, 575–604.

Higgins, E. T. (1987). Self-discrepancy: A theory relating self and affect. *Psychological Review*, 94, 319–340.

Higgins, E. T. (1999). Persons and situations: Unique explanatory principles or variability in general principles? In D. Cervone & Y. Shoda (Eds.), *The coherence of personality: Social-cognitive bases of consistency, variability, and organization* (pp. 61–93). New York: Guilford Press.

Hilton, J. L., & von Hippel, W. (1996). Stereotypes. *Annual Review of Psychology*, 47, 237–271.

Hirsch, P. (2005). Apostle of freedom: Alfred Adler and his British disciples. *History of Education*, 34, 473–481.

Hoffman, D. (2003). Sandor Ferenczi and the origins of humanistic psychology. *Journal of Humanistic Psychology*, 43, 59–86.

Hoffman, L., Stewart, S., Warren, D. M., & Meek, L. (2015). Toward a sustainable myth of self: An existential response to the postmodern condition. In K. J. Schneider, J. F. Pierson, & J. F. T. Bugental (Eds.), *The handbook of humanistic psychology: Theory, research, and practice* (2nd ed., pp. 105–133). Los Angeles, CA: Sage.

Holmes, J. G. (2000). Social relationships: The nature and function of relational schemas. *European Journal of Social Psychology*, 30, 447–495.

Holmes, J. G. (2002). Interpersonal expectations as the building blocks of social cognition: An interdependence theory perspective. *Personal Relationships*, *9*, 1–26.

Holt, R. R. (2005). A lifelong attempt to understand and assess personality. *Journal of Personality Assessment*, *84*, 3–15.

Homans, G. C. (1961). *Social behaviour: Its elementary forms*. New York: Harcourt Brace Jovanovich.

Horney, K. (1937). *The neurotic personality of our time*. New York: Norton.

Horney, K. (1966). *Feminine psychology*. New York: Norton. (Original work published 1922–37).

Hough, L. M., Oswald, F. L., & Ock, J. (2015). Beyond the Big Five: New directions for personality research and practice in organizations. *Annual Review of Organizational Psychology and Organizational Behavior*, *2*, 183–209.

Hovland, C., & Sears, R. R. (1940). Minor studies in aggression: Correlation of lynchings with economic indices. *Journal of Psychology*, *9*, 301–310.

Howard, J. A. (2000). Social psychology of identities. *Annual Review of Sociology*, *26*, 367–393.

Howitt, D., & Owusu-Bempah, K. (1994). *The racism of psychology: Time for change*. Hemel Hempstead, UK: Harvester Wheatsheaf.

Hull, C. (1943). *Principles of behavior*. New York: Appleton-Century-Crofts.

Hull, C. L., Hovland, C. I., Ross, R. T., Hall, M., Perkins, D. T., & Fitch, F. B. (1940). *Mathematico-deductive theory of rote learning*. New Haven, CT: Yale University Press.

Hyde, J. S., & Kling, K. C. (2001). Women, motivation, and achievement. *Psychology of Women Quarterly*, *25*, 364–378.

Ickes, W. (1985). Sex-role influences on compatibility in relationships. In W. Icked (Ed.), *Compatible and incompatible relationships* (pp. 187–208). New York: Springer-Verlag.

Ickes, W., Snyder, M., & Garcia, S. (1997). Personality influences on the choice of situations. In R. Hogan, J. Johnson, & S. Briggs. (Eds.), *Handbook of personality psychology* (pp. 165–195). San Diego, CA: Academic Press.

Innis, N. K. (1992). Tolman and Tryon: Early research on the inheritance of the ability to learn. *American Psychologist*, *47*, 190–197.

Jacobsen, B. (2007). What is happiness? The concept of happiness in existential psychology and therapy. *Existential Analysis*, *18*, 39–50.

Jahoda, M. (1958). *Current concepts of positive mental health*. New York: Basic Books.

James, W. (1902). *The varieties of religious experience*. Glasgow, UK: Collins.

James, W. (2010). *The principles of psychology* (Vol.'s 1 & 2). Mansfield Center, CT: Martino Publishing. (Original work published 1890).

Jamison, D. F. (2010). Fanon revisited: Exploring the relationship between African-centered psychology and Fanonian psychology. *The Journal of Pan African Studies*, *3*, 179–193.

Jardim, L. L., Costa Pereira, M. E., & de Souza Palma, M. (2011). Fragments of the other: A psychoanalytic approach to the ego in schizophrenia. *International Forum of Psychoanalysis*, *20*, 159–166.

Joffe, P. E., & Naditch, M. P. (1977). Paper and pencil measures of coping and defense processes. In N. Haan (Ed.), *Coping and defending: Processes of self-environmental organization* (pp. 280–294). New York: Academic Press.

John, O. P., Donahue, E. M., & Kentle, R. L. (1991). *The Big Five Inventory— Versions 4a and 5a*. Berkeley, CA: University of California.

Jones, A. (2001). Absurdity and being-in-itself. The third phase of phenomenology: Jean-Paul Sartre and existential psychoanalysis. *Journal of Psychiatric and Mental Health Nursing*, *8*, 367–372.

Jones, E. E. (1998). Major developments in five decades of social psychology. In S. T. Fiske, D. T. Gilbert, & G. Lindzey (Eds.), *The handbook of social psychology* (4th ed., Vol. 1, pp. 3–57). Boston, MA: McGraw-Hill. (Original work published 1985).

Jones, H. (2015). The vision of William James. *Journal for Spiritual and Consciousness Studies*, *38*, 121–129.

Jones, J. M. (1997). *Prejudice and racism* (2nd ed.). New York: McGraw-Hill.

Jones, M. C. (1924a). A laboratory study of fear: The case of Peter. *The Pedagogical Seminary*, *31*, 308–315.

Jones, M. C. (1924b). The elimination of children's fears. *Journal of Experimental Psychology*, *7*, 382–392.

Jung, C. G. (1916). *Psychology of the unconscious: A study of the transformations and symbolisms of the libido, a contribution to the history of the evolution of thought*. London: Kegan Paul Trench Trubner. (Original work published 1912).

Jung, C. G. (1971). *Psychological types*. London: Routledge. (Original work published 1921).

Juni, S. (2009). Conceptualization of hostile psychopathy and sadism: Drive theory and object relations perspectives. *International Forum of Psychoanalysis*, *18*, 11–22.

Karasu, T. B. (2001). The advanced practice of psychotherapy. *Harvard Review of Psychiatry*, *9*, 118–123.

Karniol, R., & Ross, M. (1996). The motivational impact of temporal focus: Thinking about the future and the past. *Annual Review of Psychology*, *47*, 593–620.

Kelly, G. A. (1955). *The psychology of personal constructs* (Vol.'s 1 & 2). New York: Norton.

Kelley, H. H. (1979). *Personal relationships: Their structures and processes*. Hillsdale, NJ: Erlbaum.

Kelley, H. H., Holmes, J. G., Kerr, N. L., Reis, H. T., Rusbult, C. E., & Van Lange, P. A. M. (2003). *An atlas of interpersonal situations*. New York: Cambridge University Press.

Kelley, H. H., & Thibaut, J. W. (1978). *Interpersonal relations: A theory of interdependence*. New York: Wiley.

Kenrick, D. T., Neuberg, S. L., & White, A. E. (2013). Relationships from an evolutionary life history perspective. In J. A. Simpson & L. Campbell (Eds.), *The Oxford handbook of close relationships* (pp. 13–38). Oxford: Oxford University Press.

Kensit, D. A. (2000). Rogerian theory: A critique of the effectiveness of pure client-centred therapy. *Counselling Psychology Quarterly*, *13*, 345–351.

Kernberg, O. F. (1967). Borderline personality organization. *Journal of the American Psychoanalytical Organization*, *15*, 641–685.

Kernberg, O. F. (1970). Actors in the psychoanalytic treatment of narcissistic personalities. *Journal of the American Psychoanalytic Association*, *18*, 51–85.

Kernberg, O. F. (1975). *Borderline conditions and pathological narcissism*. New York: Aronson.

Kernberg, P. F. (1994). Mechanisms of defense: Development and research perspectives. *Bulletin of the Menninger Clinic*, *58*, 55–87.

Kierkeboen, G. (2001). Sources of Damasio's error – A reply to Damasio. *Journal of the History of the Neurosciences*, *10*, 195–196.

Kierkoboen, G. (2001). Descartes' embodied psychology: Descartes' or Damasio's error? *Journal of the History of the Neurosciences*, *10*, 173–191.

Kihlstrom, J. F. (2004). Unity within psychology, and unity between science and practice. *Journal of Clinical Psychology*, *60*, 1243–1247.

Kihlstrom, J. F., & Harackiewicz, J. M. (1990). An evolutionary milestone in the psychology of personality. *Psychological Inquiry*, *1*, 86–100.

Kim, J. O., & Mueller, C. W. (1978). *Factor analysis: Statistical methods and practical issues*. Beverly Hills, CA: Sage.

Kirsch, I., Lynn, S. J., Vigorito, M., & Miller, R. R. (2004). The role of cognition in classical and operant conditioning. *Journal of Clinical Psychology*, *60*, 369–392.

Kiser, S. (2007). Sacred dialectic: The centrality of paradox in the worldview of Rollo May. *The Humanistic Psychologist*, *35*, 191–201.

Klaif, C. H. (1985). Developments in the psychoanalytic concept of the self: A Jungian view. *Journal of Analytical Psychology*, *30*, 251–260.

Klee, G. D. (2005). The resurrection of Wilhelm Reich and orgone therapy. *The Scientific Review of Mental Health Practice: Objective Investigations of Controversial and Unorthodox Claims in Clinical Psychology, Psychiatry, and Social Work*, *4*, 6–8.

Kleiger, J. H. (1993). The enduring Rorschach contributions of David Rapaport. *Journal of Personality Assessment*, *61*, 198–205.

Klein, M. (1927). Symposium on child analysis. *International Journal of Psychoanalysis, 8*, 339–391.

Koffka, K. (1935). *Principles of Gestalt psychology*. New York: Harcourt & Brace.

Kohut, H. (1971). *The analysis of self*. New York: International Universities Press.

Kohut, H. (1977). *The restoration of the self*. New York: International Universities Press.

Koltko-Rivera, M. E. (2006). Rediscovering the later version of Maslow's hierarchy of needs: Self-transcendence and opportunities for theory, research, and unification. *Review of General Psychology, 10*, 302–317.

Koole, S. L., & Kuhl, J. (2003). In search of the real self: A functional perspective on optimal self esteem and authenticity. *Psychological Inquiry, 14*, 43–49.

Kornfeld, A. D. (1989). Mary Cover Jones and the Peter case: Social learning versus conditioning. *Journal of Anxiety Disorders, 3*, 187–195.

Kuhl, J. (2000). A functional-design approach to motivation and self-regulation: The dynamics of personality systems interactions. In M. Boekaerts, P. R. Pintrich, & M. Zeidner (Eds.), *Handbook of self-regulation* (pp. 111–169). San Diego, CA: Academic Press.

Kuhl, J., & Quirin, M. (2011). Seven steps towards freedom and two ways to lose it: Overcoming limitations of intentionality through self-confrontational coping with stress. *Social Psychology, 42*, 74–84.

Kuhl, J., Quirin, M., & Koole, S. L. (2015). Being someone: The integrated self as a neuropsychological system. *Social and Personality Psychology Compass, 9*, 115–132.

Kunce, L. J., & Shaver, P. R. (1994). An attachment-theoretical approach to caregiving in romantic relationships. In K. Bartholomew & D. Perlman (Eds.), *Attachment processes in adulthood: Advances in personal relationships* (Vol. 5, pp. 205–238). London: Jessica Kingsley.

Kurzweil, E. (1981). Jacques Lacan: French Freud. *Theory and Society, 10*, 419–438.

Kwan, V. S. Y., & Herrmann, S. D. (2015). The interplay between culture and personality. In M. Mikulincer & P. R. Shaver (Eds.), *APA handbook of personality and social psychology* (Vol. 4: Personality processes and individual differences, pp. 553–574). Washington, DC: American Psychological Association.

Lacan, J. (1977). *Ecrits: A selection*. New York: Norton. (Original work published 1966).

Laing, R. D. (1960). *The divided self: An existential study in sanity and madness*. Harmondsworth: Penguin.

Langle, A. A., & Kriz, J. (2015). The renewal of humanism in European psychotherapy: Developments and applications. In K. J. Schneider, J. F. Pierson, & J. F. T. Bugental (Eds.), *The handbook of humanistic psychology: Theory, research, and practice* (2nd ed., pp. 373–385). Los Angeles, CA: Sage.

Leary, D. E. (2004). On the conceptual and linguistic activity of psychologists: The study of behaviour from the 1890s to the 1990s and beyond. *Behavior and Philosophy*, *32*, 13–35.

Leary, T. (1957). *Interpersonal diagnosis of personality*. New York: Ronald.

Leary, M., & Tangney, J. P. (2012). The self as an organizing construct in the behavioral and social sciences. In M. Leary & J. P. Tangney (Eds.), *Handbook of self and identity* (2nd ed., pp. 1–18). New York: Guilford Press.

Lee, J. A. (1973). *Colours of love: An exploration of the ways of loving*. Toronto: New Press.

Lee, J. A. (1976). Forbidden colors of love: Patterns of gay love and gay liberation. *Journal of Homosexuality*, *1*, 401–418.

Lee, K., & Ashton, M. C. (2004). Psychometric properties of the HEXACO Personality Inventory. *Multivariate Behavioral Research*, *39*, 329–358.

Lee, K., & Ashton, M. C. (2006). Further assessment of the HEXACO personality inventory: Two new facet scales and an observer report form. *Psychological Assessment*, *18*, 182–191.

Lefcourt, H. M. (1991). Locus of control. In J. P. Robinson, P. R. Shaver, & L. S. Wrightsman (Eds.), *Measures of personality and social psychological attitudes* (pp. 413–499). San Diego, CA: Academic Press.

Lenney, E. (1991). Sex roles. In J. P. Robinson & P. R. Shaver (Eds.), *Measures of personality and social psychological attitudes* (pp. 573–660). San Diego, CA: Academic Press.

Lerwill, C. (2009). On the origins of human nature. *Psychologist*, *22*, 988–990.

LeUnes, A. (1983). Little Albert from the viewpoint of abnormal psychology textbook authors. *Teaching of Psychology*, *10*, 230–231.

Levenson, H. (1973a). Multidimensional locus of control in psychiatric patients. *Journal of Consulting and Clinical Psychology*, *41*, 397–404.

Levenson, H. (1973b). Reliability and validity of the I, P, and C scales: A multidimensional view of locus of control. In *Proceedings from the American Psychological Association Convention*. Montreal.

Levenson, H. (1974). Activism and powerful others: Distinctions within the concept of internal-external control. *Journal of Personality Assessment*, *38*, 377–383.

Levenson, H. (1981). Differentiating among internality, powerful others, and chance. In H. Lefcourt (Ed.), *Research with the locus of control construct* (Vol. 1, pp. 15–63). New York: Academic Press.

Lewin, K. (1936). *Principles of topographical psychology*. New York: McGraw-Hill.

Lilienfeld, S. O., & Andrews, B. P. (1996). Development and preliminary validation of a self-report measure of psychopathic personality traits in noncriminal population. *Journal of Personality Assessment*, *66*, 488–524.

Lorr, M., & McNair, D. M. (1963). An interpersonal behavior circle. *Journal of Abnormal and Social Psychology*, *67*, 68–75.

Lorr, M., & McNair, D. M. (1965). Expansion of the interpersonal behavior circle. *Journal of Personality and Social Psychology*, *2*, 823–830.

Lubbe, T. (2008). A Kleinian theory of sexuality. *British Journal of Psychotherapy*, *24*, 299–316.

Lucas, R. E., & Diener, E. (2015). Personality and subjective well-being: Current issues and controversies. In M. Mikulincer & P. R. Shaver (Eds.), *APA handbook of personality and social psychology* (Vol. 4, pp. 577–599). Washington, DC: American Psychological Association.

MacDonald, G., & Leary, M. R. (2012). Individual differences in self-esteem: A review and theoretical integration. In M. R. Leary & J. P. Tangney (Eds.), *Handbook of self and identity* (2nd ed., pp. 354–377). New York: Guilford Press.

MacDonald, S. G. (2001). The real and the researchable: A brief review of the contribution of John Bowlby (1907–1990). *Perspectives in Psychiatric Care*, *37*, 60–64.

Mackintosh, N. J. (1986). Tolman and modern conditioning theory. *British Journal of Psychology*, *77*, 517–523.

Magnusson, D., & Endler, N. S. (1977). *Personality at the crossroads*. Hillsdale, NJ: Erlbaum.

Maldonado-Torres, N. (2017). Frantz Fanon and the decolonial turn in psychology: From modern/colonial methods to the decolonial attitude. *South African Journal of Psychology*, *47*, 432–441.

Malone, J. C. (2014). Did John B. Watson really "found" behaviorism? *The Behavior Analyst*, *37*, 1–12.

Mandin, P. (2007). The contribution of system and object-relation theories to an understanding of the therapeutic relationship in social work practice. *Journal of Social Work Practice*, *21*, 149–162.

Mandler, G. (2002). Origins of the cognitive (r)evolution. *Journal of the History of the Behavioral Sciences*, *38*, 339–353.

Mann, C. (2000). Fromm's impact on interpersonal psychoanalysis: A well kept secret. *International Forum for Psychoanalysis*, *9*, 199–205.

Marcia, J. E. (1966). Development and validation of ego-identity status. *Journal of Personality and Social Psychology*, *3*, 551–558.

Marcia, J. E. (1967). Ego identity status: Relationship to change in self-esteem, "general maladjustment", and authoritarianism. *Journal of Personality*, *35*, 119–133.

Marcus, E. R. (1999). Modern ego psychology. *Journal of the American Psychoanalytic Association*, *47*, 843–871.

Marcus-Newhall, A., Pedersen, W. C., Carlson, M., & Miller, N. (2000). Displaced aggression is alive and well: A meta-analytic review. *Journal of Personality and Social Psychology*, *78*, 670–689.

Margolis, M. L. (1984). *Mothers and such: Views of American women and why they changed*. Berkeley, CA: University of California Press.

Markey, P. M., & Markey, C. N. (2009). A brief assessment of the interpersonal circumplex: The IPIP-IPC. *Assessment*, *16*, 352–361.

Markus, H., & Kitayama, S. (1991). Culture and the self: Implications for cognition, emotion, and motivation. *Psychological Review*, *98*, 224–253.

Markus, H., & Zajonc, R. B. (1985). The cognitive perspective in social psychology. In G. Lindzey & E. Aronson (Eds.), *Handbook of social psychology* (3rd ed., pp. 137–229). New York: Random House.

Markus, H. R. (2008). Pride, prejudice, and ambivalence: Toward a unified theory of race and ethnicity. *American Psychologist*, *63*, 651–670.

Marx, K. (1990). *The economic and philosophic manuscripts of 1844*. New York: International Publishers. (Original work published 1932).

Maslow, A. H. (1954). *Motivation and personality*. New York: Harper & Row.

Maslow, A. H. (1962). *Toward a psychology of being*. New York: Van Nostrand.

Maslow, A. H. (1968). *Toward a psychology of being* (2nd ed.). New York: Van Nostrand Reinhold.

Maslow, A. H. (1969). The farther reaches of human nature. *Journal of Transpersonal Psychology*, *1*, 1–9.

Massey, R. F. (1988). Adler's missing quadrant: Berne's solution. *Individual Psychology*, *44*, 447–452.

Matsumoto, D. (1999). Culture and self: An empirical assessment of Markus and Kitayama's theory of independent and interdependent self-construals. *Asian Journal of Social Psychology*, *2*, 289–310.

May, R. (1953). *Man's search for himself*. New York: Norton.

May, R. (1969). *Love and will*. New York: Norton.

May, R. (1991). *The cry for myth*. New York: Norton.

May, R. (1994). *The discovery of being*. New York: Norton. (Original work published 1983).

May, R. (1996). *The meaning of anxiety*. New York: Norton. (Original work published 1950).

May, R. (1999). *Freedom and destiny*. New York: Norton. (Original work published 1981).

May, R., Angel, E., & Ellenberger, H. F., Eds. (1958). *Existence*. New York: Basic Books.

McAdams, D. P. (1980). A thematic coding system for the intimacy motive. *Journal of Research in Personality*, *14*, 413–432.

McAdams, D. P. (1997). A conceptual history of personality psychology. In R. Hogan, J. Johnson, & S. R. Briggs (Eds.), *Handbook of Personality* (pp. 3–39). New York: Academic Press.

McAdams, D. P. (2010). The problem of meaning in personality psychology from the standpoints of dispositional traits, characteristic adaptations, and life stories. *Japanese Journal of Personality*, *18*, 173–186.

McAdams, D. P., Albaugh, M., Farber, E., Daniels, J., Logan, R. L., & Olson, B. (2008). Family metaphors and moral intuitions: How conservatives and liberals narrate their lives. *Journal of Personality and Social Psychology, 95,* 978–990.

McAdams, D. P., & Bryant, F. B. (1987). Intimacy motivation and subjective mental health in a nationwide sample. *Journal of Personality, 55,* 395–413.

McAdams, D. P., Diamond, A., de St. Aubin, E., & Mansfield, E. D. (1997). Stories of commitment: The psychosocial construction of generative lives. *Journal of Personality and Social Psychology, 72,* 678–694.

McAdams, D. P., & Manczak, E. (2015). Personality and the life story. In M. Mikulincer & P. R. Shaver (Eds.), *APA handbook of personality and social psychology* (Vol. 4: Personality processes and individual differences, pp. 425–446). Washington, DC: American Psychological Association.

McAdams, D. P., & Powers, J. (1981). Themes of intimacy in behavior and thought. *Journal of Personality and Social Psychology, 40,* 573–587.

McAdams, D. P., Reynolds, J., Lewis, M., Patten, A., & Bowman, P. J. (2001). When bad things turn good and good things turn bad: Sequences of redemption and contamination in life narrative, and their relation to psychosocial adaptation in midlife adults and in students. *Personality and Social Psychology Bulletin, 27,* 472–483.

McClelland, D. C. (1966). Longitudinal trends in the relation of thought to action. *Journal of Consulting Psychology, 30,* 479–483.

McClelland, D. C. (1987). *Human motivation.* New York: Cambridge University Press. (Original work published 1985).

McClelland, D. C., Atkinson, J. W., Clark, R. A., & Lowell, E. L. (1953). *The achievement motive.* New York: Appleton-Century-Crofts.

McCrae, R. (2009). The Five-Factor Model of personality traits: Consensus and controversy. In P. J. Corr & G. Matthews (Eds.), *The Cambridge handbook of personality psychology* (pp. 148–161). Cambridge: Cambridge University Press.

McCrae, R. R., & Costa, P. C., Jr. (1985). Using Norman's "adequacy taxonomy": Intelligence and personality dimensions in natural language and in questionnaires. *Journal of Personality and Social Psychology, 49,* 710–721.

McCrae, R. R., & Costa, P. T., Jr. (1986). Clinical assessment can benefit from recent advances in personality psychology. *American Psychologist, 41,* 1001–1003.

McCrae, R. R., & Costa, P. T., Jr. (1989). More reasons to adopt the Five-Factor Model. *American Psychologist, 44,* 451–452.

McCrae, R. R., & Costa, P. T., Jr. (1997). Personality trait structure as a human universal. *American Psychologist, 52,* 509–516.

McCrae, R. R., & Costa, P. T., Jr. (2008). The five factor theory of personality. In O. P. John, R. W. Robins, & L. A. Pervin (Eds.), *Handbook of personality: Theory and research* (pp. 159–181). New York: Guilford Press.

McDonald, M., & Wearing, S. (2013). A reconceptualisation of the self in humanistic psychology: Heidegger, Foucault and the sociocultural turn. *Journal of Phenomenological Psychology*, *44*, 37–59.

McLaughlin, N. (1998a). How to become a forgotten intellectual: Intellectual movements and the rise and fall of Erich Fromm. *Sociological Forum*, *13*, 215–246.

McLaughlin, N. (1999). Origin myths in the social sciences: Fromm, the Frankfurt School and the emergence of critical theory. *Canadian Journal of Sociology*, *24*, 109–139.

McLaughlin, N. G. (1998b). Why do schools of thought fail? Neo-Freudianism as a case study in the sociology of knowledge. *Journal of the History of the Behavioral Sciences*, *34*, 113–134.

McNulty, J. K. (2013). Personality and relationships. In L. Campbell & J. A. Simpson (Eds.), *Oxford handbook of close relationships* (pp. 535–552). Oxford: Oxford University Press.

McSherry, A. (2013). Jacques Lacan's theory of the subject as real, symbolic and imaginary: How can Lacanian theory be of help to mental health nursing practice? *Journal of Psychiatric and Mental Health Nursing*, *20*, 776–781.

Mead, G. H. (1967). *Mind, self and society from the standpoint of a social behaviorist*. Chicago, IL: University of Chicago Press. (Original work published 1934).

Medina, M. (2008). Everyday courage: Living courageously without being a hero. *Existential Analysis*, *19*, 280–299.

Merkur, D. (2010). *Explorations of the psychoanalytic mystics (Contemporary Psychoanalytic Studies, vol. 11)*. Tijinmuiden, The Netherlands: Rodopi Press.

Meronen, P. (1999). The return of narcissism: Heinz Kohut in the context of the history of ideas. *International Forum of Psychoanalysis*, *8*, 211–220.

Mikulincer, M., & Shaver, P. R. (2016). *Attachment in adulthood: Structure, dynamics, and change* (2nd ed.). New York: Guilford Press.

Milavec, A. (2006). How acts of discovery transform our tacit knowing powers in both scientific and religious inquiry. *Zygon*, *41*, 464–486.

Miller, N. E., & Dollard, J. (1941). *Social learning and imitation*. New Haven, CT: Yale University Press.

Miller, N. E., & Dollard, J. (1950). *Personality and psychotherapy*. New York: McGraw-Hill.

Millon, T. (1996). *Disorders of personality: DSM-IV and beyond*. New York: Wiley.

Milton, M. J. (1993). Existential thought and client centered therapy. *Counselling Psychology Quarterly*, *6*, 239–248.

Mischel, W. (1968). *Personality and assessment*. New York: Wiley.

Mischel, W. (1973). Toward a cognitive social learning reconceptualization of personality. *Psychological Review*, *80*, 252–283.

Mischel, W. (1999). Personality coherence and dispositions in a cognitive-affective personality system (CAPS) approach. In D. Cervone & Y. Shoda (Eds.), *The coherence of personality: Social-cognitive bases of consistency, variability, and organization* (pp. 37–60). New York: Guilford Press.

Mischel, W. (2004). Toward an integrative science of the person. *Annual Review of Psychology, 55,* 1–22.

Mischel, W., & Shoda, Y. (1995). A cognitive-affective system theory of personality: Reconceptualizing situations, dispositions, dynamics, and invariance in personality structure. *Psychological Review, 102,* 246–268.

Mitchell, S. A., & Harris, A. (2004). What's American about American psychoanalysis? *Psychoanalytic Dialogues, 14,* 165–191.

Molouki, S., & Pronin, E. (2015). Self and other. In M. Mikullincer & P. R. Shaver (Eds.), *APA handbook of personality and social psychology* (Vol. 1: Attitudes and social cognition, pp. 387–414). Washington, DC: American Psychological Association.

Montuori, A., & Purser, R. (2015). Humanistic psychology in the workplace. In K. J. Schneider, J. F. Pierson, & J. F. T. Bugental (Eds.), *The handbook of humanistic psychology: Theory, research, and practice* (2nd ed., pp. 723–734). Los Angeles, CA: Sage.

Moore, J. (2013). Sketch: Three views of behaviorism. *Psychological Record, 63,* 681–692.

Morf, C. C., & Mischel, W. (2012). The self as a psycho-social dynamic processing system: Toward a converging science of self-hood. In M. R. Leary & J. P. Tangney (Eds.), *Handbook of self and identity* (2nd ed., pp. 21–49). New York: Guilford Press.

Morgan, C. D., & Murray, H. A. (1935). A method for investigating fantasies. *Archives of Neurological Psychiatry, 34,* 289–306.

Moss, D. (2015). The roots and genealogy of humanistic psychology. In K. J. Schneider, J. F. Pierson, & J. F. T. Bugental (Eds.), *The handbook of humanistic psychology: Theory, research, and practice* (2nd ed., pp. 3–18). Los Angeles, CA: Sage.

Munafo, M. R. (2009). Behavioural genetics: From variance to DNA. In P. J. Corr & G. Matthews (Eds.), *The Cambridge handbook of personality psychology* (pp. 287–304). Cambridge, UK: Cambridge University Press.

Murray, H. A. (1938). *Explorations in personality.* New York: Oxford University Press.

Mussen, P., & Eichorn, D. (1988). Mary Cover Jones (1896–1987). *American Psychologist, 43,* 818.

Myers, D. G., & Diener, E. (1995). Who is happy? *Psychological Science, 6,* 10–19.

Myers, D. G., & Diener, E. (2018). The scientific pursuit of happiness. *Perspectives on Psychological Science, 13,* 218–225.

Myers, I. B. (1962). *The Myers-Briggs type indicator: Manual*. Palo Alto, CA: Consulting Psychologists Press.

Neary, R. S., & Zuckerman, M. (1976). Sensation seeking, trait and state anxiety, and the electrodermal orienting reflex. *Psychophysiology*, *13*, 205–211.

Noppeney, U. (2001). Kurt Goldstein – A philosophical scientist. *Journal of the History of the Neurosciences*, *10*, 67–78.

Nunnally, J. C., & Bernstein, I. H. (1994). *Psychometric theory* (3rd ed.). New York: McGraw-Hill.

Nussbaum, M. (2006). Winnicott on the surprises of the self. *Massachusetts Review*, *47*, 375–393.

O'Connell, A. N. (1980). Karen Horney: Theorist in psychoanalysis and feminine psychology. *Psychology of Women Quarterly*, *5*, 81–93.

O'Dell, J. W. (1978). *Letters from Jenny* revisited: The computer content analysis redone. *Journal of Clinical Psychology*, *34*, 161–164.

Omar, S. M. (2009). Fanon in Algeria: A case of horizontal (post)-colonial encounter? *Journal of Transatlantic Studies*, *7*, 264–278.

Ozer, D. J., & Reise, S. P. (1994). Personality assessment. *Annual Review of Psychology*, *45*, 357–388.

Parker, S., & Davis, E. (2009). The false self in Christian contexts: A Winnicottian perspective. *Journal of Psychology and Christianity*, *28*, 315–225.

Paulhus, D. L., & Williams, K. M. (2002). The Dark Triad of personality: Narcissism, Machiavellianism, and psychopathy. *Journal of Research in Personality*, *36*, 556–563.

Paunonen, S. V., & Hong, R. Y. (2015). On the properties of personality traits. In M. Mikulincer & P. R. Shaver (Eds.), *APA handbook of personality and social psychology* (Vol. 4: Personality processes and individual differences, pp. 233–259). Washington, DC: American Psychological Association.

Pavlov, I. P. (1927). *Conditioned reflexes: An investigation of the physiological activity of the cerebral cortex*. London: Routledge and Kegan Paul.

Pavlov, I. P. (1928). *Lectures on conditioned reflexes: Twenty-five years of objective study of the higher nervous system*. New York: International Publishers. (Original work published 1926).

Pearce, R. (2011). On being a person: Sartre's contribution to psychotherapy. *Existential Analysis*, *22*, 83–95.

Pedersen, W. D., Putcha-Bhagavatula, A., & Miller, L. C. (2011). Are men and women really that different? Some of sexual strategy theory's (SST) key assumptions about sex-distinct mating mechanisms. *Sex Roles*, *64*, 629–643.

Peluso, P. R., Peluso, J., White, J., P., & Kern, R. M. (2004). A comparison of attachment theory and individual psychology: A review of the literature. *Journal of Counseling & Development*, *82*, 139–145.

Peng, J. H. (2011). Appreciation of Rollo May: A search for existential sensibilities. *Journal of Humanistic Psychology*, *51*, 516–522.

Peterson, C., & Seligman, M. E. P. (2004). *Character strengths and virtues: A handbook and classification*. Oxford: Oxford University Press.

Petty, R. E., & Brinol, P. (2015). Processes of social influence through attitude change. In M. Mikullincer & P. R. Shaver (Eds.), *APA handbook of personality and social psychology* (Vol. 1: Attitudes and social cognition, pp. 509–545). Washington, DC: American Psychological Association.

Phinney, J. S. (1990). Ethnic identity in adolescents and adults: A review of research. *Psychological Bulletin*, *108*, 499–514.

Phinney, J. S. (1992). The multigroup ethnic identity measure: A new scale for use with adolescents and you adults from diverse groups. *Journal of Adolescent Research*, *7*, 156–176.

Phinney, J. S., & Ong, A. D. (2007). Conceptualization and measurement of ethnic identity: Current status and future directions. *Journal of Counseling Psychology*, *54*, 271–281.

Pickering, A. D., Cooper, A. J., Smillie, L. D., & Corr, P. J. (2013). On the shoulders of giants. *The Psychologist*, *26*(1), 22–25.

Pietikainen, P. (2002). Utopianism in psychology: The case of Wilhelm Reich. *Journal of the History of the Behavioral Sciences*, *38*, 157–175.

Piper, W. E., Debbane, E. G., Bienvenu, J. P., & Garant, J. (1984). A comparative study of four forms of psychotherapy. *Journal of Consulting and Clinical Psychology*, *52*, 268–279.

Pitchford, D. B. (2009). The existentialism of Rollo May: An influence on trauma treatment. *Journal of Humanistic Psychology*, *49*, 441–461.

Polkinghorne, D. E. (2015). The self and humanistic psychology. In K. J. Schneider, J. F. Pierson, & J. F. T. Bugental (Eds.), *The handbook of humanistic psychology: Theory, research, and practice* (2nd ed., pp. 87–104). Los Angeles, CA: Sage.

Poll, J. B., & Smith, T. B. (2003). The spiritual self: Toward a conceptualization of spiritual identity development. *Journal of Psychology and Theology*, *31*, 129–142.

Popkewitz, T. S. (2011). Curriculum history, schooling and the history of the present. *History of Education*, *40*, 1–19.

Prado de Oliviera, L. E. (2001). The nature of the transference between Anna Freud and Melanie Klein: Learning from the controversies. *International Forum of Psychoanalysis*, *10*, 247–258.

Prager, J.-A. (2011). Darwin and his disciples. *History Review*, *71*, 32–36.

Puhakka, K. (2000). Beyond reflection: Loss and transformation of self. *The Humanistic Psychologist*, *28*, 334–342.

Quinodoz, J.-M. (2010). How translations of Freud's writings have influenced French psychoanalytic thinking. *International Journal of Psychoanalysis*, *91*, 695–716.

Quzilbash, M. (1998). Aristotle and Sartre on the human condition: Lack, responsibility and the desire to be God. *Angelaki: Journal of the Theological Humanities*, *3*, 29–37.

Rapaport, D. (1960). *The structure of psychoanalytic theory: A systematic attempt.* New York: International Universities Press.

Rapaport, D., Gill, M., & Schafer, R. (1945). *Diagnostic psychological testing* (Vol. 1). Chicago, IL: The Year Book Publishers.

Raskin, R., & Hall, C. S. (1979). A narcissistic personality inventory. *Psychological Reports*, *45*, 590.

Raskin, R., & Terry, H. (1988). A principal-components analysis of the Narcissistic Personality Inventory and further evidence of its construct validity. *Journal of Personality and Social Psychology*, *54*, 890–902.

Redfearn, J. W. T. (1983). Ego and self: Terminology. *Journal of Analytical Psychology*, *28*, 91–106.

Reed, E. S., & Gaines, S. O., Jr. (1997). Not everyone is "different-from-me": Toward an historico-cultural account of prejudice. *Journal of Black Psychology*, *23*, 245–274.

Reich, W. (1980). *Character analysis.* New York: Farrar, Straus and Giroux. (Original work published 1933).

Reis, H. T. (2007). Steps toward the ripening of relationship science. *Personal Relationships*, *14*, 1–23.

Reis, H. T., Capobianco, A., & Tsai, F.-F. (2002). Finding the person in personal relationships. *Journal of Personality*, *70*, 813–850.

Reis, H. T., Sheldon, K. M., Gable, S. L., Roscoe, R., & Ryan. R. (2000). Daily well-being: The role of autonomy, competence, and relatedness. *Personality and Social Psychology Bulletin*, *26*, 419–435.

Rendon, M. (2008). The vicissitudes of affect in Horney's theory. *International Review of Psychoanalysis*, *17*, 158–168.

Rhodewalt, F. (2012). Contemporary perspectives on narcissism and the narcissistic personality type. In M. R. Leary & J. P. Tangney (Eds.), *Handbook of self and identity* (2nd ed., pp. 571–586). New York: Guilford Press.

Richards, G. (1991). James and Freud: Two masters of metaphor. *British Journal of Psychology*, *82*, 205–215.

Ridgeway, D., & Hare, R. D. (1981). Sensation seeking and psychophysiological responses to auditory stimulation. *Psychophysiology*, *18*, 613–618.

Riegel, K. F. (1972). Influence of economic and political ideologies on the development of developmental psychology. *Psychological Bulletin*, *78*, 129–141.

Rilling, M. (2000). John Watson's paradoxical struggle to explain Freud. *American Psychologist*, *55*, 301–312.

Roberts, R., Phinney, J., Masse, L., Chen, Y., Roberts, C., & Romero, A. (1999). The structure of ethnic identity in young adolescents from diverse ethnocultural groups. *Journal of Early Adolescence*, *19*, 301–322.

Robins, R. W., & John, O. P. (1997). The quest for self-insight: Theory and research on accuracy and bias in self-perception. In R. Hogan, J. A. Johnson, & S. R. Briggs (Eds.), *Handbook of personality psychology* (pp. 649–679). New York: Academic Press.

Robinson, M. D., & Wilkowski, B. M. (2015). Personality processes and processes as personality: A cognitive perspective. In M. Mikulincer & P. R. Shaver (Eds.), *APA handbook of personality and social psychology* (Vol. 4, pp. 129–145). Washington, DC: American Psychological Association.

Robinson, T. N., Jr., & Zahn, T. P. (1983). Sensation seeking, state anxiety and cardiac and EDR orienting reactions. *Psychophysiology, 20*, 465.

Rocha, G. M. (2012). The unconscious: Ideal worker? *International Forum of Psychoanalysis, 21*, 17–21.

Rogers, C. R. (1951). *Client-centered therapy: Its current practice, implications and theory.* London: Constable.

Rogers, C. R. (1959). A Theory of therapy, personality, and interpersonal relationships as developed in the client-centered framework. In S. Koch (Ed.), *Psychology: A study of a science* (Vol. 3, pp. 184–256). New York: McGraw-Hill.

Rogers, C. R. (1961). *On becoming a person: A therapist's view of psychotherapy.* London: Constable.

Rorschach, H. (1924). *Manual for Rorschach Ink-Blot test.* Chicago, IL: Stoelting.

Rosenberg, M. (1965). *Society and the adolescent self-image.* Princeton, NJ: Princeton University Press.

Rosenberg, M. (1989). *Society and the adolescent self-image* (rev. ed.). Princeton, NJ: Princeton University Press.

Ross, L., Lepper, M., & Ward, A. (2010). History of social psychology: Insights, challenges, and contributions to theory and applications. In S. T. Fiske, D. T. Gilbert, & G. Lindzey (Eds.), *Handbook of social psychology* (5th ed., Vol. 1, pp. 3–50). Hoboken, NJ: John Wiley & Sons, Inc.

Rotter, J. B. (1954). *Social learning and clinical psychology.* Englewood Cliffs, NJ: Prentice-Hall.

Rotter, J. B. (1966). Generalized expectancies for internal versus external control of reinforcement. *Psychological Monographs, 80* (1, Whole No. 609), 1–28.

Rotter, J. B. (1967). A new scale for the measurement of interpersonal trust. *Journal of Personality, 35*, 651–665.

Rotter, J. B. (1975). Some problems and misconceptions related to the construct of internal versus external control of reinforcement. *Journal of Consulting and Clinical Psychology, 48*, 56–67.

Rowan, J. (2000). The self, the field and the either-or. *International Journal of Psychotherapy, 5*, 219–226.

Rowe, D. C. (1997). Genetics, temperament, and personality. In R. Hogan, J. Johnson, & S. Briggs (Eds.), *Handbook of personality psychology* (pp. 367–386). San Diego, CA: Academic Press.

Rubinstein, G. (2010a). Narcissism and self-esteem among homosexual and heterosexual male students. *Journal of Sex & Marital Therapy*, *36*, 24–34.

Rubinstein, G. (2010b). Response to Hartmann. *Journal of Sex and Marital Therapy*, *36*, 48.

Rusbridger, R. (2012). Affects in Melanie Klein. *International Journal of Psychoanalysis*, *93*, 139–150.

Rusbult, C. E., & Van Lange, P. A. M. (2003). Interdependence, interaction, and relationships. *Annual Review of Psychology*, *54*, 351–375.

Rusbult, C., Verette, J., Whitney, G., Slovik, L., & Lipkus, I. (1991). Accommodation processes in close relationships: Theory and preliminary evidence. *Journal of Personality and Social Psychology*, *60*, 53–78.

Rutter, M., & Silberg, J. (2002). Gene-environment interplay in relation to emotional and behavioral disturbance. *Annual Review of Psychology*, *53*, 463–490.

Ryan, R. M., & Deci, E. L. (2000a). Self-determination theory and the facilitation of intrinsic motivation, social development, and well-being. *American Psychologist*, *55*, 68–78.

Ryan, R. M., & Deci, E. L. (2000b). The darker and brighter sides of human existence: Basic psychological needs as a unifying concept. *Psychological Inquiry*, *11*, 319–338.

Ryan, R. M., & Deci, E. L. (2001). On happiness and human potentials: A review of research on hedonic and eudaimonic well-being. *Annual Review of Psychology*, *52*, 141–166.

Ryan, R. M., & Frederick, C. (1997). On energy, personality, and health: Subjective vitality as a dynamic reflection of well-being. *Journal of Personality*, *65*, 529–565.

Ryff, C. D. (1989). Happiness is everything, or is it? Explorations on the meaning of psychological well-being. *Journal of Personality and Social Psychology*, *57*, 1069–1081.

Ryff, C. D. (1995). Psychological well-being in adult life. *Current Directions in Psychological Science*, *4*, 99–104.

Ryff, C. D., & Keyes, C. L. M. (1995). The structure of psychological well-being revisited. *Journal of Personality and Social Psychology*, *69*, 719–727.

Ryff, C. D., & Singer, B. (1998a). Human health: New directions for the next millennium. *Psychological Inquiry*, *9*, 69–85.

Ryff, C. D., & Singer, B. (2008). Know thyself and become what you are: A eudaimonic approach to psychological well-being. *Journal of Happiness Studies*, *9*, 13–39.

Ryff, C. D., & Singer, B. (1998b). The contours of positive mental health. *Psychological Inquiry*, *9*, 1–28.

Salzinger, K. (2008). Skinner's *verbal behavior*. *International Journal of Psychology and Psychological Therapy*, *8*, 287–294.

Sappington, A. A. (1989). The third force and the psychology of effective functioning. *The Humanistic Psychologist*, *17*, 56–63.

Sartre, J.-P. (1956). *Being and nothingness: An essay on phenomenological ontology*. New York: Routledge. (Original work published 1943).

Sartre, J.-P. (1996). *Existential psychoanalysis*. Washington, DC: Gateway Editions. (Original work published 1953).

Saville, P., & Blinkhorn, S. (1981). Reliability, homogeneity and the construct validity of Cattell's 16 Personality Factor Questionnaire (16PF). *Personality and Individual Differences*, *2*, 325–333.

Schafer, R. (1999). Recentering psychoanalysis: From Heinz Hartmann to the contemporary British Kleinians. *Psychoanalytic Psychology*, *16*, 339–354.

Schellenberg, J. A. (1978). *Masters of social psychology*. Oxford: Oxford University Press.

Schipke, T. (2017). Narcissism, ego, and self: Kohut – A key figure in transpersonal psychology. *Journal of Transpersonal Psychology*, *49*, 3–21.

Schneider, K. J. (2011a). Humanistic psychology's chief task: To reset psychology on its rightful existential–Humanistic base. *Journal of Humanistic Psychology*, *51*, 436–438.

Schneider, K. J. (2011b). Toward a humanistic positive psychology: Why can't we just get along? *Existential Analysis*, *22*, 32–38.

Schneider, K. J. (2015). Rediscovering awe: A new front in humanistic psychology, psychotherapy, and society. In K. J. Schneider, J. F. Pierson, & J. F. T. Bugental (Eds.), *The handbook of humanistic psychology: Theory, research, and practice* (2nd ed., pp. 73–81). Los Angeles, CA: Sage.

Schuerger, J. M., Zarella, K. L., & Hotz, A. S. (1989). Factors that influence the temporal stability of personality by questionnaire. *Journal of Personality and Social Psychology*, *56*, 777–783.

Schunk, D. H. (1991). Self-efficacy and academic motivation. *Educational Psychologist*, *26*, 207–231.

Seligman, M., & Csikszentmihalyi, M. (2000). Positive psychology: An introduction. *American Psychologist*, *55*, 5–14.

Sellers, R. M., Rowley, S. A. J., Chavois, T. M., Shelton, J. N., & Smith, M. A. (1997). Multidimensional inventory of black identity: A preliminary investigation of reliability and construct validity. *Journal of Personality and Social Psychology*, *73*, 805–815.

Sellers, R. M., Smith, M. A., Shelton, J. N., Rowley, S. A. J., & Chavous, T. M. (1998). Multidimensional model of racial identity: A reconceptualization of African American racial identity. *Personality & Social Psychology Review*, *2*, 18–39.

Shadel, W. G., Cervone, D., Niaura, R., & Abrams, D. B. (2004). Developing an integrative social-cognitive strategy for personality assessment at the level of the individual: An illustration with regular cigarette smokers. *Journal of Research in Personality*, *38*, 394–419.

Shahar, G. (2011). Projectuality versus eventuality: Sullivan, the (ambivalent) intentionalist. *Journal of Psychotherapy Integration*, *21*, 211–220.

Shapiro, D. (2002). Theoretical reflections on Wilhelm Reich's *Character Analysis*. *American Journal of Psychotherapy*, *56*, 338–346.

Sheehy, N. (2004). *Fifty key thinkers in psychology*. London: Routledge.

Sheldon, K. M., & Schuler, J. (2015). Agency and its discontents: A two-process perspective on basic psychological needs and motives. In M. Mikulincer & P. R. Shaver (Eds.), *APA handbook of personality and social psychology* (Vol. 4: Personality processes and individual differences, pp. 167–187). Washington, DC: American Psychological Association.

Sherby, L. B. (2007). Rediscovering Fairbairn. *Contemporary Psychoanalysis*, *43*, 185–203.

Shiner, R. L. (2015). The development of temperament and personality traits in childhood and adolescence. In M. Mikulincer & P. R. Shaver (Eds.), *APA handbook of personality and social psychology* (Vol. 4: Personality processes and individual differences, pp. 85–105). Washington, DC: American Psychological Association.

Shiner, R. L., Buss, K. A., McClowry, S. G., Putnam, S. P., Saudino, K. J., & Zentner, M. (2012). What is temperament now? Assessing progress in temperament research on the twenty-fifth anniversary of Goldsmith et al. (1987). *Child Development Perspectives*, *6*, 436–444.

Shostrom, E. (1964). An inventory for the measurement of self-actualization. *Educational and Psychological Measurement*, *24*, 207–218.

Shostrom, E. L. (1975). *Personal orientation dimensions*. San Diego, CA: EdITS/ Educational and Industrial Testing Service.

Shulman, G. (2010). The damaged object: A "strange attractor" in the dynamical system of the mind. *Journal of Child Psychotherapy*, *36*, 259–288.

Sidanius, J., & Pratto, F. (1999). *Social dominance: An intergroup theory of social hierarchy and oppression*. New York: Cambridge University Press.

Silvia, P. J., & Eddington, K. M. (2012). Self and emotion. In M. R. Leary & J. P. Tangney (Eds.), *Handbook of self and identity* (2nd ed., pp. 425–445). New York: Guilford Press.

Simpson, J. A., & Campbell, L. (2013). The waving of the relationship flag. In J. A. Simpson & L. Campbell (Eds.), *The Oxford handbook of close relationships* (pp. 825–827). New York: Oxford University Press.

Skinner, B. F. (1938). *The behaviour of organisms: An experimental analysis*. London: D. Appleton Century Company.

Skinner, B. F. (1950). Are theories of learning necessary? *Psychological Review*, *57*, 193–216.

Skinner, B. F. (1953). *Science and human behavior*. New York: Simon and Schuster.

Skinner, B. F. (1957). *Verbal behavior*. New York: Appleton-Century-Crofts.

Skinner, B. F. (1974). *About behaviorism*. New York: Knopf.

Sleeth, D. B. (2006). The self and the integral interface: Toward a new understanding of the whole person. *The Humanistic Psychologist, 34*, 243–261.

Slife, B. D., & Barnard, S. (1988). Existential and cognitive psychology: Contrasting views of consciousness. *Journal of Humanistic Psychology, 28*, 119–136.

Slochower, J. (2011). Analytic idealizations and the disavowed: Winnicott, his patients, and us. *Psychoanalytic Dialogues, 21*, 3–21.

Smiler, A. P. (2011). Sexual strategies theory: Built for the short term or the long term? *Sex Roles, 64*, 603–612.

Smith, C. U. M. (2010). Darwin's unsolved problem: The place of consciousness in an evolutionary world. *Journal of the History of the Neurosciences, 19*, 105–120.

Smith, G. M. (1967). Usefulness of peer ratings of personality in education research. *Educational and Psychological Measurement, 27*, 967–984.

Smith, G. T., & Guller, L. (2015). Psychological underpinnings to impulsive behavior. In M. Mikulincer & P. R. Shaver (Eds.), *APA handbook of personality and social psychology* (Vol. 4: Personality processes and individual differences, pp. 329–350). Washington, DC: American Psychological Association.

Snyder, M., & Cantor, M. (1998). Understanding personality and social behavior: A functionalist strategy. In D. T. Gilbert, S. T. Fiske, & G. Lindzey (Eds.), *The handbook of social psychology* (4th ed., Vol. 1, pp. 635–679). Boston, MA: McGraw-Hill.

Snyder, M., & Ickes, W. (1985). Personality and social behavior. In G. Lindzey & E. Aronson (Eds.), *Handbook of social psychology* (3rd ed., Vol. 2, pp. 883–947). New York: Random House.

Son, A. (2006). Relationality in Kohut's psychology of the self. *Pastoral Psychology, 55*, 81–92.

Soto, C. J., & John, O. P. (2014). Traits in transition: The structure of parent-reported personality traits from early childhood to early adulthood. *Journal of Personality, 82*, 182–199.

South, S. C., Reichborn-Kjennerud, T., Eaton, N. R., & Krueger, R. F. (2015). Genetics of personality. In M. Mikulincer & P. R. Shaver (Eds.), *APA handbook of personality and social psychology* (Vol. 4: Personality processes and individual differences, pp. 31–60). Washington, DC: American Psychological Association.

Spence, J. T. (1985). Gender identity and its implications for the concepts of masculinity and femininity. In T. B. Sonderegger (Ed.), *Nebraska symposium on motivation, 1984* (pp. 59–95). Lincoln, NE: University of Nebraska Press.

Spence, J. T. (1993). Gender-related traits and gender ideology: Evidence for a multifactorial theory. *Journal of Personality and Social Psychology*, *64*, 624–635.

Spence, J. T., Deaux, K., & Helmreich, R. L. (1985). Sex roles in contemporary American society. In G. Lindzey & E. Aronson (Eds.), *Handbook of social psychology* (Vol. 2, pp. 149–178). New York: Random House.

Spence, J. T., Helmreich, R., & Stapp, J. (1973). A short version of the Attitudes toward Women Scale (AWS). *Bulletin of the Psychonomic Society*, *2*, 219–220.

Spence, J. T., Helmreich, R., & Stapp, J. (1974). The personal attributes questionnaire: A measure of sex role stereotypes and masculinity-femininity. *JSAS Catalog of Selected Documents in Psychology*, *4*, 43–44.

Spence, J. T., & Helmreich, R. L. (1978). *Masculinity and femininity*. Austin: University of Texas Press.

Spence, J. T., Helmreich, R. L., & Holahan, C. K. (1979). Negative and positive components of psychological masculinity and femininity, and their relationship to self-reports of neuroticism and acting out behavior. *Journal of Personality and Social Psychology*, *37*, 1673–1682.

Spence, J. T., Helmreich, R. L., & Sawin, L. L. (1980). The Male-Female Relations Questionnaire: A self-report inventory of sex role behaviors and preferences and its relationships to masculine and feminine personality traits, sex role attitudes, and other measures. *JSAS Catalog of Selected Documents in Psychology*, *10*, 87.

Spence, K. W. (1956). *Behavior theory and conditioning*. New Haven, CT: Yale University Press.

Sperry, M. (2003). Putting our heads together: Mentalizing systems. *Psychoanalytic Dialogues*, *23*, 683–699.

Spillius, E. B. (2009). On becoming a British psychoanalyst. *Psychoanalytic Inquiry*, *29*, 204–222.

Stagner, R. (1937). *Psychology of personality*. New York: McGraw-Hill.

Stagner, R. (1948). *Psychology of personality* (2nd ed.). New York: McGraw-Hill.

Stagner, R. (1961). *Psychology of personality* (3rd ed.). New York: McGraw-Hill.

Stagner, R. (1974). *Psychology of personality* (4th ed.). New York: McGraw-Hill.

Steele, H., & Steele, M. (1998). Attachment and psychoanalysis: Time for a reunion. *Social Development*, *7*, 92–119.

Steinberg, N. (2010). Hidden gifts of love: A clinical application of object relations theory. *International Journal of Psychoanalysis*, *91*, 839–858.

Stephenson, M. (2012). Finding Fairbairn – Discovery and exploration of the work of Ronald Fairbairn. *Psychodynamic Practice*, *18*, 465–470.

Stevens, R. (2008). *Sigmund Freud: Examining the essence of his contribution*. London: Palgrave.

Stewart, H. (2003). Winnicott, Balint, and the independent tradition. *American Journal of Psychoanalysis*, *63*, 207–217.

Still, A. (1986). E. C. Tolman: A centenary symposium. *British Journal of Psychology*, *77*, 513–515.

Strickland, B. R. (1989). Internal-external control expectancies: From contingency to creativity. *American Psychologist*, *44*, 1–12.

Strohl, J. E. (1998), Transpersonalism: Ego meets soul. *Journal of Counseling & Development*, *76*, 397–403.

Stryker, S., & Statham, A. (1985). Symbolic interaction and role theory. In G. Lindzey & E. Aronson (Eds.), *Handbook of social psychology* (3rd ed., Vol. 1, pp. 311–378). New York: Random House.

Sugarman, A., & Kanner, K. (2000). The contribution of psychoanalytic theory to psychological thinking. *Psychoanalytic Psychology*, *17*, 3–23.

Sullivan, H. S. (1953). *The interpersonal theory of psychiatry*. New York: Norton.

Sullivan, H. S. (1954). *The psychiatric interview*. New York: Norton.

Sullivan, H. S. (1966). *Conceptions of modern psychiatry*. New York: Norton. (Original work published 1947).

Sullivan, J. L., & Transue, J. E. (1999). The psychological underpinnings of democracy: A selective review of research on political tolerance, interpersonal trust, and social capital. *Annual Review of Psychology*, *50*, 625–650.

Sussal, C. M. (1992). Object relations family therapy as a model for practice. *Clinical Social Work Journal*, *20*, 313–321.

Swann, W. B., Jr. (1983). Self-verification: Bringing social reality into harmony with the self. In J. Suls & A. G. Greenwald (Eds.), *Psychological perspectives on the self* (Vol. 2, pp. 33–66). Hillsdale, NJ: Erlbaum.

Swann, W. B., Jr., & Bosson, J. K. (2010). Self and identity. In S. T. Fiske, D. T. Gilbert, & G. Lindzey (Eds.), *Handbook of social psychology* (5th ed., Vol. 1, pp. 589–628). Hoboken, NJ: John Wiley & Sons, Inc.

Sweeney, J. A., Clarkin, J. F., & Fitzgibbon, M. L. (1987). Current practice of psychological assessment. *Professional Psychology: Research and Practice*, *18*, 377–380.

Tabachnick, B. G., & Fidell, L. S. (2007). *Using multivariate statistics* (5th ed.). Boston, MA: Allyn and Bacon.

Tajfel, H. (1981). *Human groups and social categories*. Cambridge, MA: Cambridge University Press.

Tajfel, H., & Turner, J. C. (1979). An integrative theory of intergroup conflict. In W. G. Austin & S. Worchel (Eds.), *The social psychology of intergroup relations* (pp. 33–37). Monterey, CA: Brooks/Cole.

Tajfel, H., & Turner, J. C. (1986). The social identity theory of intergroup behavior. In S. Worchel & W. G. Austin (Eds.), *Psychology of intergroup relations* (pp. 7–24). Chicago, IL: Nelson-Hall.

Tantam, D. (2015). The contribution of female existential philosophers to psychotherapy. *Existential Analysis*, *26*, 36–48.

Taormina, R. J., & Gao, J. H. (2013). Maslow and the motivation hierarchy measuring satisfaction of the needs. *The American Journal of Psychology, 126,* 155–177.

Tate, C. C. (2013). Addressing conceptual confusions about evolutionary theorizing: How and why evolutionary psychology and feminism do not oppose each other. *Sex Roles, 69,* 491–502.

Tauvon, L. (2001). A comparison of psychoanalytic and psychodramatic theory from a psychodramatist's perspective. *Counselling Psychology Quarterly, 14,* 331–355.

Taylor, E. (1991). William James and the humanistic tradition. *Journal of Humanistic Psychology, 31,* 56–74.

Taylor, E. (1999). William James and Sigmund Freud: "The future of psychology belongs to your work." *Psychological Science, 10,* 465–469.

Taylor, E. (2000). "What is man, psychologist, that thou art so unmindful of him?" Henry A. Murray on the historical relation between classical personality theory and humanistic psychology. *Journal of Humanistic Psychology, 40,* 29–42.

Taylor, E. (2010). William James and the humanistic implications of the neuroscience revolution: An outrageous hypothesis. *Journal of Humanistic Psychology, 50,* 410–429.

Tellegen, A. (1982). *Multidimensional personality questionnaire.* Minneapolis, MN: University of Minnesota Press.

Terman, L. M., & Miles, C. C. (1936). *Sex and personality: Studies in masculinity and femininity.* New York: McGraw-Hill.

Thibaut, J. W., & Kelley, H. H. (1959). *The social psychology of groups.* New York: Wiley.

Thompson, C. M. (1953). Towards a psychology of women. *Pastoral Psychology, 4,* 29–38.

Thomson, J. A. K. (1955). *The ethics of Aristotle: The Nicomachean ethics.* Harmondsworth: Penguin.

Thorndike, E. L. (1905). *The elements of psychology.* New York: A. G. Seiler.

Thorndike, E. L. (1911). *Animal intelligence: Experimental studies.* New York: Macmillan.

Thorndike, E. L. (1917). *Thorndike arithmetics* (Books, 1, 2, & 3). Chicago, IL: Rand McNally.

Tiedemann, J. (1989). Measures of cognitive styles: A critical review. *Educational Psychologist, 24,* 261–275.

Titchener, E. B. (1902). *Experimental psychology: A manual of laboratory practice.* New York: MacMillan & Co.

Todes, D. P. (1997). Pavlov's physiological factory. *Isis, 88,* 205–246.

Tolman, E. C. (1924). The inheritance of maze-learning ability in rats. *Journal of Comparative Psychology, 4,* 1–18.

Tolman, E. C. (1932). *Purposive behavior in animals and men*. New York: Century.

Tolman, E. C. (1938). The determinants of behavior at a choice point. *Psychological Review*, *45*, 1–41.

Tolman, E. C. (1948). Cognitive maps in rats and men. *Psychological Review*, *55*, 189–208.

Tonkin, M., & Fine, H. J. (1985). Narcissism and borderline states: Kernberg, Kohut, and psychotherapy. *Psychoanalytic Psychology*, *2*, 221–239.

Tosi, D. J., & Lindamood, C. A. (1975). The measurement of self-actualization: A critical review of the Personal Orientation Inventory. *Journal of Personality Assessment*, *39*, 215–224.

Trapnell, P. D., & Paulhus, D. L. (2012). Agentic and communal values: Their scope and measurement. *Journal of Personality Assessment*, *94*, 39–52.

Trivers, R. L. (1972). Parental investment and sexual selection. In B. Campbell (Ed.), *Sexual selection and the descent of man 1871-1971* (pp. 136–179). Chicago, IL: Aldine.

Tudor, K. (2010). Person-centered relational therapy: An organismic perspective. *Person-Centered & Experiential Psychotherapies*, *9*, 52–68.

Tupes, E. C., & Christal, R. E. (1961). Recurrent personality factors based on trait ratings. *USAF ASD Technical Report*, 61–97.

Umana-Taylor, A. J. (2012). Ethnic identity. In S. J. Schwartz, K. Luyckx, & V. L. Vignoles (Eds.), *Handbook of identity theory and research* (pp. 755–774). New York: Springer-Verlag.

Umana-Taylor, A. J., Yazedijan, A., & Bamaca-Gomez, M. (2004). Developing the ethnic identity scale: Using Eriksonian and social identity perspectives. *Identity: an International Journal of Theory and Research*, *4*, 9–38.

Unger, R. K. (1979). Toward a redefinition of sex and gender. *American Psychologist*, *34*, 1085–1094.

Van Dijken, S., van der Veer, R., van Ijzendoorn, M., & Kuipers, H.-J. (1998). Bowlby before Bowlby: The sources of an intellectual departure in psychoanalysis and psychology. *Journal of the History of the Behavioral Sciences*, *34*, 247–269.

Van Lange, P. A. M., & Balliet, D. (2015). Interdependence theory. In M. Mikulincer & P. R. Shaver (Eds.), *APA handbook of personality and social psychology* (Vol. 3: Interpersonal relations, pp. 65–92). Washington, DC: American Psychological Association.

Verkuyten, M. (2005). *The social psychology of ethnic identity*. Hove, UK: Psychology Press.

Vernon, P. E., & Allport, G. W. (1931). A test for personal values. *Journal of Abnormal and Social Psychology*, *26*, 231–248.

von Hilsheimer, G., & Quirk, D. A. (2006). Origin of EEG biofeedback for remediating misbehavior. *The Behavior Analyst Today*, *7*, 492–507.

Wade, N. J., Sakurai, K., & Gyoba, J. (2007). Wither Wundt? *Perception, 36,* 163–166.

Wahlsten, D. (1999). Single-gene influences on brain and behavior. *Annual Review of Psychology, 50,* 599–624.

Walker, E., Kestler, L., Bollini, A., & Hochman, K. M. (2004). Schizophrenia: Etiology and course. *Annual Review of Psychology, 55,* 401–430.

Walkey, F. H. (1979). Internal control, powerful others, and chance: A confirmation of Levenson's factor structure. *Journal of Personality Assessment, 43,* 532–535.

Wallace, A. R. (1869). *The Malay Archipelago.* London: Macmillan.

Wallerstein, R. S. (2002). The growth and transformation of American ego psychology. *Journal of the American Psychoanalytic Association, 50,* 135–169.

Walsh, R., Teo, T., & Baydala, A. (2014). *A critical history and philosophy of psychology: Diversity of context, thought, and practice.* Cambridge: Cambridge University Press.

Warner, M. S. (2009). Defense or actualization? Reconsidering the role of processing, self and agency within Rogers' theory of personality. *Person-Centered & Experiential Psychotherapies, 8,* 109–126.

Wasserman, E. A., & Miller, R. R. (1997). What's elementary about associative learning? *Annual Review of Psychology, 48,* 573–607.

Watson, D., Clark, L. A., & Tellegen, A. (1988). Development and validation of brief measures of positive and negative affect: The PANAS scales. *Journal of Personality and Social Psychology, 54,* 1063–1070.

Watson, J. B. (1913). Psychology as the behaviorist views it. *Psychological Review, 20,* 158–177.

Watson, J. B. (1916). The place of the conditioned reflex in psychology. *Psychological Review, 23,* 89–116.

Watson, J. B. (1924). *Behaviorism.* New York: People's Institute Publishing Company.

Watson, J. B., & Raynor, R. (1920). Conditioned emotional reactions. *Journal of Experimental Psychology, 3,* 1–14.

Wegner, D. M., & Bargh, J. A. (1998). Control and automaticity in social life. In D. T. Gilbert, S. T. Fiske, & G. Lindzey (Eds.), *Handbook of social psychology* (4th ed., Vol. 1, pp. 446–496). Boston, MA: McGraw-Hill.

Weiner, B. (2010). The development of an attribution-based theory of motivation: A history of ideas. *Educational Psychologist, 45,* 28–36.

Wertz, F. J. (2015). Humanistic psychology and the qualitative research tradition. In K. J. Schneider, J. F. Pierson, & J. F. T. Bugental (Eds.), *The handbook of humanistic psychology: Theory, research, and practice* (2nd ed., pp. 259–274). Los Angeles, CA: Sage.

West, S. G., & Finch, J. F. (1997). Personality measurement: Reliability and validity issues. In R. Hogan, J. A. Johnson, & S. R. Briggs (Eds.), *Handbook of personality psychology* (pp. 143–164). San Diego, CA: Academic Press.

Westen, D. (1992). The cognitive self and the psychoanalytic self: Can we put our selves together? *Psychological Inquiry*, *3*, 1–13.

Westen, D., & Chang, C. (2000). Personality pathology in adolescence: A review. *Adolescent Psychiatry*, *25*, 61–100.

Wheeler, M., Kern, R. M., & Curlette, W. L. (1986). Factor analytic scales designed to measure Adlerian lifestyle themes. *Journal of Individual Psychology*, *42*, 1–16.

Whitbourne, S. K., & Waterman, A. S. (1979). Psychosocial development in young adulthood: Age and cohort comparisons. *Developmental Psychology*, *15*, 373–378.

White, S. C., Gaines, S. O., Jr., & Jha, S. (2012). Beyond subjective well-being. *Journal of International Development*, *24*, 763–766.

White, W. F. (1993). From S-R to S-O-R: What every teacher should know. *Education*, *113*, 620–629.

Wicker, A. W. (1969). Attitudes versus actions: The relationship of verbal and overt behavioral responses to attitude objects. *Journal of Social Issues*, *25*, 41–78.

Wiggins, J. S. (1979). A psychological taxonomy of trait-descriptive terms: The interpersonal domain. *Journal of Personality and Social Psychology*, *37*, 395–412.

Wiggins, J. S. (1991). Agency and communion as conceptual coordinates for the understanding and measurement of interpersonal behavior. In W. M. Grove & D. Ciccetti (Eds.), *Thinking clearly about psychology: Vol. 2. Personality and psychopathology*. (pp. 89–113). Minneapolis, MN: University of Minnesota Press.

Wiggins, J. S. (1995). *Interpersonal adjective scales professional manual*. Lutz, FL: Psychological Assessment Resources, Inc.

Wiggins, J. S. (1997). Circumnavigating Dodge Morgan's interpersonal style. *Journal of Personality*, *65*, 1069–1086.

Wiggins, J. S., & Broughton, R. (1985). The Interpersonal Circle: A structural model for the integration of personality research. In R. Hogan & W. H. Jones (Eds.), *Perspectives in personality: Vol. 1* (pp. 1–47). Greenwich, CT: JAI Press.

Wiggins, J. S., & Holzmuller, A. (1978). Psychological androgyny and interpersonal behavior. *Journal of Consulting and Clinical Psychology*, *46*, 40–52.

Wiggins, J. S., & Pincus, A. L. (1992). Personality: Structure and assessment. *Annual Review of Psychology*, *43*, 473–504.

Wiggins, J. S., Steiger, J. H., & Gaelick, L. (1981). Evaluating circumplexity in personality data. *Multivariate Behavioral Research*, *16*, 263–289.

Wiggins, J. S., Trapnell, P., & Phillips, N. (1988). Psychometric and geometric characteristics of the Revised Interpersonal Adjective Scales (IAS-R). *Multivariate Behavioral Research*, *23*, 517–530.

Wiggins, J. S., & Trapnell, P. D. (1997). Personality structure: The return of the Big Five. In R. Hogan, J. Johnson, & S. Briggs (Eds.), *Handbook of personality psychology* (pp. 737–765). San Diego, CA: Academic Press.

Windholz, G., & Lamal, P. A. (1986). Priority in the classical conditioning of children. *Teaching of Psychology*, *13*, 192–195.

Winnicott, D. (1931). *Clinical notes on disorders of childhood*. London: Heinemann.

Winston, A., Laikin, M., Pollack, J., Samstag, L., McCullough, L., & Muran, C. (1994). Short-term psychotherapy of personality disorders. *American Journal of Psychiatry*, *151*, 190–194.

Winter, D. G. (1997). Allport's life and Allport's psychology. *Journal of Personality*, *65*, 723–731.

Wood, W., & Eagly, A. H. (2010). Gender. In S. T. Fiske, D. T. Gilbert, & G. Lindzey (Eds.), *Handbook of social psychology* (5th ed., Vol. 1, pp. 629–667). New York: Wiley.

Wrightsman, L. S. (1981). Personal documents as data in conceptualizing adult personality development. *Personality and Social Psychology Bulletin*, *7*, 367–385.

Wrightsman, L. S. (1991). Interpersonal trust and attitudes toward human nature. In J. P. Robinson, P. R. Shaver, & L. S. Wrightsman (Eds.), *Measures of personality and social psychological attitudes* (pp. 374–412). San Diego, CA: Academic Press.

Wundt, W. (1910). *Principles of physiological psychology*. London: Swan Sonnenschein & Co. (Original work published 1874).

Wundt, W. (1973). *An introduction to psychology*. New York: Arno Press. (Original work published 1911).

Yarkoni, T. (2015). Neurobiological substrates of personality: A critical overview. In M. Mikulincer & P. R. Shaver (Eds.), *APA handbook of personality and social psychology* (Vol. 4: Personality processes and individual differences, pp. 61–83). Washington, DC: American Psychological Association.

Yee, A. H., Fairchild, H. H., Weizmann, F., & Wyatt, G. E. (1993). Addressing psychology's problem with race. *American Psychologist*, *48*, 1132–1140.

York, G. K., III. (2009). Localization of language function in the twentieth century. *Journal of the History of the Neurosciences*, *18*, 283–290.

Zehr, D. (2000). Portrayals of Wundt and Titchener in introductory psychology texts: A content analysis. *Teaching of Psychology*, *27*, 122–126.

Zeiler, K. (2013). A phenomenology of excorporation, bodily alienation, and resistance: Rethinking sexed and racialized embodiment. *Hypatia*, *28*, 69–84.

Zerbe, K. J. (1990). Through the storm: Psychoanalytic theory in the psychotherapy of anxiety disorders. *Bulletin of the Menninger Clinic*, *54*, 171–183.

Zuckerman, M. (1969). Theoretical formulations. In J. P. Zubek (Ed.), *Sensory deprivation* (pp. 407–432). New York: Appleton-Century-Crofts.

Zuckerman, M. (1971). Dimensions of sensation seeking. *Journal of Consulting and Clinical Psychology*, *36*, 45–52.

Zuckerman, M. (1984). Sensation seeking: A comparative approach to a human trait. *Behaviour and Brain Sciences*, *7*, 413–471.

Zuckerman, M. (1990). The psychophysiology of sensation seeking. *Journal of Personality*, *58*, 313–339.

Zuckerman, M., & Cloninger, R. C. (1996). Relationships between Cloninger's, Zuckerman's and Eysenck's dimensions of personality. *Personality and Individual Differences*, *21*, 283–285.

Zuckerman, M., Eysenck, S. B. G., & Eysenck, H. J. (1978). Sensation seeking in England and America: Cross-cultural, age, and sex comparisons. *Journal of Consulting and Clinical Psychology*, *46*, 139–149.

Zuroff, D. C. (1986). Was Gordon Allport a trait theorist? *Journal of Personality and Social Psychology*, *51*, 993–1000.

INDEX